THE EUROPEAN UNION SERIES

General Editors: Neill Nugent, William E. Paterson, Vincent Wright

The European Union series is designed to provide an authoritative library on the European Union ranging from general introductory texts to definitive assessments of key institutions and actors, policies and policy processes, and the role of member states.

Books in the series are written by leading scholars in their fields and reflect the most up-to-date research and debate. Particular attention is paid to accessibility and clear presentation for a wide audience of students, practitioners and interested general readers.

The series consists of four major strands:
- general textbooks
- the major institutions and actors
- the main areas of policy
- the member states and the Union

Published titles

Michelle Cini and Lee McGowan
Competition Policy in the European Union

Renaud Dehousse
The European Court of Justice

Desmond Dinan
Ever Closer Union? An Introduction to the European Community

Wyn Grant
The Common Agricultural Policy

Justin Greenwood
Representing Interests in the European Union

Alain Guyomarch, Howard Machin and Ella Ritchie
France in the European Union

Fiona Hayes-Renshaw and Helen Wallace
The Council of Ministers

Simon Hix and Christopher Lord
Political Parties in the European Union

Brigid Laffan
The Finances of the European Union

Janne Haaland Matláry
Energy Policy in the European Union

Neill Nugent
The Government and Politics of the European Union (Third Edition)

John Peterson and Margaret Sharp
Technology Policy in the European Union

European Union Series
Series Standing Order
ISBN 0–333–71695–7 hardcover
ISBN 0–333–69352–3 paperback
(*outside North America only*)

You can receive future titles in this series as they are published by placing a standing order. Please contact your bookseller or, in the case of difficulty, write to us at the address below with your name and address, the title of the series and the ISBN quoted above.

Customer Services Department, Macmillan Distribution Ltd
Houndmills, Basingstoke, Hampshire RG21 6XS, England

Forthcoming

Simon Bulmer and Drew Scott
European Union Economics Policy and Politics

Simon Hix
The Political System of the European Union

John Peterson and Elizabeth Bomberg
Decision-Making in the European Union

Ben Rosamond
Theories of European Integration

Richard Sinnott
Understanding European Integration

•   •   •   •

Simon Bulmer and Wolfgang Wessels
The European Council (Second Edn)

David Earnshaw and David Judge
The European Parliament

Neill Nugent
The European Commission

Anne Stevens
The Administration of the European Union

•   •   •   •

David Allen and Geoffrey Edwards
The External Economic Relations of the European Union

Laura Cram
Social Policy in the European Union

Wyn Grant, Duncan Matthews and Peter Newell
The Greening of the European Union?

Martin Holland
The European Union and the Third World

Malcolm Levitt and Christopher Lord
The Political Economy of Monetary Union

Anand Menon
Defence Policy and the European Union

James Mitchell and Paul McAleavey
Regionalism and Regional Policy in the European Union

Jörg Monar
Justice and Home Affairs in the Eueopean Union

Hazel Smith
The Foreign Policy of the European Union

Mark Thatcher
The Politics of European High Technology

Rüdiger Wurzel
Environmental Policy in the European Union

•   •   •   •

Simon Bulmer and William E. Paterson
Germany and the European Union

Phil Daniels and Ella Ritchie
Britain and the European Union

Other titles planned include

European Union: A Brief Introduction
The History of the European Union
The European Union Source Book
The European Union Reader
The Political Economy of the European Union

•   •   •   •

Political Union
The USA and the European Union

•   •   •   •

The European Union and its Member States
Reshaping the States of the Union
Italy and the European Union
Spain and the European Union

Technology Policy in the European Union

John Peterson
and
Margaret Sharp

First published 1998 by
MACMILLAN PRESS LTD
Houndmills, Basingstoke, Hampshire RG21 6XS
and London
Companies and representatives throughout the world

ISBN 0–333–65642–3 hardcover
ISBN 0–333–65643–1 paperback

A catalogue record for this book is available from the British
Library.

This book is printed on paper suitable for recycling and made from
fully managed and sustained forest sources

10	9	8	7	6	5	4	3	2	1
07	06	05	04	03	02	01	00	99	98

Printed in Hong Kong

Published in the United States of America 1998 by
ST. MARTIN'S PRESS, INC.,
Scholarly and Reference Division,
175 Fifth Avenue, New York, N.Y. 10010

ISBN 0–312–21641–6

To Calum for being such a good boy
and to Tom for being so patient

Contents

List of Exhibits, Tables and Figures

Figures

Preface

Many authors begin their prefaces with a statement about how the book took much longer to write than it should have. We really mean it! We have been fortunate to have had such a patient publisher, the equanimity to put up with each other's (often sharp) criticisms, and the sheer will not to give up on several occasions when that seemed the logical thing to do.

John Peterson's contribution to this book draws heavily on interviews and other materials collected as part of an ESRC-funded study of EU decision-making (R000235829). His collaborator on that study (and on much else), Elizabeth Bomberg, provided crucial support to the work that ultimately yielded this book. Margaret Sharp's contribution has been funded throughout by the ESRC STEEP Centre at the Science Policy Research Unit, University of Sussex. We also have received able and much-appreciated assistance on this project from Janet French and Ricardo Gomez.

Throughout the book, we have drawn on our earlier published work. Chapter 2 and parts of Chapter 4 expand and update Sharp and Shearman (1987). Parts of Chapter 5 are based on Peterson (1993b: Chapter 3; 1997a). Early sections of Chapter 6 draw heavily on (while also updating) Peterson (1995b).

We owe a very large debt to the EU and national officials and MEPs we interviewed in connection with this study. At the same time, we feel it necessary to note that Margaret Sharp's participation on a major European Commission (1996a) study into research policy and cohesion meant that we had access to rich and interesting data on national receipts from EU-funded research. However, most of our requests to use this data in this book were refused by the Commission. It is difficult not to feel disappointed and frustrated that we cannot tell our readers all we know. Nonetheless, we hope that we have provided a fair picture of who gets what from European technology policy.

We are in considerable debt to colleagues who read earlier versions of some or all of this book, including Luca Guzzetti, Wayne Sandholtz, Nicholas Ziegler, and John Zysman. Our publisher Steven Kennedy was gentle but persistent in prodding us along, and we are grateful to him for not giving up on us. The series editors gave us useful feedback on our original proposal and Vincent Wright offered very astute comments on the manuscript itself. Of course, we are fully responsible for any errors or omissions.

Finally, our own partnership has not always been easy, but ultimately it has been enormously pleasurable and always productive. This book probably would never have been completed if either of us had set out to write it by ourselves. Thus, our biggest debt is owed to each other.

JOHN PETERSON
MARGARET SHARP

List of Abbreviations

ABB — Asea Boveri Brown
AIR — Agro-Industrial Research
AT&T — American Telephone & Telegraph
BAe — British Aerospace
BAP — Biotechnology Action Programme
BEP — Biomolecular Engineering Programme
BRIDGE — Biotechnology Research for Innovation, Development and Growth in Europe
BRITE — Basic Research in Industrial Technologies for Europe
BSE — bovine spongiform encephalopathy
CAD/CAM — Computer-Aided Design/Computer-Aided Manufacturing
CAP — Common Agricultural Policy
CEPT — Conference of European Post and Telecommunications administrations
CERD — European Research and Development Committee
CERN — Centre Européen Recherche Nucléaire
CGCT — Compagnie General des Communications Téléphoniques
CGE — Compagnie Generale d'Electricité
CII — Compagnie Internationale d'Information
COST — Co-operation in Scientific and Technology
CRAFT — Cooperative Research Action for Technology
CREST — Comité de la Recherche Scientifique et Technique
CSCE — Conference on Security and Co-operation in Europe
CUBE — Concertation Unit for Biotechnology in Europe
DEBENE — DEutschland-BElgium-NEtherlands
DG — Directorate-General (European Commission)
DRAM — Dynamic Random Access Memory
DTI — Department of Trade and Industry (United Kingdom)

EC	European Community
ECLAIR	European Collaborative Linkage of Agriculture and Industry Research
ECSC	European Coal and Steel Community
ECU	European Currency Unit
EEC	European Economic Community
EFA	European Fighter Aircraft
EFTA	European Free Trade Association
ELDO	European Launcher Development Organization
EMBO	European Molecular Biology Organisation
EMU	Economic and Monetary Union
EP	European Parliament
ERDA	European Research and Development Agency
ESA	European Space Agency
ESF	European Science Foundation
ESPRIT	European Strategic Programme in Information Technologies
ESRO	European Space Research Organization
ESTA	European Science and Technology Assembly
ETSI	European Telecomunications Standards Institute
EU	European Union
EURAM	European Research in Advanced Materials
EUREKA	European Research Co-ordinating Agency
EUROTRAC	European Experiment on Transport and Transformation of Environmentally Relevant Trace Constituents in the Troposphere over Europe
FAMOS	Flexible Automated Manufacturing
FAST	Forecasting and Assessment of Science and Technology
FDI	foreign direct investment
FLAIR	Food Linked Agro-Industrial Research
GATT	General Agreement on Tariffs and Trade
GDP	Gross Domestic Product
GEC	General Electric Company (UK)
GNP	Gross National Product
HDTV	high-definition television
HEIs	higher education institutions
HLG	High-Level Group
IBM	International Business Machines

ICL	International Computers Limited
ICT	information and communications technology
IGC	intergovernmental conference
ILL	Institut Lave Langevin
IPTS	Institute for Prospective Technological Studies
IRDAC	Industrial Research and Development Advisory Committee
ISDN	integrated services digital networking
IT	information technology
ITER	International Thermo-Nuclear Reactor
ITT	International Telephone and Telegraph
ITTF	Information Technologies Task Force
JESSI	Joint European Silicon Structures Initiative
JOULE	Non-Nuclear Energies and Rational Use of Energy
JRC	Joint Research Centre
JET	Joint European Torus
MAC	Multiplexed Analogue Components
MEPs	members of the European Parliament
MITI	Ministry of International Trade and Industry (Japan)
MNCs	multinational corporations
MS-DOS	Microsoft Disc Operating System
NAFTA	North American Free Trade Area
NATO	North Atlantic Treaty Organization
NEC	Nippon Electric Corporation
NIP	National Information Points
NPCs	National Project Coordinators
OECD	Organization for Economic Cooperation and Development
ONP	Open Network Provision
OSI	Open Standards Interconnection
PAL	Phase Alternation by Line
PC	personal computer
PET	Planning Exercise in Telecommunications
PHARE	Poland and Hungary: Aid for the Restructuring of Economies
POST	Parliamentary Office of Science and Technology
PTT	Post, Telephone and Telecommunications
QMV	qualified majority voting
RACE	Research in Advanced Communications for Europe
RAM	random-access memory

RCA	Radio Company of America
R&D	research and development
RTD	research and technological development
SCIENCE	Stimulation des Coopérations Internationales et des Echanges Nécessaires aux Chercheurs en Europe
SDI	Strategic Defense Initiative
SEA	Single European Act
SEPSU	Science and Engineering Policy Studies Unit (UK Royal Society and Fellowship of Engineering)
SME	small or medium-sized enterprise
SPAG	Standards Promotion and Application Group
SPES	Stimulation Programme for Economic Sciences
TABD	Transatlantic Business Dialogue
TENs	Trans-European Networks
TMR	Training and Mobility of Researchers
TSER	targeted socio-economic research
UNICE	European Union of Employers' Confederations
VCR	videocassette recorder
VALUE	Valorisation and Utilisation for Europe
VLSI	Very Large-Scale Integration
WTO	World Trade Organization

1

Introduction

Technological change is transforming economic, political and social life on the eve of the new millennium, at the same time as European integration is entering a new and uncertain phase. The claim that technology, and the science that underpins it, 'is not just the stage manager, but the playwright in the story of our century' is not simply a platitude (May 1995: i). Profound changes have been unleashed by the development of the cotton gin, automobile and silicon chip. We lack solid counterfactuals, but a good argument can be made that the accelerating pace of technological change in the late 1990s makes it a more important determinant of the way in which economies, polities and societies are organised than ever before.

Against this broad backdrop, the European Union (EU) has developed an important role in technology policy, or policy that seeks 'to influence the decisions of firms (and public agencies and enterprises) to develop, commercialise or adopt new technologies' (Mowery 1992: 29). At first glance, technology policy seems to be a relatively uncontroversial concern of the EU. In economic terms, the EU's ambitions to create a single market have made the Union the logical level of government at which to promote or regulate technological change. In policy terms, research programmes have become an established part of the Union's repertoire.

In political terms, technology policy offers new opportunities to the EU. For example, the 'information society' – a broad initiative to promote the diffusion of new information technologies – became one of the European Commission's 'big ideas' under the presidency of Jacques Santer. It was sold both as a way to modernise European industry *and* to renew Europe's democratic culture. The

1

Commission made much of estimates that only half of European white-collar workers regularly used a computer at work in 1997, compared with 80 per cent of their American counterparts. It also argued that the information society gave Europe a chance to recover Thomas Paine's vision of global communications between free and equal citizens (see Katz 1996). The perception that Europe – alongside the United States (US) – enjoyed a comparative advantage in this venture was stoked by the admission of a Japanese telecommunications minister that not only did he lack an electronic mail address, he did not know what e-mail was (*Financial Times*, 22 January 1996). In short, an EU role in technology policy can be justified by both competitive challenges and advantages that, in relative global terms, are more or less shared by all its member states.

Nevertheless, the politics of EU technology policy remain lively and contentious. They reflect wider debates about the proper role of the Union in European political and economic life. The purpose of this book is to provide an authoritative – yet accessible – assessment of the development, size and impact of policies that promote technological innovation at the European level, as well as a critique of their direction.

What this book is about

As our title implies, our book is about public policies designed to promote technological innovation, or the 'application of science and technology in a new way, with commercial success' (OECD 1971: 11). More specifically, we are concerned with collaborative efforts at the European level to promote innovation and its diffusion. We are less concerned with science policy, which aims more broadly to expand and advance systematised knowledge about the natural world. We are somewhat more concerned with industrial policy, or 'the activities of governments which are intended to develop or retrench various industries in a[n] . . . economy in order to maintain global competitiveness' (Johnson 1984: 7), since the application of new technology is an increasingly important prerequisite of competitiveness. Our emphasis is on technology policy in the civilian realm. We leave it to others make sense of European collaborative efforts in the defence sector (see Walker and Gummett 1993; Taylor 1994; Hayward 1997). We are not primarily concerned with national tech-

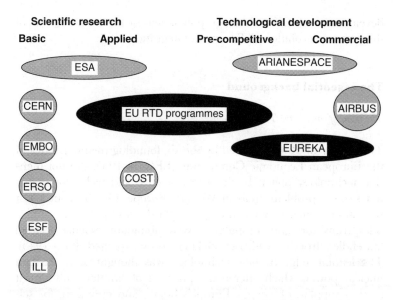

FIGURE 1.1   The place of EU research and technological development (RTD) programmes and EUREKA in relation to other joint European science and technology initiatives

nology policies in Europe, but do examine them in the context of collaborative programmes and policies.

Figure 1.1 presents a stylised map that helps to identify the territory we are proposing to explore. From left to right, it presents an array of joint or collaborative European science and technology initiatives. They range from those concerned with basic science on the left, such as the European particle physics laboratory CERN, to Airbus on the right, which is at the competitive end of the scale and concerned with making and selling new civilian aircraft. Our book is primarily about the area in the centre of the map, which represents applied scientific research and technological development.

We offer a broad view of the political economy of European technology policy, but we are preoccupied mostly with EU programmes to promote collaborative research and technological development (RTD) and the EUREKA programme, shown in the diagram by the two darker shaded ellipses. Our aim is to provide a comprehensive picture of theory, practice and performance of collaborative RTD efforts. We begin in this chapter by outlining the origins and development of EU technology policy against the broad canvas of the post-war evolution of European integration.

The essential background

The point of entry – the Treaty of Rome

The Treaty of Rome, ratified by the six founding member states of the European Economic Community (EEC) in 1957, did not mention technology policy. In the 1950s science and technology were not seen as problem areas in Western Europe. On the contrary it was an era when new technologies – plastics and polymers, antibiotics, transistors and computers – were abundant. Science seemed 'an endless frontier' with rich pickings to be exploited (Bush 1945). The leading edge of new technology was thought to be civilian nuclear power, which offered the prospect of limitless and almost costless supplies of energy. Europe's hopes, and optimism, for science and technology were reflected not in the EEC Treaty, but in the separate European Atomic Energy Community (Euratom) Treaty, which aimed to pool European nuclear experience and capabilities.

This optimism did not last long. By the 1960s, celebration of the limitless frontiers of science and technology had given way to anxieties about a 'technology gap' that loomed between the United States and Europe. US multinational companies were perceived to be in the vanguard of a new technological imperialism, and Europe seemed increasingly subservient. The French in particular were thwarted in their aspirations to become a (military) nuclear power by American refusals to grant export licences on large, number-crunching computers. France, in turn, led a European revolt against US dependence, but also elected to go it alone and develop its own distinctly national capacity in nuclear and computer technologies. Other European states followed the French lead. The Euratom Treaty, which had originally held out hope for the joint development of new reactors, rapidly fell prey to a new 'techno-nationalism' as Community aspirations were sacrificed to the pursuit of purely national objectives. The technology policy void in the Treaty of Rome was rapidly filled by national governments.

The failure of national champions

The 1960s and especially the 1970s thus became the age of the 'national champion'. As computers and electronics emerged as *the* new and vital areas of technology, French, British, Italian and even West German governments tried to limit their technological dependence on the US by offering their own companies subsidies, soft loans and arranged marriages. Large national players were granted effective monopoly rights on public contracts in the defence and telecommunications sectors. Few questions were asked about their long-term abilities to deliver the goods. Far from promoting the development of new technologies, 'national champion' policies fragmented markets and isolated companies from competition. By the early 1980s, the technology gap, if anything, had widened.

Meanwhile, two new and daunting external challenges emerged. First, deregulation in the United States unleashed both AT&T, the world's largest telecommunications company, and IBM, the world's largest computer company and already a major player in Europe, from restrictions that had limited their abilities to attack foreign markets. Both companies sought new alliances to facilitate their entry into European telecommunications markets (Dang Nyugen 1985).

Second, Japanese electronics firms, which had rapidly and singlemindedly entered the European consumer electronics markets in the 1970s, began planning wider operations in Europe. Seemingly effortless Japanese advances in the components (chips) sector and the withdrawal of many European producers from attempts to compete aroused new fears about Europe's lagging technological competitiveness. Voluntary export restraints, tariffs and anti-dumping duties did little to stem the tide. Instead, they encouraged inward foreign investment by non-European firms, bringing them into the home markets of the erstwhile national champions.

The Davignon initiatives

Against this backdrop, Etienne Davignon, the European Commissioner for Industry from 1977 to 1985 (and also RTD from 1981 to 1985), organised a new 'Round Table' of top industrialists from the European electronics industry (see Table 1.1). All of its members represented large, politically powerful firms from the

TABLE 1.1

The 'Big 12' Round Table of Industrialists (1982)

ICL	AEG	Thomson	Olivetti
(UK)	(West Germany)	(France)	(Italy)
GEC	Siemens	Bull	STET
(UK)	(West Germany)	(France)	(Italy)
Plessey	Nixdorf	CGE-Alcatel	Philips
(UK)	(West Germany)	(France)	(Netherlands)

Community's largest member states. Davignon's message was quite simple: given the gravity of threats from the US and Japan, the European electronics industry had to either improve its performance or collapse. The deal he offered was simple: the Community would develop new programmes to help firms update their industrial knowledge and techniques if they would give up their cosy, protected national niches and attack foreign markets as European-based multinationals. One important outcome was the European Strategic Programme for Information Technology, or ESPRIT.

ESPRIT was deliberately modelled on Japan's Very-Large Scale Integration (VLSI) programme, as were several national programmes in Europe such as the British Alvey project (Keliher 1987; Oakley and Owen 1989). The VLSI formula was to promote precompetitive, generic research that had wide applications across many economic sectors. Research was undertaken collaboratively by firms, research institutes and universities. Bringing research organisations together to work on collaborative projects would stimulate transnational linkages, awareness of market opportunities beyond home borders and greater understanding of developments in the global economy. A related concern was to make firms recognise that production was becoming an increasingly collaborative exercise, and in particular that academic–industry linkages needed to be strengthened and extended.

ESPRIT also served as a model for subsequent programmes, such as the telecommunications programme RACE (Research in Advanced Communications for Europe) and the BRITE programme (Basic Research in Industrial Technologies for Europe), which aimed at diffusing new industrial technologies. More specialist programmes in biotechnology and medicine also were developed at the Community level. All shared five common characteristics:

- First, they were genuinely collaborative. Funded projects had to involve firms and/or research institutes from at least two EU countries.
- Second, funding was on a shared-cost basis for industrial partners. Industry generally met at least 50 per cent of the research costs.
- Third, the Commission laid down broad priorities for EU programmes, but only after extensive consultation with technical experts and user groups.
- Fourth, applications for funding were judged by independent experts and accepted on the basis of academic or technological excellence.
- Fifth, all projects were 'pre-competitive' – that is, concerned in principle with generic or general research, and not research specific to a particular product or process.

EUREKA

The EUREKA programme came into existence soon after ESPRIT, but as a very different creature. It was launched not as an EU programme, but as a loose intergovernmental initiative designed to promote 'near-market' research: that is, R&D leading to 'products, processes and services having a world-wide market potential' in a relatively short period of time (EUREKA Secretariat 1985: 1). EUREKA employed a 'bottom-up' methodology with research organisations themselves responsible for designing projects. The overwhelming share of public funding was provided by national governments (as opposed to the EU).

EUREKA was the brainchild of the French president, François Mitterrand, and his (then) close adviser, Jacques Attali, who proposed the initiative as an alternative to European participation in the Reagan administration's Strategic Defence Initiative (SDI) in 1985. With civil rather than military aims, the French argued that EUREKA would ensure that Europe's best technologies and researchers were not 'poached' by the Pentagon. In the event, EUREKA became an umbrella mechanism for mostly small R&D projects. It never realised Mitterrand's vision of a programme for large, centralised and highly subsidised *grands projets*.

In its early years, EUREKA was often criticised bitterly by Commission officials, who viewed it as detracting from political sup-

port for the Community's own programmes (see Peterson 1993b).
Yet the programme survived and flourished. EUREKA's ostensible
focus on 'near-market' R&D meant that it complemented – at least
in theory – the emerging range of pre-competitive Community programmes. Most EUREKA projects were small, but the initiative did
incorporate large initiatives piloted by Big 12 firms, such as Joint
European Submicron Silicon Initiative (JESSI) into the next generations of microchips, and the high-definition television (HDTV) project to develop the television standards and hardware of the future.
EUREKA thus provided something of a respite to some of Europe's
erstwhile national champions.

The Single European Act and Maastricht Treaty

The response of the Commission and European governments to the
'technology gap' was not only to promote and fund collaboration,
but also to force Europe's national champions to confront more
competition. Ratified in 1987, the Single European Act (SEA) set in
train the '1992 Project' to create a single European market by
removing all barriers to the free movement of goods, services, capital and people in the EU within five years. For the first time, the
Community was given competence in research and technology by
the SEA. The Maastricht Treaty (ratified in 1993) further defined
this competence.

Both Treaties made it clear that the twin objectives of EU policy
were, first, to strengthen Europe's science and technology capabilities and, second, to promote its competitiveness at an international
level. The Maastricht Treaty further specified that the Union's RTD
policies had to serve other objectives, such as 'cohesion' – that is, the
narrowing of the wealth gap between the EU's richest and poorest
regions. After Maastricht, the Commission acquired powers to take
the lead in coordinating national RTD policies if it seemed useful to
do so.

Both Treaties required the Community to develop a forward strategy for its research and technology activities. The result was the
multiannual Framework programme, covering all the Community's
RTD activities. Framework I was launched in 1984. Ten years later,
Framework IV (1994–8) was the first to be negotiated through the
new Maastricht Treaty provisions of 'co-decision' involving the
European Parliament (EP). No sooner were its fine details agreed,

than work began on preparing for the Framework V programme (1999–2002).

The Framework programmes gave coherence to the European Union's RTD efforts, but the compartmentalisation of its activities has remained highly entrenched. Semi-autonomous fiefdoms that fiercely defend their own budgets have developed over time in many areas of research. As such, it proved impossible to bring all activities into the Framework programme until after the Maastricht Treaty was ratified. Only then did the Commission (with support from the EP) manage to bring spending for research in energy, Eastern and Central Europe, and other international programmes into the Framework IV budget.

The size and shape of EU programmes

The evolution of the Framework programme

Table 1.2 compares the main lines of expenditure in successive Framework programmes. A substantial reduction in spending on energy (mainly reflecting declining support for nuclear power in the mid-1980s) is notable, as is the smaller share of funding earmarked for information and communications technology (ICT) in the Framework IV programme. Support for the life sciences has increased steadily, but it is still less than half the total spent on ICT. The growing importance of the human capital and mobility programme, designed to promote the exchange of researchers between member states, is also striking.

RTD must be placed in the context of the EU's general budget. Table 1.3 details all Community RTD expenditures since 1984. It shows that total annual spending approached 3 billion ECU by the mid-1990s. This figure compared with nearly 42 billion ECU expenditure on agriculture and more than 31 billion ECU spent under the structural funds (for regional development) – the two major takers from the Community budget. Thus, spending on research came (a distant) third in terms of total expenditure, although the Commission generally enjoyed more discretion in the spending of research funds than in spending for agricultural or regional development.

EU spending on research accounted for about 4 per cent of the

TABLE 1.2

RTD priorities and the Framework programmes

Framework programme Years	I 1984–7	II 1987–91	III 1990–4	IV 1994–8
Total million ECUs (adjusted to 1992 prices)	3 750	5 396	6 600	12 300[d]
	Priorities (%)			
ICT[a]	25	42	38	28
Industrial Technologies[b]	11	16	15	16
Environment	7	6	9	9
Life Sciences	5	7	10	13
Energy	50	22	16	18
Other[c]	2	7	12	14
Total	100	100	100	100

[a]   Information and Communications Technologies.
[b]   Includes industrial processes and new materials.
[c]   Includes human capital and mobility, development, diffusion and
      exploitation and social economic research.
[d]   See note to table 7.1 (p. 190).

Source: Commission (1994) appendix table IV.2.

Union's total budget by the mid-1990s (see Table 1.3). The Framework programme equalled only a very small share of total government spending on RTD in member states, and a very much smaller percentage of all RTD expenditures (public and private). Thus, although EU spending on research has grown, the total remains small in relative terms, especially when spread between 15 member states. Even when the Framework programme, EUREKA and all other forms of RTD cooperation in the Union (such as CERN, the European Space Agency, and so on) are included, they add up to only about 13 per cent of total public sector investment in research (Ruberti 1997: 13).

The question of national receipts from the Framework programme remains highly contentious. The Commission takes great care to guard its own statistics on who gets what. The larger member states – Germany, the UK, France and Italy – naturally receive the most EU research funding in absolute terms. However, smaller northern countries – Belgium, Denmark, the Netherlands and

TABLE 1.3

EU commitment to RTD 1984–98

	EU RTD spending MECU (1992 prices)	EU RTD spending as% EU budget	EU RTD spending as % of member states' total RTD spending (public and private)	EU RTD spending as % of member states' government spending on R&D
1984	848.4	2.1	0.5	1.1
1988	1 373.9	2.6	1.1	2.3
1990	1 946.9	3.9	1.2	2.7
1992	2 842.3	4.6	1.5	3.3
1994	2 637.3	3.8	1.7	3.8
1996[a]	3 066.0	4.2	n/a	n/a
1998[a]	2 800.9	3.5	n/a	n/a

n.a. = not available
[a] Projected

Source: EUROSTAT, Commission (1994).

Ireland – tend to receive more on a per capita basis. The poorer ('cohesion') countries, especially Spain, Greece and Portugal, have attacked an apparent bias towards the northern, richer countries. Yet, in relation to their (generally small) national budgets for RTD, southern countries do quite well out of the Framework programme. Adding in subsidies for RTD available from the structural funds, the EU contribution can amount to well over 50 per cent of total public spending on research in some of the poorer member states.

Equally contentious is the question of whether the significance of Union RTD expenditures belies their absolute size. In the cohesion countries, EU funding clearly has made a sizeable extra contribution to public spending on innovation. In the advanced industrialised economies of northern Europe, the Union's contribution in monetary terms has been marginal. Yet, in the case of France, Larédo (1995: 3) found that:

Nearly all heavy R&D spenders in industry, most French high-tech SMEs (small and medium-sized enterprises) and most large public research laboratories [were involved in EU-funded research]. When coupled with the average involvement of participating units (a fifth of their research capabilities), this clearly points to a major involvement of the French research system.

In short, the significance of the collaborative programmes in the context of Europe's total research effort cannot be measured strictly in monetary terms.

RTD and competitiveness

There are many ways of measuring the impact of European collaborative programmes, but the SEA and Maastricht Treaty offered a clear yardstick: the Union's RTD policy was intended 'to strengthen the scientific and technological basis of Community industry and to encourage it to become more competitive at the international level'. If increased competitiveness has remained the primary goal of European technology policy, the EU's policy agenda has changed over time. In 1983, when ESPRIT was first set in train, the burning issue for policy-makers was how to close the 'technology gap'. In the 1990s, the key policy issue became unemployment and the EU's failure to match either the fast growth-rates of South-East Asia or the faster employment creation of the US. Europe's inability to create jobs was viewed as a symptom of its declining competitiveness.

Unemployment was the main focus of the Commission's (1993) White Paper on 'Growth, Competitiveness and Employment'. It highlighted low rates of investment in the EU and macroeconomic policies that constrained structural change. Above all, the Commission (1993: 49) argued that:

> The depth of the present crisis is largely due to insufficient progress in adapting the structures of the Community's economy to the changing technological, social and international environment . . . Only through the structural adaptation of industry can the twin requirements of higher productivity and more jobs be achieved.

This argument put technology and technology policy in the front line of EU policy-making. It also directly challenged member states 'to accelerate structural change rather than to slow it down' (Commission 1993: 49).

A number of indicators allow us to assess Europe's ability to respond to structural change, and thus improve its competitive performance. Trade flows are a traditional method of measuring competitiveness. By identifying those sectors that are relatively R&D intensive, it is possible to separate figures for 'high tech' sectors from other, more traditional sectors. Taken as a whole, the EU's performance has been poor. A relatively low percentage of total EU exports – 17 per cent – were high-tech products in the early 1990s, compared with the US (31 per cent) and Japanese (27 per cent) totals (Commission 1992b).

Thus, the EU as a whole ran a persistent deficit on high-tech trade. However, performance varied across countries. Germany and France had surpluses in their high-tech trade, with Germany enjoying a 16 per cent share of all high-tech export markets between 1982 and 1992 (Commission 1994: 51). German strength lay in the chemicals, pharmaceutical and motor vehicles sectors. France was strong in aerospace, as was the UK, whose pharmaceutical sector was world-class. However, as Table 1.4 shows, compared with its competitors in the so-called Triad (Japan and the US), Europe remained weak in the sectors crucial to economic modernisation and the information society: electronics, office equipment and data processing.

Table 1.5 compares R&D expenditures in the EU, the US and Japan in the mid-1990s. Once again, the EU is not cast in a favourable light. R&D as a percentage of GDP was lower than for many of Europe's competitors. Significantly, the proportion of R&D

TABLE 1.4

European performance in technology-intensive sectors

Sector	Europe's ranking in Triad	Trade balance trend
Aerospace	2	Stable
Chemicals	1	Increasing
Pharmaceuticals	1	Increasing
Electrical equipment	3	Stable
Data processing and office equipment	3	Falling
Electronics	3	Falling
Motor vehicles	2	Stable
Scientific instruments	2	Falling

Source: Commission (1994).

TABLE 1.5

R&D indicators for the Triad – 1995

	EU 15	USA	Japan
Total R&D expenditures ($m)	127 643	191 526	81 514
Total R&D expenditures as % of GDP	1.85	2.29	2.98
Total R&D expenditures per inhabitant ($)	343	494	649
% of total R&D expenditures financed by governments	39.1	36.4	22.8
% of total R&D expenditures financed by industry	52.7	58.7	67.1

Source: OECD (1997).

financed by industry in Europe was low, indicating less willingness on the part of the private sector to attempt innovation. Again, however, there was considerable variation across the Union. In 1995 Germany and France each had a ratio of total (gross) R&D to GDP of 2.3 per cent. Sweden's ratio was 3.6 per cent; the UK's was 2.1 per cent, whereas Italy only managed 1.2 per cent and Greece a paltry 0.6 per cent.

The share of R&D funded by business also varied considerably. In Germany, 59 per cent was financed by the private sector. Sweden and the UK had roughly similar figures, but in Greece and Portugal less than 30 per cent of R&D expenditure came from business.

Finally, with increasing emphasis being put on human capital, Europe as a whole compared badly with its rivals in terms of education and training. However, (see Table 1.6) again the picture in terms of numbers of scientists and engineers varied from country to country. Germany, France and Sweden were all beginning to approach levels attained in the US and Japan.

The 1995 Green Paper on Innovation

The EU's competitive position was well summarised in the Commission's (1995a: 7) *Green Paper on Innovation*:

European industry has recently improved its competitiveness, particularly vis-à-vis its major competitors, the United States and Japan . . . Nevertheless, major and disquieting weaknesses remain:

TABLE 1.6

R&D scientists and engineers

	Total researchers[a] Full-time equivalents (000)s	Total researchers[a] per thousand labour force				
	1994	1971	1975	1981	1991	1994
Germany	229.8[b]	3.3	3.8	4.4	6.1	5.8[b]
Spain	47.9	0.6	0.6	1.4	2.6	3.0
France	149.2	2.8	2.9	3.6	5.2	5.9
Italy	75.7	1.5	1.8	2.3	3.1	3.3
Sweden	29.4[b]	2.5	3.6	4.1	5.9	6.8[b]
United Kingdom	146.0	3.3	n.a.	4.8	4.6	5.1
EU 15	777.6[b]	n.a.	n.a.	n.a.	4.5	4.7[b]
US	962.7[b]	6.1	5.5	6.2	7.6	7.4[b]
Japan	658.9	3.7	4.6	5.4	9.2	9.9

[a]   These figures only include researchers who have at least a first level
university degree. It does not include technicians.
[b]   1993 Figures.
n.a. not available.

Source: OECD.

a lower degree of specialisation in both high tech sectors and sectors with high growth rates; a lower presence in geographical
markets which show strong development; productivity which is
still inadequate; *a research and development effort which remains disparate
and fragmented; insufficient capacity to innovate, to launch new products and
services, to market them rapidly on world markets and, finally, to react rapidly
to changes in demand.* [Emphasis added.]

   In other words, by the mid-1990s the EU's key competitive problem was its inability to manage innovation. In particular, the
Commission argued, Europe seemed unable to commercialise and
diffuse new technologies.

   Yet, the solutions put forward in the Green Paper reflected the
traditional schizophrenia between the 'hands-on' and the 'hands-
off' schools of technology policy. On the one hand, the Green Paper
prominently profiled the new 'Task Forces' created in 1995 by the
incoming Commissioner for Research (and former French prime
minister) Edith Cresson. The Task Forces were meant to organise
and catalyse ambitious research projects designed to create the 'car

of the future' or develop new viral vaccines. Soon, it was promised, they would begin 'mobilising all the expertise necessary and . . . concentrating the budgetary resources available so that industry can respond more effectively' (Commission 1995a: 21).

On the other hand, the Commission's main proposed lines of action in the Green Paper were more diffusion-oriented than mission-oriented. The emphasis was on human resources, labour mobility and obstacles to enterprise. The Commission stressed the importance of industry financing and the need to realise the value of assets tied up in know-how rather than bricks and mortar.

In the event, the Commission's (1997b) *First Action Plan for Innovation*, the official follow-up to the Green Paper, made little reference to the Task Forces. Its emphasis was on fostering 'an innovation culture' and 'a framework conducive to innovation'. Whatever Cresson's ambitions to 'direct' the Union's research efforts, most of the Commission's proposed actions, in practical terms, required implementation by national or even sub-national authorities.

The changing focus of EU technology policy

By 1996–7, the future of technology policy in the EU had become a subject of intense debate, particularly after negotiations started on the shape of the Framework V programme. The 1995 Green Paper marked a clear – and generally effective – attempt by Cresson and the Commission to set the agenda for the negotiations. Despite its tendency towards schizophrenia, the Green Paper gave EU technology policy a new *raison d'être*: Europe's inability to manage innovation meant that the focus of policy had to shift away from producers to users. The policies introduced by Davignon in the early 1980s had been all about enhancing Europe's ability to *produce* new technologies. By the late 1990s, the new goal of EU policy was enhancing European abilities to *use* new technologies.

The changing political economy of RTD

What underlay this switch in the focus from producers to users? If we are to understand recent changes in European technology policy, we must make sense of the broad and rapidly changing context in which it is made and implemented. Since the Framework programme and EUREKA were created in the mid-1980s, the political economy of research and technological development has changed dramatically. In particular, five new features of the global economic landscape are worth highlighting.

First, *the end of the Cold War has altered the way in which 'security' is defined, and enhanced the importance of innovation in civilian technologies.* As Soviet power declined in the 1980s, military competition between states became less salient than rivalries to foster rising standards of living, economic growth and good jobs. As large-scale war became more unimaginable, Western governments increasingly focused their attention on 'economic security', and particularly the competitiveness of their national firms. Innovation in civilian (as opposed to military) technologies – particularly those driving the world's fastest-growing industries such as telecommunications and biotechnology – became viewed as the key to prosperity, falling unemployment and even political survival.

Innovation and security became linked in a surprising number of contexts. For example, the European Union's audio-visual policy sought to preserve a European identity in the face of the globalisation of mass (mostly American) culture and new technologies for delivering it. For the French and others, preserving European culture and independence in the technologies that comprised the 'new media' became matters of 'security'. More generally, the EU took on the role of agent in promoting economic security. Collaborative research programmes such as the Framework programme and EUREKA – which had initially been sold as specific and targeted – became viewed as general tools in the efforts of European governments to promote economic competitiveness and, ultimately, economic security.

A second broad change in the political economy of RTD arises from *globalisation, and the erosion of national control over economic policy generally, and technology policy specifically.* No other post-war development in international political economy has been analysed as extensively – with such a lack of clarity – as globalisation. Simply defined, globalisation is a set of processes that result in the increased interdependence of previously separate national economies.

A number of factors accelerated the pace of globalisation in the 1980s: the opening up of capital markets and increased cross-border investment; the modernisation of infrastructures in telecommunications and transport; the emergence of 'information based' economies, in which trade increasingly is in information more than physical goods; increases in the number of alliances between firms; and new regional and global projects to free trade, such as the North American Free Trade Area (NAFTA), the World Trade Organization (WTO), and, of course, the EU itself. Many multinational companies (MNCs) responded by globalising their activities: decentralising their productive and distributive capacities and effectively becoming local producers in specific markets.

Technological change was accelerated by globalisation, as markets opened and competitors looked to innovation as a means of gaining market advantage. With macroeconomic policy options becoming increasingly limited, many Western governments shifted the focus of policy from the macro to the microlevel, where they sought to influence the performance of firms and industries. Here, too, globalisation raised a fundamental question for all governments: which firms were they trying to influence? Governments wanted to assist their own 'national' firms, but the identities of firms were increasingly blurred. Governments began to ask 'who is us?' (Reich 1991). In Europe, the question eventually became: 'Who are EU?' (Strange 1998).

A third broad change arises from globalisation: a *widening of disparities between more and less technologically advanced countries*. Many multinational companies have globalised production, but few have shifted research and development (R&D) capabilities or corporate headquarters away from their traditional home bases (Patel 1995). The reason is simple: while technology (in terms of machines and blueprints) is mobile, technological competence is not. Increasingly, it has become recognised that the capacity to innovate is cumulative: innovation begets more innovation. The key factor is the knowledge and skills acquired over time by the people who work in research. While the firm may shift production facilities (plant and machinery) overseas, people tend not to move (Sharp and Pavitt 1993). It is not easy to pick up new, state-of-the-art technologies without the knowledge and skills required to make good use of them.

The political effects of this pattern of technological development are powerful. More intense competition, between more firms, to push forward the development of ever more sophisticated technologies means that countries (and firms) that start with less sophisticated technological competence may be left behind, and find it very difficult to catch up. The process of competition merely reinforces the advantage of those in the lead and takes them further down the learning curve. To illustrate the point, the primary effect of the development of the Internet, arguably, is to widen the wealth gap between rich and poor in global terms. By the mid-1990s, of the 15 000 or so networks on the global Internet, only 42 were in Muslim countries, and 29 of those were in Turkey or Indonesia (Nye and Owens 1996).

The tendency for technological development to reinforce existing competitive advantages has powerful repercussions for the EU, given its mission to promote cohesion. By the mid-1990s, the Framework programme had begun to yield relatively stable policy networks in specific technological sectors, such as IT or the life sciences. They tended to be dominated by the same firms and research organisations over time. The danger was that new players – particularly from less advanced member states – were being excluded. The work of Gambardella and Garcia (1995) on BRITE, for example, noted a strong tendency for the North to link with North, and South with South, with élite institutions tending to form their own exclusive networks. If EU programmes were subsidising the formation of cosy, exclusive networks dominated primarily by large, northern firms and well-endowed research institutes, was the Framework programme a good use of resources? Or did EU spending on research, in the derisive words of one Spanish diplomat, amount to 'cohesion funding for the rich'? (Interview, November 1996.)

A fourth change in the political economy of RTD concerns *new industrial structures and their implications for innovation*. States are increasingly unable to influence the activities of large, oligopolistic MNCs whose businesses and internal structures are global in scale. However, while many multinational companies have globalised their activities, they have decentralised their productive and distributive capacities. The term 'corporation' even seems a misnomer for many firms, which have become tightly controlled webs of local operations (see Zysman and Schwartz 1998).

The trend towards 'delayering' (getting rid of middle management levels) in MNCs has had even wider implications. Most MNCs need close links to 'supply chains' of small and medium-sized enterprises (SMEs) who supply specialist services. These small firms have become viewed as crucial to providing added value and good jobs in a geographical area, while a critical mass of SMEs is seen as an important 'carrot' in attracting large investments by

MNCs. The results of most SME policies have been modest. Many – including the EU's – seem based on inflated assumptions about the ability of SMEs to generate jobs (see Clay *et al.* 1996). Nevertheless, in Europe as elsewhere, the development of an innovative, thriving coterie of SMEs is an important new focus of technology policies.

A fifth and final change is that it has become clear, as never before, that *technologies become diffused widely only if they are embraced widely by citizens in democratic societies.* Technology policies – which traditionally have been producer-driven – need to take account of the *demand* side. A broad and similar lesson may be drawn from the cases of nuclear power in the 1970s, cattle growth hormones in the 1980s and gene technologies in the 1990s: new technologies will not catch on unless they are viewed by citizens as safe, ethical and consumer-friendly. Successful diffusion depends just as much on social attitudes as it does on technology. Governments may sometimes help by 'preparing' markets to assimilate new technologies. The case of mobile phones in Scandinavia illustrates the point: Sweden (followed by Finland) has the highest rate of penetration of mobile phones of any country in the world. The Scandinavian firms, Nokia and Ericsson, have benefited enormously from public measures to promote diffusion of the technology.

In short, diffusion needs to be approached in broad, sociological terms. Both governments and firms must recognise that technology and society need to move in step: the diffusion of innovations involves constant change and a reciprocal moulding process between technologies on one hand and societies on the other. Yet, technology policy is a uniquely technocratic area of policy in which experts are powerful and the general public is not. Efforts by the Commission under Cresson to make EU-funded research more socially relevant and sensitive to the 'needs of society' reflect a new and general enthusiasm for open debates about how technology policy can serve broad social needs.

Policy dilemmas for the EU

The broad changes in the political economy of RTD that we have highlighted create new dilemmas for EU policy-makers.

- *Are the EU's technology policy goals and structures still appropriate? How far have they really adapted to the process of globalisation?*

On the face of it, seeking to promote competitiveness, strengthening the EU's science base, trying to ensure cohesion, while recognising the social goals of RTD, may seem a crowded agenda. However, it is one well adapted to the global framework within which technology policy must be made. Beneath the surface are many conflicts and tensions that have yet to be resolved. Increasingly, for example, concerns about cohesion have penetrated debates about the proper direction of EU technology policy. The Union has had profound difficulties balancing two competing policy imperatives. On one hand, it seeks to foster 'European excellence', regardless of where that excellence is geographically located. On the other, it must ensure '*juste retour*', and achieve a distribution of funding that is politically sensitive and aims, in part, to ensure greater cohesion between richer and poorer member states.

Moreover, it is questionable how far EU policies have really adapted to globalisation. Robert Reich (1991), the Clinton administration's first Secretary of Labor, offers a simple policy prescription for a globalised world. If states want to attract investments by MNCs and encourage them to innovate, they must make large public investments, first, in human capital through training and education, and, second, in infrastructures and institutions that support human capital (see also Strange 1998). Yet, responsibilities for education, training and basic science in the EU remain firmly at the national level. Member states resist, usually quite fiercely, any incursion on these areas of competence by Brussels. Meanwhile, the delays and difficulties of the Trans-European Networks (TENs) reflect a general reluctance to organise large-scale infrastructure investments at the level of the European Union.

The debate of the late 1990s about the future of European technology policy was stoked by the clear need to shift from the production-oriented policies of the early Framework programmes to diffusion-oriented policies more appropriate to meeting pressures from global competition. Nevertheless, this policy shift raised new questions about the EU's established policy role and methods. For example, diffusion-oriented policies implied a new concern with downstream applications of technology, or 'direct effects' in terms of new product and process technologies. The accepted logic of pre-competitive restraints on EU-funded research thus became subject to new challenges. Moreover, the Commission's practice of setting priorities for EU programmes itself became open to new questions: would the 'bottom-up' EUREKA approach be preferable to the EU's 'top-down' methods (Larédo 1995)? Were some EU tasks more appropriately delegated to lower tiers of government? In response to strong pressures to 'do something' for small firms, for example, the Commission tried gamely to develop an 'SME policy'. Increasingly, however, the Commission had trouble countering the argument that national or even subnational governments were far better placed to help small firms whose circumstances varied enormously between member states and regions.

It was also questionable whether the EU possessed appropriate policy instruments. The Union had shed its chauvinistic attitudes of the 1980s. Nevertheless, it became an open question whether it was desirable for EU programmes to continue subsidising collaboration between *European* firms and researchers, when other players in the field, particularly from the US or Japan, might better provide access to leading edge technology. Was it time to rethink the shared-cost, collaborative ethos upon which the Framework programme had been built?

Cresson's advocacy of a more vigorous EU research effort seemed designed to shift the agenda from technology policy *per se* to the wider issue of 'economic security'. However, this shift only raised a further policy dilemma:

- *Does it make sense to 'sell' EU technology policy to (often reluctant) member states as a means to achieve competitiveness, and economic security, at the risk of raising unrealistic expectations?*

Arguably, given the modest EU share of all European spending on research and the pre-competitive restrictions that remain in place, the Union's technology policy cannot hope to make a large or even tangible difference in terms of European competitiveness or employment. Its potential impact has certainly always been minimal compared with EU trade, competition or regulatory policies. Yet, it remains tempting for the Commission to oversell EU technology policy as a formula for kick-starting Europe's economies. A close advisor to Cresson insisted that:

We now have two industry-minded Commissioners [Cresson and the Industry Commissioner, Martin Bangemann] working on research. Both are concerned about the contribution of R&D to industry, and both want to shake up the bureaucracy and shorten the process from research to result. The Task Forces and Green Paper are meant to create a laboratory for Framework V. Above all, the Task Forces are designed to make the fruits of R&D more visible to society (interview, November 1995).

Yet the Green Paper and the Action Plan contained little that was new. The Task Forces were given ambitious remits, but few resources and only vague co-ordinating responsibilities. The Commission insisted that its main purpose was to catalyse national actions and promote the diffusion of information among European research communities, thus lowering transaction costs in the process of innovation. Still, it was impossible not to suspect the Commission of wishing to seize on general concerns about economic security in a more globalised and competitive economy to expand the Union's RTD competence and resources. It was perhaps too much to expect that the potential impact of EU technology policy would not be oversold in the process.

Meanwhile, real doubts emerged about how easily the Commission could change the focus of EU policy, even if it wanted to. The policy dilemma became:

- *How can a user-friendly, 'social-needs-driven' policy be reconciled with the established, technocratic and closed style of EU research policy-making?*

The Framework programme and EUREKA were originally designed to close the 'technology gap' between Europe and its major competitors. Over time, large producer interests became well entrenched in collaborative programmes such as ESPRIT, often with the encouragement and support of the Commission. The obstacles to a truly diffusion-oriented policy – that is, one that focused on the demand side and sought to spread the benefits of innovation to a much wider group of firms – were considerable. As a Commission official acknowledged:

The big companies have done a good job of getting together and pushing their own ideas through. The [Big 12] Roundtable illustrates a simple idea: it's much easier for the Commission if it wants an opinion from the big IT companies in Europe to go to the Roundtable for it. With all the good will in the world in approaching SMEs and getting more of them to participate, there is no easy way of finding them, there is no easy way of talking to them because there is no single forum for these people. (Interview, DG XIII, November 1994)

Technology policy is already a political football at the EU level. The dilemma for the Commission, in moving to a policy with a different group of beneficiaries, is that it will lose the crucial political support of large firms. Networks of technology producers, which generally have allied with the Commission in lobbying national governments for more RTD resources at the EU level, have become a force for inertia at a time when policy clearly needs to change.

In short, if technology policy offers new opportunities to the EU in the twenty-first century, it also poses daunting challenges. How to reconcile conflicting aims and objectives? How to limit ambitions to what is truly feasible? How to prevent 'capture' of today's policy by yesterday's beneficiaries? How to develop new instruments of policy adapted to new tasks? The aim of this book is not to answer all of these questions, although we return to them in Chapter 10 and offer some views along the way. Our primary purpose is to provide a measured, balanced and objective discussion of the issues in order to inform the policy debate.

The plan of the book

We begin our analysis by fleshing out the historical context, which we have sketched only briefly here, in Chapter 2. The story of early attempts to collaborate at the European level, the failure of most, and the lessons learned is a fascinating one, which is germane to understanding why so much progress towards developing a European competence in R&D was made so quickly in the 1980s. Still, the reader who is primarily interested in contemporary European programmes may wish to skim or skip this chapter.

Chapter 3 sets the scene for later chapters by surveying models of technological change, political integration and EU policy-making that help us make sense of the emergence of European technology policies. Chapter 4 examines the origins and development of the EU's Framework programme and confronts the apparent contradiction between competition and collaboration at the heart of the 1992 project. Chapter 5 focuses on EUREKA and explains why it emerged and developed more as a rival than as a complement to the EU's collaborative research programmes.

Developments in the 1990s are the focus for our subsequent chapters. In Chapter 6, we link the difficult negotiations on the Framework IV programme to the political crisis that surrounded the ratification of the EU's Maastricht Treaty. Chapter 7 brings the analysis up to date by analysing the present state of the 'European Technological Community'. Chapter 8 augments the economic and political focus of most of our book with a detailed policy analysis of RTD decision-making.

Our concluding chapters bring our story full circle. Chapter 9 squarely confronts the question: precisely what has been achieved by the European technology programmes? Chapter 10 offers a final assessment and critique of the current direction of European technology policy, and revisits the question of whether the policy dilemmas posed by the new political economy of technology change are amenable to solutions at the European level, or not.

2

The Historical Backdrop

The emergence of a legal and political mandate for European technology policies in the 1980s was a product of both worrying competitive trends and the general reinvigoration of European integration. However, the actual design of new policies was much influenced by early experiments in research and technological collaboration in Europe in the 1960s and 1970s. Most of these experiments either failed or succeeded only in the long term. Still, many valuable – if often quite painful – lessons were learned from them.

Our focus here is on early policy experiments in three 'big science' sectors – nuclear energy, civil aviation and space. We begin by explaining why these sectors were prime candidates for European collaboration in the 1960s. We then examine debates about the Community's policy role and explain why European collaboration in 'big science' sectors was mostly organised outside the framework of the EU itself. We conclude by identifying lessons learned from the early experiments, and how they informed the subsequent construction of EU technology policy.

The exigencies of big science

Nuclear energy, civil aviation and space have always been 'prestige technologies' in which governments have had strong interests. Until the era of privatisation and liberalisation in the 1980s, states were also the primary – usually only – customers in these sectors. The pursuit of supersonic transport through Concorde, for example, was 'in scale and complexity . . . comparable to the USA's Apollo moonshot programme' (Clark and Gibson 1976: 2).

Crucially, the early stages of technological development in these sectors coincided with a period of strong economic growth in Europe. The boom years of the 1960s facilitated relatively generous public funding. The implicit assumption was that big was beautiful: it was taken for granted that advantages gained from exploiting economies of scale would far outweigh the disadvantages of complex, bureaucratic controls. In each of these sectors, too, we find echoes of some of the major underlying political themes of the day: European dependence on US technology, European governments jostling for position, the cosseting of national champions, and the policy ambitions of the European Commission.

Within each of these sectors there were also specific features favouring collaboration. Industrialists in the aerospace industry recognised the need for collaborative solutions from an early stage. The scale and complexities inherent in both civil and military aerospace were beyond the capabilities of any single European firm. Meanwhile, no government was prepared to see its own national champion disappear. Although a European framework did not emerge in all areas of aviation, it seemed a promising option for many projects, both civilian and military. Collaboration also seemed well suited to the space sector, as purely national options were recognised as untenable in view of the massive investments needed. In nuclear power, the potential dangers associated with waste and accidents militated in favour of international regulation and a collective search for peaceful applications. Thus a European framework appeared especially appropriate.

From a functionalist point of view, these sectors seemed prime candidates for sectoral integration in line with Monnet's vision of integration proceeding both horizontally (via the broad programme of the Common Market) and vertically, sector by sector. Yet, tension between West German free market scruples and (in particular) French interventionism constantly hampered integrated European efforts in these sectors. For example, West Germany was only persuaded to join the Euratom programme because it was sold as a package with the Treaty of Rome, with the guarantee of the opening up of French and Italian markets to German exports. Within Euratom, the Germans repeatedly favoured indirect action programmes that involved contracting R&D projects out to national laboratories. In contrast, the French and others preferred direct programmes, which involved the Community's own in-house Joint

Research Centre (JRC) laboratories. Political disagreements about what *kind* of European framework was most appropriate persisted in all of these sectors. The relatively neat, simple solution of granting the EC a mandate for action remained a non-starter.

The role of the European Community

A European Technological Community?

The three treaties establishing the European Communities – the European Coal and Steel Community (ECSC) Treaty of 1951, and the Treaties of Rome 1957 establishing the European Economic Community (EEC) and the European Atomic Energy Authority (Euratom) – allowed for the financing of R&D only in the fields of coal and steel, nuclear research and agriculture. Otherwise, until 1987 and the ratification of the Single European Act, Community actions relating to science and technology had to be undertaken under Article 235 of the Treaty of Rome:

> If action by the Community should prove necessary to attain . . . and this Treaty has not provided the necessary powers, the Council shall, acting unanimously on a proposal from the Commission, and after consulting the European Parliament, take appropriate measures.

Predictably, actions proposed under Article 235 often led to protracted negotiations lasting several years.

Yet, as early as the 1960s a debate arose over extending Community competence to technology and technological collaboration. Views were heavily influenced by the perceived emergence of a 'technology gap' between Europe and its competitors (especially the USA), as outlined above all by Servan-Schreiber (1967). Driven more by political calculations than close economic analysis, the debate gave rise to proposals for a European Technological Community. The Italians, for instance, toyed with the concept of a 'technological Marshall Plan', while the French proposed that the European Commission begin a study of the national industrial and research policies of the EEC Six with a view to developing common policies (see Guzzetti 1995: 35–9).

The question of the UK's membership of the EEC was part of the same debate. Britain's own view was that its technological expertise constituted its strongest hand as an applicant. This view was endorsed not only by the Commission (1967) but also by a Council of Europe (1967: 30) report, which was 'doubtful whether a European Technological Community could go it alone without the United Kingdom'. With the benefit of hindsight, it seems ironic that the UK was perceived to be the cornerstone of such a community given its relative economic decline over this period (see Gamble 1990). Yet, at the time British leadership of a European Technological Community aptly reflected the image of modernisation via the 'white heat of technology' promoted by the UK's Prime Minister, Harold Wilson. Indeed, Wilson (1971: 300) believed that his 1967 proposal for 'a drive to create a new technological community' in Europe and a later, similar plan put forward along with the UK's second formal application to join the EEC played a crucial role in convincing other Europeans that Britain 'meant business'.

A variety of proposals were considered as to the form a European Technological Community should take. Two of the more influential views emanated from Jean Monnet's Action Committee for a United States of Europe and Christopher Layton's (1969) book *European Advanced Technology: A Programme for Integration*. Monnet called for a new institution to promote technological cooperation to be established in conjunction with the Commission. Layton's plans focused on fifteen specific policy areas ranging from basic science to legal and financial support. His suggestions also included a European merger-promoting agency, common public purchasing, Community industrial R&D contracts, a European Advisory Council and a Technology Assessment Centre. Many of these ideas were later incorporated in Commission proposals that laid the foundations for what subsequently emerged as, on the one hand, a Community industrial policy, and on the other, its science and technology policies.

Industrial policy

While the EEC Treaty did not provide explicitly for science and technology, it did provide a range of policy powers that could be used to determine the regulatory framework and market conditions for European industry. They ranged from competition policy to the free movement of capital and labour and the EEC's customs union. They were not, however, subsumed into a general framework for industrial policy.

At the beginning of 1964, the EEC Council of Ministers set up a Medium Term Economic Policy Committee composed of experts from member states and representatives of the Commission. The aim was to begin to coordinate the (very different) economic policies that then held sway across the Six, focusing on the medium to long term. This initiative led, first, to the establishment of the Maréchal group to look at ideas for the coordination of policies on science and technology; and, second, to the establishment of a new Directorate-General for Industrial Affairs (DG III) in 1966–7. Within a few years, the debate had moved on to the point where the Commission (1970) decided the time was ripe for the tabling of an ambitious memorandum that became known as the Colonna Report. It called for the elimination of technical barriers to trade and the opening up of public purchasing; the harmonisation of European legal, fiscal and financial frameworks; the encouragement of transnational mergers; measures to speed industrial readjustment and adaptation; and a Community position on multinational corporations (Sharp and Shearman 1987: 26–27).

Not all of these policy aims were consistent with one another. While DG III promoted trans-European mergers, DG IV (Competition) scrutinised them with considerable scepticism. There were sharp disagreements among member states – particularly West Germany and France – over the Colonna Report's underlying philosophy. The Commission attempted to break the deadlock in 1971 with a proposal for an Industrial Policy Committee, to be convened jointly by the Council of Ministers and the Commission. However, it failed in the face of French opposition to the Commission's proposed role and the Council's preoccupation with (the 1973) enlargement. Meanwhile, proposals (also contained in the Colonna Report) for the creation of a European R&D Committee (CERD) and a European R&D Agency (ERDA) met with a cool response, especially from West Germany. Only towards the end of the 1970s, when Europe faced crises in its steel, ship-building and textiles industries, was DG III able to carve out a more active, assertive role for itself, and then mostly in declining industries.

Science and technology policy

The Maréchal Committee, created in 1965 to review national scientific and technological policies, reported to the first-ever meeting of the EEC Council of Science Ministers in 1967. It was given the green light to examine seven broad technological sectors – transport, oceanography, metallurgy, environmental problems, meteorology, and data processing and telecommunications – and explore (what appeared to be good) opportunities for collaborative research. Suggestions included plans for a high performance computer, standardisation of software, electronic applications for the motor car, a giant hovercraft and a gas turbine engine for trains (Sharp and Shearman 1987: 27).

However, these plans were shelved as the Community became consumed by the debate over Britain's application for EC membership and France's refusal to include the four candidate countries (the UK, Ireland, Denmark and Norway) in the exercise. Eventually, in December 1968, the Committee resumed its work under the leadership of Pierre Aigrain, French Delegate-General for Scientific and Technical Research. Over forty projects for European-owned companies (to avoid encouraging further US penetration) were put forward under the sectoral headings already identified. Comments were invited from the four applicant countries, together with Switzerland, Sweden, Austria, Spain and Portugal, and later from Finland, Greece, Yugoslavia and Turkey, in recognition of the importance of examining the technological issues in a broad European context. In November 1971 an outline plan was agreed for a programme of Cooperation in Science and Technology (COST). Seven initial projects were put in train at a cost of $21.5 million.

Such was the beginning of what became the COST programme. It survived into the 1990s to become a useful, if low key, framework for the preparation and implementation of European projects involving applied scientific research. Each of its nineteen members (all the European OECD member states and a representative of the Commission) enjoyed the same rights, whether or not a member of the European Community. The EC as an entity also participated in COST actions and projects. In 1989 COST was extended to include most Eastern and Central European countries. By then its projects spanned ten broad research areas, ranging from informatics and agriculture to oceanography and meteorology. By the mid-1990s it was estimated to be coordinating projects worth 400 million ECU (Commission 1994: 266).

However, COST was never really a Community programme. Its methodology remained strictly intergovernmental: it was given no independent organisation, but rather took the form of an international association with jointly determined obligations. For each project, cooperation was negotiated in a single, purpose-built agreement. Any member country could propose a COST project, and all research was be funded nationally, not by the Commission, although Community funding could be used to help meet the costs of coordination.

To summarise, early efforts to develop common industrial and technology policies were hampered by the tough policy choices facing Western Europe and the difficulties of securing consensus and launching joint actions. When progress was made, the agenda and membership were flexibly defined, and the detailed work did not command a high political profile. Above all, the lack of agreement on the overall thrust of industrial policy and the proper scope of the Community's competence meant that little came of proposals for a European Technological Community.

The nuclear sector

The experience of Euratom

The initial main objective of the European Atomic Energy Community (EURATOM) was to encourage the creation and growth of a European atomic industry based on a broadly conceived common programme of research (see Williams 1973; Guzzetti 1995). Four branches of the Joint Research Centre (JRC) were set up to coordinate activities in the field – at Karlsruhe (West Germany), Ispra (Italy), Geel (Belgium) and Petten (the Netherlands). Areas of research covered by Euratom agreements included fast breeder reactors, high-temperature gas reactors, nuclear ship propulsion, and nuclear applications in agriculture and medicine. In addition, Euratom took on important responsibilities for regulating civil nuclear energy and materials and ensuring safeguards.

The Commission's role in the early stages was essentially one of coordinator and facilitator. It tried to bring together the work of individual member states and avoid duplication of effort, while promoting the exchange of ideas and using the JRC to plug any gaps that emerged from the totality of national efforts. As a tide of optimism about the future potential of nuclear power swept across Europe, Euratom was transformed from a research programme into an industrial programme. By 1963 its main aim was no longer research and regulation, but the development of a new type of reactor that, it was hoped, would decisively strengthen Europe's competitive position *vis-à-vis* the Americans.

The shift from research to reactor design immediately brought problems, especially with Euratom's financial arrangements. No member state was prepared to sacrifice its own (national) programme. Nor was any prepared to back attempts to develop a common, distinct, European model. By 1967, the development of a joint nuclear reactor on a Community basis had been abandoned.

As Roger Williams (1973: 39) observed, Euratom's basic problem lay in the fact that, as both an organisation and set of objectives, it was based on mistaken assumptions. A predicted fuel shortage failed to materialise, while the novelty, potential and defence implications of nuclear power ensured a jealous guarding of national programmes. Euratom was effectively crippled when the French military denied it any effective role or influence in France's own nuclear development programme. More generally, firms running European power plants were in strong competition with each other and preferred to exploit their historic links with US firms rather than cooperating with their European counterparts. Deeply rooted patterns of national procurement, standards and regulation encouraged such conservatism. Given the high hopes that spurred its creation, Euratom was a major disappointment to enthusiasts of European technological collaboration

Fast breeder reactors

By 1968 the general context for collaboration had changed. The industrial application of fast breeder reactors was then considered imminent and Franco-German competition was intense. France withdrew from the Euratom programme to pursue its own national Phénix programme, leaving Germany, Belgium and the Netherlands to sign an intergovernmental agreement to construct their prototype, the SNR 300 in a collaboration known as the Debene (DEutschland-BElgium-NEtherlands) programme. Although the governmental go-ahead for construction of the SNR 300 was given in March 1972, the reactor took a very long time to complete. A major constraint was inherent in the German licensing system, which anti-nuclear groups exploited to good effect. One consequence was large cost escalations, which finally forced the Belgian and Dutch governments to impose a ceiling on their contributions, and Germany to accept the lion's share of the costs (Shearman 1986).

Still, the 1970s witnessed a gathering momentum of collaboration in the fast breeder reactor sector. In 1973, French, Italian and German utility companies agreed to collaborate on the construction of two new industrial power stations – the Superphénix in France and SNR 2 in Germany. With the Debene SNR 300 so much delayed, hopes focused largely on the French Superphénix programme, which aimed to exploit the benefits of reduced costs, more rapid technological development and a wider market. A joint Franco-Italian industrial partnership was established in 1978 to collaborate on its design. Subsequently, a reconfigured collaboration was agreed in a new Memorandum of Understanding in 1984, between France, Britain and Germany, for the construction over the next three decades of three European reactors. By this stage, the UK had decided against further investment in its own reactor design. Nevertheless, a combination of economic constraints, technological complexity and receding prospects for commercialisation dogged Superphénix, and it was essentially abandoned in 1997.

Fusion research

Nuclear fusion is shorthand for experimental techniques designed to generate virtually pollution-free energy by mimicking the sun. Research into plasma physics and high temperature fusion started in the 1950s and was incorporated into the Euratom Treaty in 1958. At that time, activities at the Community level consisted mainly of exchange of information between national programmes, but as time went by the Commission increasingly became involved in sponsoring research activities, mainly by contracting out research to its various associated national laboratories. The long life span and uncertainties of the research, and the heavy investments required in equipment and manpower, made a sharing of activities the only sensible route. Over time, the EU's fusion programme involved a wide spectrum of laboratories across Europe, including Sweden (prior to its membership of the EU) and Switzerland (a non-member). Euratom provided grants for the exchange of scientists and, from an early point, a real European dimension emerged in the programme.

The West European approach to fusion research from the late 1960s onwards focused on advancing and scaling up the so-called Tokamak reactors, developed initially by the Soviet Union. Negotiations in the 1970s over the design and location (in Germany or the UK) of a new facility based on the Tokamak design were long and fraught. Eventually the UK (Culham) was chosen and the Joint European Torus (JET) programme got underway in 1978. The project was completed on time and to budget by 1983, when the reactor began experiments. In 1991, for the first time ever in a laboratory, fusion power in the megawatt range was produced at JET for a few seconds. By 1997, JET had achieved the breakthrough of producing sufficient power to supply a small town (for one second). While these achievements might seem modest ones to the layperson, they acted to vindicate a programme that was pursuing profoundly difficult technical goals and showed that, in many areas of physics performance and fusion technology, Europe was in the vanguard of research and development (Shaw 1997; Guzzetti 1995: 61–6).

Although the first JET programme formally came to an end in 1992, the EU programme of research into fusion continued, with activities focusing on the development of safe, environmentally sound, prototype reactors – the so-called Next Step activities. The main effort was tied into the international programme ITER (International Thermo-Nuclear Reactor) with the US, Russia and Japan. As before, it involved both collective research on the part of a great number of nationally-based laboratories associated with the fusion programme, and work at the joint undertaking at Culham. Considerable uncertainties surrounded ITER, particularly given its huge cost (estimated variously at 5 to 9 billion ECU) and US concerns about its budget. Nevertheless, Community expenditures (which formed a part of Framework programme expenditures from 1987 onwards) amounted to over 200 million ECU a year (Commission 1994: 217).

In short, looking across the nuclear sector as a whole, there has been a mixed record of collaboration. Progress towards combined European efforts has been held back repeatedly by clashes of national philosophy and interest. Even though a clear Community competence has existed in this sector for longer than in any other, with the exception of fusion research, some of the most important achievements have been organised outside the EU itself.

The aviation sector

Early experiments in collaboration

In the 1960s it was apparent that small-scale producers had no chance of competing in the major civil aviation markets alongside American producers such as Boeing or McDonnell Douglas, who benefited from large-scale US civil and defence aerospace programmes. As a result, European governments and industry were forced to look to collaboration. The Franco-German Transall and Atlantic projects of the 1950s marked the first tentative steps down this road. The Anglo-French Concorde was the first attempt at a joint project entailing a large-scale technical challenge. Experience was consolidated with the Anglo-French helicopter package and Jaguar project, which were successful, and the Anglo-French Variable Geometry combat aircraft, which was not. By the end of the 1960s, confidence in European collaboration had increased to the point where the UK, Germany and Italy could launch the Tornado, the first truly challenging aircraft project to be undertaken by three as opposed to two partners.

Broad lessons were learned from these projects, which may seem obvious today but were less so at the time. Concorde was especially important because of the major psychological impact it had on British perceptions of European collaboration. After the Anglo-French Treaty was signed in 1962, both parties were bound to the project by treaty obligations and domestic political considerations. After major redesigns, and huge cost escalations, only 14 Concorde aircraft were actually produced – 7 each for British Airways and Air France. All had to be subsidised heavily in terms of both capital and running costs. However, the Concorde experience gave British Aerospace and Aérospatiale sharpened awareness of the methodology of collaboration, which was to prove crucial in judgements by both companies and governments about the structure of successor projects.

Airbus

With the post-war development of the jet engine, the cost of developing and launching new aircraft increased dramatically. In turn, this caused major changes in industrial structure. The production of a new generation of jet aircraft was only economical in markets where scale economies could be exploited to the full. One effect was that American producers enjoyed huge cost advantages over their European rivals by exploiting their large civil and military market. The solution to Europe's competitive decline, as urged by the British Plowden Report of 1965 (UK Government 1965: 92–3), was comprehensive European collaboration. The report called for the creation of 'a European aircraft industry, with Europe as its basic market', dismissing collaboration with American firms on the grounds that they had no need to collaborate.

Thus was born Airbus Industrie. Eventually, it was agreed that Rolls-Royce would provide the engine design and the French would lead in airframe design. West Germany became a full partner and joined the UK and France in signing a Memorandum of Understanding in September 1967 to develop the A300 aircraft. The three national airlines were each to buy 25 of the aircraft and no party was to support a competing project. Total development costs were estimated at £190m with an in-service date targeted for 1973 (Shearman 1997: 299).

Problems emerged quite quickly. Changes in the A300 design escalated programme costs, and the British pulled out of the consortium in 1968. The French and Germans were left to develop the new, smaller A300B: a twin-engined, mid-range aircraft that neatly filled a gap in the market left by the US manufacturers (Boeing, Lockheed and McDonnell Douglas), who concentrated their efforts on the long-haul market (Tyson 1992: 188).

Unfortunately the delivery of the A300B coincided with the 1973–4 recession. By March 1974 only 20 aircraft had been sold. The West German government worried about escalating costs, but the determination of the French and the importance of Airbus to the German industry prevented cutbacks. The company was able to weather the recession by producing 'whitetails': aircraft that no airline had yet ordered (hence no airline logo on the tail-fin) but which were financed by public funds. When the global economy recovered in 1975, Airbus had an inventory lead over its American competitors and could deliver from stock. Its sales that year exceeded those of the American-built DC10 and the Lockheed 1011 combined (Hayward 1989: 53–5).

However, Airbus Industrie clearly needed to follow the lead of Boeing and McDonnell Douglas and develop a family of airliners if it was to compete. By the mid-1970s, Airbus had developed a second aircraft, the A310. The Spanish firm Casa along with the Dutch company Fokker became associates, a move that helped cover costs. Meanwhile, the British government favoured cooperation with Boeing, but the British airframe industry preferred a European strategy. Forced to decide, the British government eventually announced in 1978, as the A310 was launched, that British Aerospace (BAe) would rejoin Airbus Industrie as a full partner from January 1979. Within a year, Airbus-manufactured planes had been bought by 40 airlines: a total of 292 aircraft had been sold, with 157 options (Shearman 1997: 300). Nevertheless, American producers still accounted for 85 per cent of the world's operational commercial jets (Tyson 1992: 189).

The next Airbus, the 150-seat A320, introduced several innovations (including fly-by-wire technology) that were designed to expand Airbus's market share by cutting its fuel consumption and personnel requirements. The problem was to persuade government sponsors to invest 1.5 billion ECU at a time when launch costs on the A300 and A310 were still to be repaid. As ever, the French were strong supporters of the new venture, but the West German and British governments remained non-committal until early 1984, by which time the A320 had acquired a total of 88 sales and options.

The Airbus consortium, however, had even more ambitious plans. In 1987 it launched the A330/A340 programme. These new models shared the same basic Airbus airframe, but the A330 had two engines to fly 330 passengers 5000 miles; the A340 had four engines and fewer seats but could fly 7000 miles non-stop. The two aircraft showed a common development programme and were launched in the mid-1990s. By this time, Airbus Industrie had achieved its target of 30 per cent of the world market for large airliners, mainly at the expense of McDonnell Douglas (Hayward 1994: 163).

There is little dispute about the success of Airbus Industrie in the market place. It has helped Europe to maintain a world class aerospace industry and outclassed its American rivals in important respects. Collaboration had been essential to Airbus's success, with the respective partners progressively integrating the production process as they advanced down the learning curve of cooperation and developed trust in each other's capabilities. This dynamic of cooperation led Martin Bangemann, European Commissioner for Industry for most of the 1990s, to describe Airbus as '*the* model' for European industrial cooperation (quoted in Hayward 1994: 63). Nevertheless, as German pressures in the mid-1990s for a greater share of assembly operations illustrated, the *juste retour* mentality still lay just below the surface. Airbus remained an inter-firm and inter-governmental consortium, with agreed production shares reflecting financial commitments to the consortium. Despite European concerns about the merger of McDonnell Douglas and Boeing, and subsequent moves to transform Airbus into an actual limited company by the year 2000, it was unlikely ever to be free of hard bargaining between self-interested states and firms.

The space sector

Early activities in European collaboration in the space sector involved the emergence of two European frameworks: the European Launcher Development Organisation (ELDO) and the European Space Research Organisation (ESRO). Both were foils in a generally comprehensive attempt to develop a common European space policy. Established in 1962, ELDO aimed to challenge the US monopoly over rocket launchers. ESRO was a non-commercial scientific organisation that aimed to promote collaboration in space research and related technologies.

ESRO prompted a spirited and, at this date, rare attempt at European collaboration in electronics. In 1969, the Eurodata consortium – involving ICL, CII, Philips, AEG-Telefunken, Saab and Olivetti – was established to tender for ESRO's computer requirements. However, the consortium collapsed under pressure from the West German government, largely because Siemens had been left out. A subsequent attempt in 1973 to bring Siemens, CII and Bull together under the Unidata umbrella was similarly unsuccessful, with tension between the French and the German governments undermining the alliance (Dosi 1983: 233).

Meanwhile, weak governmental commitment to ELDO was reflected in long delays and constant bickering between the French

and British. In contrast, ESRO was quite successful in fostering collaboration in basic scientific research. In any event, by 1970 a
Franco-German partnership managed to launch the Symphonie
satellite using the ELDO launcher and ESRO's telemetry. Although
not commercially viable, Symphonie did have the effect of facilitating the development of a more coherent European space policy.
The European Space Conference in 1973 merged ELDO and
ESRO into one and agreed a new programme (Krige *et al.* 1997:
203–4).

The European Space Agency (ESA) thus became the primary
framework for civilian space collaboration in Western Europe. Its
membership was wide, extending to most countries in Western
Europe including the UK, with Canada participating as a 'cooperating member'. Governments and public agencies were the prime
contractors, because many of the early applications were used to
provide public goods or acted as trailblazers for commercial applications. ESA became the cornerstone of most national programmes.
The specialised character of space technology, and of ESA as a
functionally-oriented framework, helped produce a coherence of
purpose. The result was a closely-knit community of policy-makers,
scientists, engineers and industrialists.

ESA managed two types of research programme – mandatory
and optional. The mandatory programme, to which all members
were obliged to contribute, funded the overhead costs of the organisation and the basic science programme, which extended from earth
observation satellites to space probes. In the 1990s, it employed
approximately 2000 scientists, accounting for about 20 per cent of
ESA's annual 3 billion ECU budget. The remaining 80 per cent of
the budget consisted of optional items to which member states
signed up as they wished, with rules on contribution and expenditure based explicitly on *juste retour*. For example, France's 50 per cent
interest in Ariane was rewarded by the placement of half of all contracts in France (Commission 1994: 267–8). The main programme
within the 'optional' category was the Ariane space programme,
consuming over 50 per cent of the budget. Ariane was the most
obvious and visible success of ESA, despite the setback in 1996,
when a prototype Ariane 5 rocket blew up on launch. The optional
budget also supported Europe's contributions towards manned
space stations and telecommunications satellite systems.

Like Airbus, ESA became something of a model framework for

technological collaboration, thanks partly to its success in achieving European autonomy in space. However, its success is easily over-stated. Proactive French leadership had much to do with ESA's early achievements, especially Ariane. In the 1990s, considerable tension built up between the main players, with the UK and Germany each taking a more assertive line. Moreover, the ESA had a minimal role once collaboration moved from the experimental to the commercial, with Arianespace effectively managing commercial launches.

Arguably ESA is no more than a conglomeration of interest groups, and as such is not a particularly effective vehicle for promot-ing the collective interests of the European space industry, especially in competition with American suppliers. It has neither the instru-ments nor the legal power to control market conditions within Europe for satellite telecommunications and broadcasting. It natu-rally hits difficulties whenever it approaches the boundary between civil and military applications, where its charter and the sensitivities of its neutral members inhibit development. All in all, given these features, it is surprising how much ESA has achieved in promoting the development of European space capabilities.

The lessons learned

Early experiments in European technological collaboration thus produced a mixed collection of ventures and outcomes. Attempts to develop collaboration on a (European) Community basis, promoted by the Commission, had largely disappointing results. Arguments between governments, differences of national policies and priorities, and difficulties in establishing effective management formulae were all major constraints. Even so, the European Communities in gener-al, and Euratom in particular, did much to frame the debates and promote transnational contacts. Efforts to create a European Technological Community were not successful, but they bore fruit later in the form of specific consortia such as ESA and JET, and in the new programmes in the 1980s.

Meanwhile, initiatives on a restricted basis among a few partners began to emerge as the primary means of promoting collaboration. Concorde, although a commercial failure, succeeded on technologi-cal and organisational levels. It was an important ice-breaker for reluctant French and British aviation companies and provided valuable opportunities for systems and electronics companies to work together. Its psychological legacy was significant, not least in the way the project alerted financiers (public and private) to the high risks of such investments and highlighted the need to think rigorously about the commercial implications of collaboration. More broadly, differences in language, educational training, national procedures and policies were shown not to be insuperable barriers.

Genuinely common objectives – or at least compatible self-interests – were essential foundations for success. The proposed European reactor, for example, foundered on this rock. Yet, complex projects such as Tornado were successfully managed at the international level. JET, Airbus and ESA all reached quite mature phases of collaboration. All involved a step-by-step progression, and demonstrated the importance of mutual trust between partners. Each illustrated the strength and utility of functionally specific frameworks for collaboration in sectors where go-it-alone national approaches were simply not viable.

Perhaps above all, the 1960s and 1970s showed that European technological collaboration was not easy, especially when national policies were dominated by 'national champions'. A strong Franco-German axis was often crucial, although continuing tensions between French interventionism and German commitment to the free market often inhibited the emergence of a collective European approach. However, in technological collaboration, as in nearly all other facets of European integration, experience showed that when France and Germany decided to do something together, Europe was almost always changed.

In this context, an equally striking theme of the 1960s and 1970s was the recurrent ambivalence of British governments and companies towards European collaboration. When the British joined in, they often did so late and as a junior partner. If things went badly, they often chose to drop out and blame the captain. Then, when things started to go well, they asked to be readmitted.

In the background throughout was the relationship between the USA and Europe. The acceptable extent of US penetration of the European market, how to access US technology without becoming dependent, and whether European initiatives should include American partners became key questions. They were carried through to the 1980s, with the added complications of powerful

Japanese competition, the rise of South-East Asia and a new complex of questions surrounding the process of globalisation.

Lessons from collaborative experience led ultimately to principles or criteria to guide future collaborative ventures. One such criterion concerned the rate of commercial return on investment, both public or private. While Airbus and Arianespace were considered commercial successes, in both cases the amount of public funding sunk in development costs was vast, as the Americans were only too anxious to point out in relation to Airbus (see Neven and Seabright 1995). Moreover, both would have collapsed had this ready source of 'patient' capital not been available, just as many US projects, from the microchip to the Boeing 747, would have collapsed but for 'patient' capital in the form of US military expenditure. On the other hand, fast breeder reactors illustrated only too well the degree to which high-profile, long-term projects could swallow resources and yield nothing beyond transient 'jobs for the boys'.

There were, however, demonstrable learning curves in collaboration itself. In the Airbus programme, for example, the A300 was the first step in a collaborative learning curve that established Airbus Industrie as the centre for large-scale civil aircraft production in Europe. The A320 confirmed that Airbus was a force to be reckoned with in global competition. The mixed records of ELDO and ESRO were in their turn critical in determining the shape of ESA, which ended up being far more effective. Even fast breeder reactor collaboration revealed a learning curve, although a technological and managerial one rather than commercial one and one that essentially perished amid the harsh commercial realities of the 1980s.

Similarly, the interweaving of governmental and industrial roles proved significant. As one commentator on Airbus remarked, its achievements were 'largely the result of bilateral or trilateral contacts and negotiations between both officials and industrialists. Both were indispensable' (Layton 1986: 189). At the same time, one of the most important lessons of early European experiments was the need to build in scope for review and reappraisal, even withdrawal. Without such provisions, the political logic of collaboration ran the risk of encouraging expensive white elephants, or at least of discouraging adaptation and innovation. Once created, new policy networks in specific sectors of technology threatened to run away with policy, unless they were subject to explicit political controls.

Thus, Europe's early postwar experiments in collaborative R&D produced few technological or commercial successes, but *did* at least yield a clear set of principles to guide the subsequent construction of new European programmes. The 1980s proved to be a decade in which the scepticism of earlier years receded, and renewed faith emerged in the ability of industrial collaboration to give a fillip to Europe's competitiveness. The early 1980s witnessed a rash of government-backed initiatives to stimulate joint R&D between companies, at both national and Community levels. It is relatively easy to demonstrate how past lessons informed their construction. To explain, in theoretical terms, *why* they were constructed is a more complex analytical task, which we confront in Chapter 3.

3

Competition, Collaboration and Integration

The lessons learned from early collaborative R&D experiments had begun to sink in by the time new debates arose in the 1980s about Europe's (apparently) declining technological competitiveness, and what to do about it. By the middle of the decade, a critical mass of European governments had been persuaded to believe that the continent's competitive crisis required a general relaunch of the Community and a radical programme of deregulation and liberalisation. The EU's enhanced policy role as a promoter of innovation was, in important respects, boosted by the 1992 project. A crucial element of the project was a political commitment to reduce state aids to industry, an important slice of which subsidised R&D. Partly because they promised to compensate for new restrictions on national policy actions, the Framework programme and EUREKA became viewed as important policy tools in a more general effort to kick-start Europe's high-tech industries out of the doldrums of the national champion days.

The relaunch of European integration via the 1992 project provoked new theoretical debates about why and under what circumstances states opted for cooperation instead of national solutions. Different economic and political theories offer alternative explanations both for the transformation of the European Community and the emergence of European technology policy. In this chapter, we survey these models before considering (in later chapters) the emergence and development of the Framework programme and EUREKA.

The economics of technology policy

Against the backdrop of the 'new' political economy of RTD noted in Chapter 1, technological innovation has become an increasingly complex process. It typically involves many economic and social factors, and a wide range of individuals and firms. It is a *process* because it is about the transformation of knowledge and information into new ways of doing or making things. Private firms play an especially important part in the process because they are (usually) the key institutions for transforming knowledge into commercially viable products and processes.

Technology policy is about promoting technological innovation. As such, it falls within the wider scope of industrial policy. Traditionally, economists have had little time for intervention by public authorities to promote innovation. Adam Smith and his contemporaries promoted the doctrine of *laissez-faire* mainly because they perceived the costs of interfering with the workings of markets to be much greater than the costs to society of leaving markets to operate in their own way. In particular, Smith worried that governments that intervened would be 'captured' by special interest groups with narrow, selfish agendas. Modern neoclassicals remain highly sceptical of any form of intervention. The notion that governments can best guess what is, or is not, good for industry is an anathema to this school of thought.

Technology policy and market failure

The one area where even neoclassicals accept the need for intervention is where there are market failures. The most obvious case is that of monopoly or monopolistic practices, when it is widely accepted that the state should intervene and regulate in order to prevent the abuse of monopoly power. Basic research is seen as another case of market failure because there is no incentive for a private firm or individual to invest in it. Its output – scientific knowledge – once discovered, is available for anyone to use. Firms cannot stop people from using knowledge or ideas in the same way as they can, for example, stop someone from owning a car unless they have paid for it. The market therefore will not provide basic research. Unless the state steps in and supports it, it will not be undertaken.

Applied research is a different matter (see Freeman and Soete

1997). The application of research to developing new products and processes yields results that can be *both* exclusive and appropriable (by patent and copyright) and can therefore make a direct contribution to profits. However, this distinction – between basic research as a public good provided by the state, and applied research as a private good – assumes that the costs of applying basic research are themselves negligible. In other words, it assumes that basic research is like a manna from heaven: it is a free good that can be picked up and used by anyone without further cost or effort.

The linear and chain-link models

The notion of scientific research as a free-flowing source of new ideas, which accumulates as a stock of knowledge on which the entire economy may draw, fits well with the *linear* model of science and technology that prevailed in the 1950s and 1960s. It neatly compartmentalised the relationships between invention (science) and innovation (technology) and suggested that research, development, production and marketing of new technologies follow a well-defined time sequence).

By the 1980s, the innovation process was perceived as being much more complex, and characterised not by linear relationships but by continuous interaction and feedback. Successful innovation depended on linkages between upstream and downstream research and on extensive feedback between the science, technology and process phases of development (see Figure 3.1).

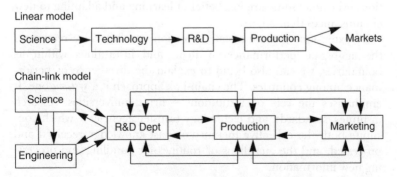

FIGURE 3.1   The linear model of innovation and the chain-link model

According to the 'chain-link' model of innovation (Kline and Rosenberg 1986), innovating firms *cannot* apply new scientific ideas without cost or effort (as implied by the free-flowing 'manna from heaven' notion). Rather, they must invest in up-to-date R&D facilities and employ scientists and engineers who understand state of the art developments. Moreover, in developing new products and processes, firms do not just pluck new scientific ideas off the shelf, but rather add to them. Their value therefore incorporates a good deal of know-how, which is 'embedded' in the firm itself. Such knowledge (for example, how to tackle a particular type of problem in a new product) is acquired over many years of practice, experiment and interaction between different parts of the firm. It is *tacit* in that it is not written down (codified) but passed on by word of mouth and learning by doing among those working in the firm. Tacit knowledge gives existing firms and organisations inherent advantages over newcomers trying to break into their industry.

The importance of the chain-link model for technology policy should not be underestimated. It describes a world in which firms are no longer the passive recipients of knowledge, but rather active participants in *learning*. Innovation requires a firm to have in-house or accessible capabilities that can understand new scientific ideas and translate them into its own production processes. Each firm has different ways of performing such translation, and develops its own routines and ideas of best practice. These routines are passed on to successive generations of manager by word of mouth and company codes of practice, which tend to change slowly over time. They help to explain the divergence in the performance of firms and institutions over time: some are just better at learning and adapting to new circumstances than others.

By extension, because a state or region's performance represents the aggregate performance of firms and institutions within its boundaries, we can also begin to explain the divergence of performance among countries. The chain-link approach is a *systemic* one. It emphasises the role of institutions – firms, universities, research institutes, standards, and technology transfer agencies – which constitute both the collective memory of past knowledge received and processed, and the guardians of routines for handling and processing new information.

Systems of innovation

Out of this systemic approach to innovation have come ideas about 'national systems of innovation' (Freeman, 1986; Lundvall, 1992; Nelson 1993). Each country has its own system of innovation, which has built up over time and embodies practices and institutions which, although adaptable, have their roots in the past and reflect elements of heritage and culture. The UK, for example, has traditionally undertaken much of its basic research in university science departments, where postgraduate students work side by side with researchers and professors. France, by contrast, conducts most of its research in specialist research institutes (often located on university campuses), and thus separates teaching from research. Germany has a mix of the two, with its highly regarded Max Planck Institutes, but a tradition of postgraduate study in universities. Germany also has a tradition of technical training through apprenticeship for non-graduates in which most firms participate.

Such national differences are reflected in the ease with which new knowledge and practices are passed on. Transferring new scientific ideas from the science base to industry is vital for innovation. Thus training graduate students in leading-edge research to work in R&D laboratories is an important means of transferring scientific knowledge (Nelson 1982). The quality of apprentice training is important in the diffusion of new engineering technologies.

In this context, the emergence of the European technology policy initiatives in the 1980s both challenged existing institutions at the national level and began to map out a new set of institutions at the supranational level. It raised questions about how far there was, or could be, a European system of innovation, and how far collaborative policy initiatives could contribute to forging such a system. It also raised questions about the adaptability of a European system. As with any set of institutions, considerable forces of inertia could be expected to emerge once such a system was established. In this regard, the economics of innovation, with its emphases on learning and adaptation, link very closely with the 'new institutionalist' approaches of a recent generation of political scientists (March and Olsen 1989; Bulmer 1994b).

Technology, trade and competition policies

The chain-link model has implications for trade and competition policies, as well as for technology policy. The model assumes that technology is knowledge and information, rather than just products and processes. It is embodied in people and institutions as much as in equipment, and passed on by learning by doing as much as through publications and blueprints. As such, the whole edifice of comparative advantage on which international trade theory is based begins to slip. Technology is no longer infinitely mobile; rather its use depends upon the 'absorptive capacity' (Cohen and Levinthal 1989) of any economy, or its mix of skills, capabilities and institutions. Sophisticated technologies need highly skilled technicians who are capable of understanding and using them. A highly educated, skilled workforce combined with an infrastructure of institutions (universities, telecoms facilities) capable of supporting high-tech activities become key assets. Government policies in relation to the provision of such capabilities and facilities are important in helping to develop competitive advantage.

In this context, dynamic economies of scale where learning by doing is important mean there are benefits in being the first firm to innovate and gain these 'first-mover' advantages. 'Strategic trade' theorists such as Krugman (1987) argue that in a world where trade is characterised more by products such as aircraft than by products such as wheat, comparative advantage becomes a very different concept from the one held by neoclassical economists. Cumulative economies of scale – increasing output to reduce the cost of each unit produced – of the sort gained by Boeing, for example, from its large military orders, can be used to justify European public action to support Airbus.

Technology policy thus becomes intertwined with both trade and competition policy. In this context, followers of Schumpeter (1947) argue that an element of monopoly profit – or, at least, an efficiently policed patent system – is necessary to support R&D activities. Others – particularly organisational scientists (Liebenstein 1987; Porter 1990) – argue that competition between large firms is necessary to stimulate innovation. Tensions between these different visions have been reflected clearly in the history of European technology policy, particularly in contrasting French and German attitudes towards intervention, and later, in the twin tracks of policy –

increased collaboration alongside increased competition – that emerged in Europe in the 1980s.

Markets, networks and collaboration

The nature of innovation networks

We have seen that systemic links arise between science and technology within the economy, and have stressed the interactive nature of those linkages. The relationships between firms and researchers, formal and informal, can be characterised as a set of networks. The chain-link model of innovation, for example, suggests that networks for given technologies or industrial sectors revolve around three main axes or 'poles' – a scientific pole, which generates knowledge, trains personnel and produces papers; a technological pole, which generates new products, pilot projects, patents, standards, and so on; and a market pole, which encompasses users, distributors, and suppliers.

The creation of linkages between the different participants involves a series of intermediaries – which may be either 'disembodied' in the form of books or equipment, or else 'embodied' in trained and experienced personnel. Such intermediaries may be needed to translate scientific ideas and information into a form that can be understood or taken up in another domain around a different pole. Again, trained scientists and engineers are necessary, not only to promote and develop new products and processes in their own field, but also to enable the diffusion of innovation to take place. In this sense they are important 'transmission agents' for scientific information (Callon 1989). Where there is ready communication between networks, information passes easily from one domain to another. In other cases, when transmission agents do not exist or are ineffective, it may be difficult for information to disseminate.

Recent developments in the European pharmaceutical industry illustrate the point. Chemists had dominated the industry since the early 1900s, and did not readily accept or appreciate the importance of new developments in biology. They did not act as effective transmission agents for these developments, and Europe's old-established (and very successful) chemical/pharmaceutical companies were slow to take up the new biotechnologies (see Galimberti 1993.)

Networks, markets and hierarchies

Whereas sociologists such as Callon (1989) look on networks in terms of linkages between people, economists look on networks as linkages between firms. Networks facilitate collaboration. The theoretical question becomes: why collaborate when the firm could either transact business through the market or, for that matter, via merger, as separate departments within the hierarchy of one firm (see Coase 1937; Williamson 1975, 1985)? From this perspective, networks constitute a hybrid form of organisation, lying half-way between markets and hierarchies.

Looking at networks and collaboration just as a hybrid form of organisation, however, fails completely to capture the dynamics of knowledge exchange. As Chesnais (1988: 84) argues:

> The [increasing] complexity of scientific and technological inputs, the uncertainty of economic conditions and the risks associated with uncertain technological trajectories have reduced the advantages of vertical and horizontal integration and made hierarchies a less efficient way of responding to market imperfections. But the need to respond to and exploit market imperfections in technology has also increased, and has pushed inter-firm agreements to the forefront of corporate strategy.

Powell (1990: 13) goes further:

> Networks can be complex: they involve neither the explicit criteria of the market nor the well-organised routines of the hierarchy. A basic assumption of network relationships is that *parties are mutually dependent upon resources controlled by another, and that there are gains to be had by pooling resources* (emphasis added).

Strategic alliances and globalisation

The term strategic alliance is often used to describe network relationships involving high-tech partners. Such alliances have become a common feature of the increasing internationalisation or globalisation of production and trading relationships since the 1970s. As was stressed in Chapter 1, globalisation has been accompanied (and indeed influenced) by profound changes in technology. The emergence of electronics and information and communications technologies (ICT) as pervasive new technologies affecting the entire socioeconomic system has had a number of important consequences. First, new technologies have demanded not only new equipment, but also *new skills and new knowledge.* Initially firms possessing the required knowledge and skills are few. Networking enables these scarce skills and resources to be shared between a number of players.

Second, the emergence of a *radical and pervasive* new technology also creates considerable *turbulence* within the economic system. The old certainties go, and in their place are a new set of uncertainties. To use again the example of the pharmaceutical industry, while the new biotechnology was opening doors to new and innovative drugs and therapies by the late 1990s, in the short run it posed great uncertainties in terms both of technical feasibility and commercial viability. Confronted by such uncertainties, existing companies sought to limit their exposure, using strategic alliances to pool risks and to hedge bets.

Third, new technologies also mean *new players,* as the cumulative advantage enjoyed by the old players in the old technologies breaks down, allowing new entrants into the game. The development of microelectronics, for example, allowed companies such as Texas Instruments, Intel and Microsoft to emerge as new global players, while the firms that had dominated the electromechanical age, such as RCA and Westinghouse, were pushed aside. The new entrants were often small companies – at least initially – closely linked to a person or group of people specialising in the new technology areas and frequently were spin-offs either from university departments or larger corporate labs, as in the cases of Apple or Netscape. The firms were highly flexible and adaptable. When successful, they grew rapidly, challenging the market dominance of the older players. Such developments intensified the pressures of competition on the older players, increasing the uncertainties and skill mismatches *and* encouraging them to seek alliances with the new entrants to help adapt and update structures.

Fourth, the emergence of new players among firms was mirrored by the *emergence of new states as key players on the international scene.* The first industrial revolution at the end of the eighteenth century saw Britain emerge as the world's dominant industrial power. It began to be challenged at the end of the nineteenth century with the rise of the (then) new industries of chemicals, steel, shipbuilding and cars. The newly industrialising countries of the era were Germany and the US. Germany's militaristic ambitions and subsequent defeat in two world wars ensured that, of the two, the United States became more dominant. Now with the approach of the third millennium, the hegemonic position of the US is being challenged by the newly emerging industrial powers of South-East Asia, first Japan and then, increasingly, China and the tiger economies of South Korea, Taiwan, Hong Kong and Singapore (Zysman and Schwartz 1998). Much of the 'networking' activity observed among firms represents a repositioning of capabilities in the light of these developments.

Finally, the gradual liberalisation of product and capital markets gave *large multinational corporations a free hand to locate activities where both costs were lowest and markets growing fastest.* Labour-intensive industries such as textiles and clothing migrated to low-cost labour countries in South-East Asia. High-tech industries often sought to establish a presence in all major markets, either by the direct establishment of subsidiaries or, when this was difficult, through links with local firms. Many strategic alliances were, in fact, mechanisms for market access rather than technology access (Senker *et al.* 1998).

These developments have been self-reinforcing. Competition increases and firms focus on innovation, which in turn drives the pace of technological change. As it accelerates, product life cycles decrease, and R&D costs and uncertainties increase. Even large multinationals hesitate to go it alone. The pace of change is such that they need constantly to access new knowledge and skills, to introduce new models and updates on old models, and yet preserve enough flexibility to move out of an area if, over time, it proves to be non-viable. For all these reasons, it makes sense not to make irreversible decisions, to limit exposure to risk and to share heavy upfront costs that may not be retrieved. Strategic partnering provides a mechanism that meets all these requirements.

It can be argued that it has all happened before. International cross-licensing between large multinationals has been around for a long time. The 1930s, another period of technological turbulence, also saw the establishment of joint agreements and research consortia in the new industries of chemicals and heavy electrical engineering (Freeman and Soete 1997). However, the late twentieth-century wave of inter-firm agreements involved much wider and more flexible arrangements. Even authors such as Porter and Fuller, who were sceptics about how much had changed, saw a qualitative difference in inter-firm relationships, and a new emphasis on operational flexibility (Porter and Fuller 1986). The question was how far such relationships were fleeting or lasting. Was this new collaborative networking model the way of the future?

There was no definitive answer to this question by the late 1990s. Nevertheless, it was clear that over the course of the 1980s and early 1990s, an increasing number of firms, particularly those in new technology areas, were involved in extensive networks. The EU's collaborative programmes and EUREKA played an important part in catalysing such partnerships. By the end of the 1990s, networking had developed its own momentum. It was arguable whether any further programme of encouragement was needed, particularly one limited to European firms.

Explaining the politics of European technology policy

If the new economics of technological change have challenged traditional, neoclassical assumptions, the *politics* of European technology policies have also provoked considerable debate among scholars interested in testing theories of political integration and decision-making. Students of EU technology policy find it useful to conceptualise the Union as a system of 'multi-level governance' (Marks *et al.* 1996a, 1996b). Understanding the EU requires 'dissecting' the Union as a political system and distinguishing between different levels of governance, where different kinds of decision are taken (see Peterson 1995a). It seems especially important to make such distinctions in technology policy because here, more than in other policy domains:

> a gulf exists between political executives and administrative agencies and each has its own distinct form of rationality. In the political realm, choices are largely determined by the will to remain in power. In the administrative realm, particularly where innovation policy is concerned, choices are largely determined by technical knowledge. Links between these two realms are often tenuous. (Peterson 1993b: 205)

The high politics of RTD

As the EU's major collaborative programmes were launched in the mid-1980s, proponents of a stronger, more integrated Europe viewed technology policy with considerable enthusiasm. Technology policy was seen as a sector ripe for an amalgamation of national policy efforts. Through fora such as the Big 12 Round Table and the Gyllenhammer Group, Europe's most powerful industrialists rallied behind new collaborative programmes. The economic arguments to support integrated policies had 'bite', particularly because EU governments were about to sign on to a radical liberalisation programme to dynamise the internal market. Collaborative, cross-border R&D would promote, or 'flank' in the EU's jargon, the internal market's completion. Public subsidies for R&D would help compensate for reduced national aids to industry.

The *strategic* justification for an EU technology policy seemed clear: national champion policies had fragmented capabilities; only by pooling efforts could the EU hope to achieve the economies of scale and critical mass needed to compete with the Americans and Japanese. In political terms, technology policy was mostly uncontroversial, technocratic and marked by problems of competitiveness that were both severe and collective. It seemed a perfect candidate-area for integration, which would beget further integration, as predicted by neofunctionalist theory.

Neofunctionalism's central assumption is that integration proceeds exponentially as successful common policies in relatively depoliticised areas create 'spillover' pressures for further integration (see Haas 1958; Lindberg 1963). Some spillover pressures are functional in that integration of one area of an economy produces technical pressures that generate demands for further integration. For example, collaborative R&D programmes lead firms to develop new technical processes together, thus creating pressures for pan-European standards. The creation of a single market unleashes pressures for a single currency.

However, neofunctionalists also identify a different, more political type of spillover: the shifting of political loyalties from the national to the European level. Supranational institutions, such as the European Commission or Parliament (EP), play a role in identifying the next steps towards integration and the benefits that might accrue. Thus, the EP's 1984 Draft Treaty on European Union or the

Commission's White Paper on the Internal Market were only the public manifestations of intensive campaigns of alliance-building and activism in search of support for a relaunch of European integration, which could restart Europe's economy. Important interest groups, such as the Big 12 Round Table, saw benefits for themselves in policy integration, and thus lobbied national governments to support the Commission's programme.

More specifically, a broad church of supporters of closer European unity became enamoured with technology policy because it seemed to offer the potential for political spillover. Research and technology policy had the potential to rid the Community of its image as a coddler of over-privileged farmers and 'sunset' industries such as steel and shipbuilding. On the contrary, technology policy offered the Commission a chance to be seen as the guardian of exciting, dynamic new economic activities that promised enhanced growth and good jobs (see Duff 1986).

Neofunctionalism at this point appeared ready to be resurrected in light of the Community's general new dynamism (see Taylor 1989; Tranholm-Mikkelsen 1991). The 1992 programme had relaunched the 'European project' to create a more politically and economically unified Europe. Under the stewardship of its President, Jacques Delors, the Commission was successful in expanding its policy role, quietly and without much fanfare, in important areas such as regional development, competition policy and social affairs, as well as technology policy (Sandholtz and Zysman 1989). Large European MNCs rallied behind first ESPRIT and then the Framework programme more generally. Polls showed a steady increase in public awareness of the EC and general enthusiasm for its objectives. The percentage of European citizens who thought their country's membership was a 'good thing' rose from 50 per cent in 1980 to 62 per cent by 1986 (Commission 1992a: 93). The neofunctionalist prediction that political spillover would lead to a transfer of political loyalties seemed plausible.

Sceptics might well have recalled Haas's (1976) notorious disavowal of neofunctionalist theory (and theorising about European integration generally) as 'obsolete' and 'no longer worth our time'. Few scholars probably remember that Haas's conclusions emerged out of a project on scientific and technological regimes. Haas noted that very little integration of technology policies (outside energy research) had occurred in Europe until the early 1970s. At that point, the Commission began to make headway only by adopting 'an approach which separates R&D from institutional questions', thus allowing governments to 'contribute and participate only in those aspects of interest to it' (Haas 1976: 55). Generally, European governments remained reluctant to put aside what Williams (1973: 143) termed their 'complex psychological halos', which led them to guard their national independence and 'sovereignty' in industrial policy. In short, technology policy witnessed very little functional integration, let alone political spillover.

For a time in the early 1980s, everything seemed to change. Large and ambitious projects combining the efforts of large Japanese multinationals in technology-intensive industries, particularly the fifth generation computer project, seemed on the verge of technical breakthroughs that far surpassed anything close to being realised in Europe. The angst-ridden debate about what Europe could do to close the new 'technology gap' began to emerge (see Marcum 1986; Pierre 1987). Collective European measures to promote innovation were further encouraged by the invitation of the Reagan administration to European firms and researchers (after most governments demurred) to take part in the US Strategic Defense Initiative (SDI). Suspicions arose that the Americans simply wished to 'cherry pick' European technologies that were more advanced than their US equivalents. Meanwhile, an extraordinarily broad consensus emerged on the desirability of the 1992 project, and the need to 'flank' it with new technology policy actions at the European level. Both the Framework programme and EUREKA were born in a sort of policy hothouse.

Still, a neofunctionalist account of EU research policy leaves quite a lot unexplained. Both the budgetary politics of the Framework programme, and the origins and launch of EUREKA, appear more amenable to realist-inspired, *intergovernmentalist* explanations. Intergovernmentalism in practice should be distinguished from intergovernmentalism in theory: even neofunctionalists assume that hardheaded, interest-driven, interstate bargaining is ubiquitous in the EU (see Stone Sweet and Sandholtz 1997). In theoretical terms, intergovernmentalists part company with neofunctionalists by insisting that European integration as a process, and EU policies as the products of it, result from intergovernmental bargaining between self-interested member states. Supranational leadership, demands for policy integration from interest groups and 'spillovers' generally are discounted. National governments are motivated by their own narrow, national interests. They rationally calculate the relative gains or losses that will accrue to their member state from different potential EU policy arrangements or outcomes. The influence of different states in bargaining is determined partly by their negotiating and coalition-forming skills, but mostly by their raw power, as measured by their relative wealth, population, and so on. In research policy, we would expect power to be a function of national technological resources, research expertise, and contributions to the EU's budget. States are 'unitary-rational' actors in EU politics, according to intergovernmentalists, as they are in international relations more generally.

More sophisticated versions of intergovernmentalist theory, particularly Moravcsik's (1993; 1995) 'liberal intergovernmentalism', conceive the preferences of national governments as arising from national economic interests, domestic politics and pressure from national interest groups. However, the overriding proposition is the same: state interests are paramount, the EU's institutions are relatively powerless and there is no reason to expect neofunctionalist 'spillovers' to occur unless a critical mass of states explicitly endorse them. In Moravcsik's (1991: 75) view, 'although supranational institutions have an important role in cementing existing interstate bargains as the foundation for renewed integration . . . the primary source of integration lies in the interests of the states themselves and the relative power that each brings to Brussels'. Intergovernmentalist assumptions appear valid when we try to make sense of the high politics of European research. After 1993, decisions on the budget for the EU's Framework programme became subject to the co-decision procedure, which gave the European Parliament (EP) a potential veto. Yet, crucially, decisions on general budgets for EU research required a *unanimous* vote by the Council of Ministers, in one (of only two, along with cultural policy) of the Maastricht Treaty's 'rogue' cases of co-decision requiring unanimity on the Council. The result was fierce intergovernmental bargaining over EU spending on research, and a Framework IV programme constructed largely on a 'Christmas tree basis' so that it offered gifts to each and every member state. Neofunctionalist predictions – which seemed credible in the mid-1980s – did not materialise.

However, the shift to qualified majority voting for future budgetary decisions, as ordained by the 1997 Amsterdam Treaty, is certainly amenable to neofunctionalist explanations. Intergovern-mentalists also have trouble explaining why the Union's budget for R&D tripled in the ten years after the signing of the Single European Act in 1985. More generally, in his perceptive analysis of the rise of collaborative European programmes, Sandholtz (1992: 9) argues that intergovernmentalists are wrong to assume that state leaders invariably base their preferences on calculations of relative gains or loss: '[r]ather, states seek a balance between their contribu-tions to the cooperative effort and the benefits they receive from it – that is, states must find a satisfactory solution to the problem of *juste retour*'. For Sandholtz, any plausible explanation of European tech-nological collaboration must focus on three factors: how demand for cooperation arises, who supplies political leadership, and what solu-tion is available to the problem of fair returns.

As a 'middle way' (between neofunctionalism and intergovern-mentalism) of understanding the politics of EU research, Sandholtz's typology deserves close examination. For instance, it is worth noting that demand for collaboration did not diminish after the original launching of EUREKA and the Framework pro-gramme. The Commission continued to supply leadership in the context of EU technology policy, even if EUREKA's existence and growth showed that it was not always followed. A crucial factor in explaining decision-making at the level of high politics appeared to be the problem of ensuring *juste retour*. By its nature, the problem did not arise within EUREKA, which national governments were free to contribute to and participate in as they saw fit.

The systemic level: the new institutionalism and RTD

The politics of technology policy are rarely dramatic or headline-grabbing. It is hard to imagine that another policy sector could be more technocratic or dominated by experts. Yet, in technology poli-cy, as in all EU policy sectors, an intermediate or 'systemic' level of decision-making exists between the level of high politics – where budgetary decisions are taken for years at a time – and the subsys-temic level, where individual programmes are managed and admin-istered. The systemic level is where the EU's institutions (and, represented within them, its member states) bargain over specific policy proposals, tabled initially by the Commission. Eventually, policies are chosen or 'set' according to one of several versions of the Community method of decision-making: the Commission proposes, the Parliament amends, and the Council votes.

At this level of analysis, the EP has played an increasingly important technology policy role, particularly under co-decision. At times, it has exercised collective judgement (which the EP must do to maximise its influence) in pushing for politically potent measures, such as more R&D funding for Eastern and Central Europe or a balanced directive on the patenting of biotechnological inventions. The Council has also shown itself able and willing to scrutinise the details of Commission proposals, and sometimes to demand major shifts in funding and priorities. At times, the Council has spent so much time and effort mulling over proposals for individual RTD programmes that start dates have had to be pushed back by as much as a year. At one point in 1991 the Commission – with considerable support from the EP – dramatically withdrew the proposals corresponding to the (five) Framework III subprogrammes near approval on the grounds that they had been amended by the Council beyond recognition (see Judge *et al.* 1994).

Yet, in the making of technology policy, the systemic level is *not* characterised by as much inter-institutional bargaining as most EU policy sectors. In practice, the Commission is usually able to get its proposals for individual programmes accepted by the Council without major changes. In the post-Maastricht period, it has worked more closely with the EP to ensure that the latter's amendments do not do violence to strategic priorities proposed by the Commission. As a lead Commission official in DG XII put it during the 'heat' of institutional negotiations on Framework IV:

> To be cynical, at the end of the day the Framework programme is not reality. The reality is the individual projects and proposals that come in. They are of course chosen by the Commission together with the committees, who have experience in adjusting things to suit the priority projects. The scientific and technical content agreed by the Council is so wide that you can make it fit a very large diversity of projects. So it's not so much the Commission determining things, as the simple continuity of individual programmes determining things (interview, February 1994).

This analysis closely reflects the assumptions of the *new institutionalism*, which has emerged as an increasingly common and sophisticated approach to EU policy-making (see Bulmer 1994a, 1994b; Pollack 1995; Pierson 1996). The new institutionalism is not really a theory, but rather a set of theoretical precepts that facilitate model-building. Its most important assumption, put simply, is that institutions *matter*: political competition does not take place in the abstract but is mediated or constrained in important respects by prevailing institutional arrangements. The new institutionalism teaches us to look carefully at the prevailing balance of power between institutions in any area of policy. At the same time, it cautions that radical policy change is unlikely because policies, and the political deals that spawn them, become *institutionalised* (see Scharpf 1988). Institutions introduce a bias towards inertia in policy content because institutions usually change more slowly than do the preferences of individual policy-makers.

The new institutionalism leads to the conclusion that the Commission effectively 'sets' EU research policy making because it has far more RTD expertise and resources than either the EP or Council. Most EU research programmes have become considerably institutionalised over time, with industrial and scientific constituencies prepared to defend them. The nature of EU-funded research, which must in principle be pre-competitive, makes it easy to argue that continuity must be preserved between successive Framework programmes because long periods of time and research effort are required before results can be achieved. In the language of the new institutionalism, the Union's RTD policy exhibits a strong path dependency: once a certain goal or path is set upon, trying to change policy is akin to turning an ocean liner around (see March and Olsen 1989).

By contrast with the Framework programme, EUREKA essentially lacks a systemic level of decision-making. Early in EUREKA's existence, its annual Ministerial Conference was required to reach crucial, 'history-making' decisions about how EUREKA would work, because so many such decisions were delayed or avoided when the initiative was launched at a political level in 1985. However, over time the conferences became a rubber stamp for approving lists of projects and made few very important policy decisions. The new institutionalism may seem to have little to offer in the way of explanation for the way in which EUREKA works, because the initiative essentially works without institutions, in the traditional sense of the term.

However, on the contrary, it could be argued that the key to understanding EUREKA is precisely its lack of institutions. It has evolved over time into a very different programme than was first envisaged by its French creators primarily because public institutions, which might be used to 'set' policy and impose control on the programme, simply do not exist. The power of private actors in determining EUREKA's content and goals is, by now, highly 'institutionalised'. The new institutionalism thus may offer more than it appears to in explaining why EUREKA is essentially a programme without policy.

The rest of the iceberg: policy networks rule?

Technology policy is a domain where, by its nature, experts and technocrats are powerful by virtue of their specialised knowledge. In contrast, politicians and political activists can be expected to focus relatively little of their time or energy on technology policy, because they both lack understanding and know that most policy issues in this realm do not fire the imaginations of ordinary citizens. In technology policy, more than other sectors, experts usually are handed broad policy mandates and left to get on with it.

The degree to which technology policy is subject to meaningful democratic controls in any political system may be questioned. To be sure, the Commission has had to adopt a stance of almost continuous evaluation of the Framework programme in order to satisfy the member states, the EP and its industrial and academic critics. Nevertheless, EU lines of accountability are often fuzzy. Its notorious 'democratic deficit' is in large measure a consequence of its lack of openness (see Williams 1991; Peterson 1995c). The main Commission services responsible for the Framework programme lean heavily on a plethora of advisory committees representing the various scientific communities they serve. These committees are open in the sense that any individual may suggest themselves for membership, and from time to time the Commission publishes an open call for new advisory experts. Nevertheless, there tends to be an inner core of advisers who constantly meet together in EU committees and other groups that dominate decision-making.

Meanwhile, the single most frequent criticism of EUREKA is that it lacks transparency. For example, partners in individual projects often do not know how much public funding their partners bring to their project. Governments themselves have been reluctant to share information on how much money they are committing to EUREKA. The wider point is that public power is weak or fragmented in European technology policy, and yet considerable public funding is committed to these initiatives.

Many important decisions that determine policy outputs are taken at this sub-systemic level after deliberations between experts, officials and industrialists or researchers. Both the Framework programme and EUREKA must bring together an eclectic range of actors – public and private, national and supranational, industrial and academic, expert and official – to decide who gets what. Outcomes are less a consequence of which interests win in inter-institutional competition at a systemic level, and more a consequence of the kind of *networks* that emerge in a certain area of technology, such as telecommunications or biotechnology. Considerable autonomy and power to determine policy is usually on offer to networks that can present a common front, while linking a wide array of actors, in European technology policy.

In light of these factors, technology policy offers fertile ground for policy network analysis. A policy network may be defined as an arena in which clusters of actors representing governments and interest groups bargain over policy. The metaphor of the policy network has become an increasingly common tool of policy analysts seeking to explain how EU policies are shaped through informal bargaining between actors, both before and after the broad outlines of policy are 'set' at a political level in EU politics. Policy networks tend to be capable of collective action when they are insular and have stable memberships. Above all, cohesive policy networks are marked by strong resource dependencies: actors within them rely heavily on each other for resources, and thus must share them in order to achieve their goals (see Rhodes 1990; Smith 1993; Peterson 1995a; 1995c). As such, policy networks are based on the same principle as innovation networks: all members gain from pooling resources.

Policy networks may be particularly powerful in technology policy, compared with other EU policy sectors, because national interests are uniquely difficult to define in a world of rapidly changing technologies and oligopolistic competition. In collaborative RTD programmes, policy networks may not only implement policy, but also come to shape the terms in which national policy-makers formulate policy strategies at home. By implication, this process of shaping may have a profound impact on negotiations over strategy at the EU level (see Ziegler 1998).

The policy networks model is by nature a model of sub-systemic decision-making. It is particularly apt as a way to explain who gets what when governments seek to promote innovation and commit resources to the task, but set very broad or vague parameters for determining who will benefit from technology policy. If we want to explain European technology policy, the policy networks model cannot give us all the answers, but it points us towards a level where many important answers lie.

Conclusion

We have ranged broadly across theoretical literatures that shed light on the political economy of European technology policy. Four particularly important insights arise from the theoretical touchstones we have introduced.

First, we have stressed the cumulative nature of the innovation system and the degree to which technology is knowledge that is passed on tacitly through learning by doing. In economics, as in politics, such a system assigns an important role to those institutions that embody cumulative learning and experience. They too have to adapt and change over time. In studying the development of European technology policy, we are confronted by the growth of a new system at the centre, and the need for diverse *national* systems of innovation to adapt to it. Not surprisingly, the process of coming together, even in the loose sense of concertation, poses problems and creates frictions.

Second, we are reminded that change of any sort creates uncertainty, and that it is in the nature of humankind to seek reassurance through friendship. Networking in both the economic and political spheres helps to lessen uncertainties. In the economic sphere, it has become an important mechanism for learning and technology (knowledge) transfer, as well as a means of spreading risks and sharing overheads. In seeking to stimulate inter-country collaboration between firms on one hand and research institutes/universities on the other, the Commission was, in the 1980s, ahead of the game.

Third, while technology policy provides succour to both

neofunctionalists *and* intergovernmentalists, it is clear that decisions concerning EU technology policy feed 'up' and 'down', affecting calculations and outcomes at other levels in a system of governance that has multiple levels. While governments bargain (hard) with each other over the broad contours and general cost of EU programmes, the nature of technology policy is such that many policy details are left to be filled in later. In approaching the EU's programmes or EUREKA, policy networks at the sub-systemic level must be an important focus of any student of EU technology policy.

Fourth and most broadly, a theory-based account of the rise of European technology policies needs to acknowledge that the politics of European efforts have been determined largely by the economics of technological innovation. The demand for policy action stems from the pressures associated with globalisation, economic turbulence, the redefinition of security and competition for technological prowess. Governments initially face demands for the protection of production capabilities and subsequently, when this proves futile, for innovation and job creation. In political terms, governments may promise (recklessly) to deliver on these demands, but find blunt and ineffective national policy instruments. Thus, they create *European* instruments, such as the Framework programme and EUREKA. However, these instruments have their own limitations: committees of experts and officials in Brussels cannot deliver technology transfer and diffusion at the national and subnational level. Therefore, as we argue in later chapters, the system of top-down direction that emerged from the early 1980s has to evolve and delegate responsibility down the line to national and regional administrations.

4

Davignon, ESPRIT and the Single European Act

If politics follows economics in technology policy, it is logical that advocates of a more united European effort in the early 1980s were able to mobilise successfully behind new programmes in the broad area of 'telematics'. The economic logic of collaboration in this sector was clear, as innovation was becoming increasingly expensive and European producers were losing market share. The most important new EC programme was ESPRIT, which was designed as a strategic programme to improve Europe's technological base. ESPRIT encouraged collaboration between companies, universities and research institutes over a wide range of areas in information technology (IT). Its sister programme in telecommunications, RACE, was intended to lay the groundwork for a new generation of optical fibre broadband communications systems expected to come into service in Europe during the 1990s. The early apparent success of these programmes helped pave the way for the Single European Act's explicit blessing for a new Treaty competence in RTD, and the incorporation of most Community initiatives into the Framework programme.

In this chapter, we examine and explain the spate of initiatives that arose in the 1980s. We focus particularly on ESPRIT and RACE, but also consider Community initiatives in other technological sectors. The emergence of the Framework programme is placed in the wider context of political agreement on the Single European Act. As such, we juxtapose the twin – apparently contradictory – tracks of European RTD policy: competition and collaboration.

The 'new' technology gap

The impetus behind a legal and political mandate for an EU technology policy in the 1980s was the re-emergence of concern about Europe's lagging technological competitiveness – this time not just *vis-à-vis* America, but also in relation to Japan. Nothing illustrates the point better than developments in semiconductor production. During the 1970s, many European producers had chosen to pull out of mainstream, memory chip production on the grounds that they could not match the US lead (see Dosi 1983; OECD 1985; Arnold and Guy 1986). Instead, European firms chose to concentrate on producing more profitable custom chips for the protected defence and telecom markets. Japanese electronics firms such as Hitachi, Toshiba, and Fujitsu chose precisely the opposite route. Having gained dominance of Western colour TV markets (see Cawson 1987), they were persuaded by the powerful Japanese Ministry of International Trade and Industry (MITI) that they needed a stronger presence in components. MITI's Very Large Scale Integration (VLSI) programme, launched in 1975, encouraged the large Japanese electronics firms to collaborate in the R&D necessary to develop the expertise to enter chip production in the early 1980s. The strategy succeeded admirably: by 1985, 5 of the top 10 manufacturers of semiconductors were Japanese. Whereas the Europeans had retreated in the face of a seemingly unassailable US lead, the Japanese had taken on the Americans and, essentially, won.

European producers were now faced by a double challenge from the US and Japan. Japan and other South-East Asian countries emerged as strong, export-oriented economies as innovation became increasingly the focal point of competition, with the frequent launch of new models accelerating product cycles and increasing R&D costs. The cost of entry into semiconductor production was a case in point. In the early 1970s, setting up a plant to manufacture mainstream memory chips cost little more than $2 million, an amount not beyond the means of a well-placed small entrepreneur. By the early 1980s the cost had shot to between $100 million and $200 million for an item with an expected product life of two years. By 1985 it had increased to $500m for an expected life of 18 months (OECD 1985). Firms sought partners to help spread the increased costs and risks.

In addition, firms feared that without participation in the leading-edge production of key components such as memory chips, skills would atrophy and re-entry at a later stage would be impossible. This logic underlay the French concept of the *'filière'*, a technology with its full complement of upstream and downstream linkages. A weak link in upstream (for example, chip production) capabilities could jeopardise competitiveness downstream (in computers) (see Dang Nguyen and Arnold 1985: 135–7). The French socialist government, installed after the election of François Mitterrand in 1981, initially promoted a highly nationalistic version of the *filière*. France was deemed to need firms with state-of-the-art capabilities at all important nodal points up and down the *filière*.

The economic crisis of 1983 led the French socialists to abandon the *filière* strategy, that had become enormously expensive as well as largely unsuccessful. Instead, France became the foremost proponent of a united EC front in the struggle to gain a larger European share in the global markets. Mitterrand and his ministers argued for the creation of strategic alliances between European firms, the amalgamation of procurement and the harmonisation of standards. In September 1983, Mitterrand called for *'un espace industriel européen'* (a European industrial 'area') and recommended new Community measures in industrial, technological and social policy. Meanwhile, Jacques Delors, French Finance Minister after 1981 and also an MEP, advocated *'géometrie variable'*, or advanced collaboration between selected Community member states in particular policy areas. These ideas emerged later in Commission proposals for a European Technological Community as well as the proposal to launch EUREKA.

Meanwhile, the failures of national champion strategies led policy-makers to rethink the Community's role in industrial R&D. The Commission set up a working group, Forecasting and Assessment in Science and Technology (FAST), which commissioned a series of 36 forward-looking reports in three main areas: work and employment, the information society and the biosociety. The synthesis report, *Eurofutures: the Challenges of Innovation* (FAST 1984: xi) set out 'a two fold task for the Community: first, to achieve a certain collaboration and division of labour in order to pursue jointly a range of options; and secondly to carry out those specific programmes where there are evident economies of scale'. Meeting the challenge from the United States and Japan became one of the main themes of the Commission's work (Sandholtz 1992: 160).

Somewhat ironically, the emergence of the EU programmes (as opposed to just studies) came at a time when there were also significant national actions in information technology. The French *filière* programme, designed by French socialists, was mirrored in many ways by the UK Alvey programme introduced by the right-wing Thatcher government. A series of British support schemes for microelectronics aimed at raising both productive capabilities and industrial awareness had been introduced before the Alvey initiative in 1982. Even the West Germans supported a succession of programmes aimed at upgrading the performance and usage of computers and components (Arnold and Guy 1986). Everyone, it seemed, was following MITI's VLSI model.

ESPRIT

The appointment of the Belgian Etienne Davignon as Commissioner for Industry in 1977 was an important step on the road to new European programmes. The problems that beset the European shipbuilding, steel and textiles industries consumed his and the Commission's attention until 1979, when focus shifted from 'sunset' to 'sunrise' industries. Under his guidance, the Commission developed a more strategic approach to the IT sector. An Information Technologies Task Force (ITTF) was established as an independent body (not under any DG), with the Commission drafting in extra hands with industrial experience. The broad outline of a programme for microelectronic technology was produced in 1979–80 and agreed by the Council in November 1981. The Commission then took the unorthodox step of inviting representatives from the major electronics companies to help draw up the detailed programme. Eventually, the exercise developed into ESPRIT (Guzzetti 1995: 77; Sandholtz 1992: 163–5).

Davignon played a vital role in developing ESPRIT. In evidence to the House of Lords Select Committee on the European Communities (1985: 169), he outlined three factors that had motivated his actions. First, he had been struck by the 'very distinctive difference in performance' between the industries of the USA, Japan and the EC. Second, he had felt that the time had come for Community competence in support for sunrise industries to be upgraded. Third, he said, he was aware of the fact that there was no real incentive for cross-border collaboration. He recognised therefore that any EC-level action needed a fresh approach.

Up to this point, the Commission had tended to work with middle-level managers in European firms, who were often unable to secure agreement for plans from higher up company hierarchies. Davignon was determined to liaise with only the very highest levels of company management, in order to secure their commitment to subsequent programmes. During 1979–80, Davignon invited the heads of Europe's 'Big 12' leading electronics and IT companies to a series of Round Table discussions. Work focused first on the idea of a series of Airbus-style joint companies to manufacture products within Europe, but these raised questions about their compatibility with competition rules. Focus therefore shifted to the pre-competitive end of collaborative research, as it was granted a block exemption from Articles 85 and 86 of the Treaty of Rome which prohibited firms from collusive actions. Industrial commitment solidified in response to two events: the looming deregulation of AT&T, which allowed the US multinational to move into international (and European) operations; and the settlement of the long-standing dispute between the US anti-trust authorities and IBM, which gave 'Big Blue' *carte blanche* to move into the telecommunications sector (Sandholtz 1992: 127–30).

Behind the scenes, and alongside the Big 12 Round Table, the influence of the Gyllenhammer Group was also important. An informal grouping of European manufacturers, such as Volvo and Pilkingtons, it kept a watching brief on general infrastructure issues affecting European industry. Meanwhile, the careful preparatory work of the Commission's DG XII paid off when its new-found industrial friends pressured their national governments to support and recognise the logic of Community action.

The first outline proposal for ESPRIT was produced in September 1980. The idea was to develop a European strategic programme based on collaboration between the major European companies, small and medium-sized firms (SMEs) as well as universities and research institutes. By May 1982, the Commission had put a firm proposal before the Council, and subsequently tabled it at the Versailles European Summit in June (Commission 1982). Political response was favourable and by the end of the year the Commission had the go-ahead for a first pilot phase costing 11.5 million ECU.

The pilot phase was an important element in the Davignon strategy. The Round Table had expressed doubts about the Commission's capacity to mount an effective programme that would not become bogged down in bureaucratic delays. Davignon thus asked for a 'toe in the water', or a pilot phase before seeking any further commitment. A call for proposals in February 1983 drew over 600 responses from 200 companies. Encouraged by this success, the Commission rapidly pushed ahead with plans for a full ten-year programme (1984–93), with an overall budget of 1.5 billion ECU.

The first call for ESPRIT proposals in early 1984 met with a huge response, and less than 25 per cent of all bids could be funded. Three-quarters of projects chosen for funding involved collaboration between firms and academic research units. ESPRIT's project list was dominated by projects involving Big 12 Round Table firms, but more than half of all participating firms were SMEs, which took part in 65 per cent of funded projects and received 14 per cent of total funding. By January 1987, a total of 1.36 billion ECU had been committed – almost the entire budget earmarked for what originally had been seen as a ten-year programme (Commission 1987a).

The popularity of ESPRIT led to immediate demands for a second, more expensive programme. Plans were delayed by protracted negotiations over the new and broader Framework programme, as mandated by the Single European Act. Finally, ESPRIT II got underway in 1988, with a projected five-year lifespan. It marked a doubling in the size of the programme, with a total spend of 3.2 billion ECU over five years split, as with ESPRIT I, fifty–fifty between the Commission (which thus contributed 1.6 billion ECU) and industry.

The third phase of ESPRIT (1990–94) was brought forward to coincide with launch of the Framework III Programme. The Community budget was 1.35 billion ECU (lower than for the ESPRIT II). In approving the programme, the Council emphasised the importance of working in conjunction with the intergovernmental EUREKA programme and particularly JESSI, its ambitious microchips initiative (Guzzetti 1995: 80).

Thus, by the 1990s, technological collaboration was widely accepted as an appropriate industrial strategy and ESPRIT had in many senses reached maturity. The programme had chalked up a number of major achievements, particularly in standardisation. A large share of ESPRIT projects addressed IT standards, such as the

Open Systems Interconnect (OSI) initiative for developing intercon-
nectability standards between different (and incompatible) operating
systems. As open systems generally gained recognition in the early
1990s, the groundwork laid in ESPRIT paid off. Technological
compatibility helped dictate patterns of future cooperation. As
Sandholtz (1992: 205) observed, '[p]rior to ESPRIT European firms
sought out American companies for technology partnerships. Because
of ESPRIT European companies now seek out European partners.'

After 1985, ESPRIT became a model for other European programmes (see Table 4.1). The next largest programme – RACE
(Research in Advanced Communications for Europe) – became the
responsibility of DG XIII (telecommunications), which also took
over responsibility for ESPRIT in 1987. Under its auspices, the
ESPRIT Task Force expanded its activities to cover both telecommunications and technology transfer/innovation. DG XII retained
responsibility for mainstream science and technology issues, including BRITE (Basic Research and Industrial Technologies for
Europe), the main programme for promoting the diffusion of new
technologies across industry, as well as Community biotechnology
programmes and the science-related mobility (personnel exchange)
programmes. DG XII also was given responsibility for the overall
planning of Community-wide R&D through the multi-annual
Framework programmes. These arrangements left plenty of scope
for lively bureaucratic politics concerning the control and direction
of EU-funded research.

RACE

By 1979, 'telematics' had become the new buzzword in the technology policy community, as it embraced the increasing integration of
microelectronics, IT and telecommunications. Commission proposals put forward under Davignon's leadership in September 1979 had
proposed work on both electronics and telecommunications, with
focus on joint standards and the longer-term development of an
integrated digital network to span the entire Community (Sandholtz
1992: 226). While Europe's telecommunications companies had not
lost market share as quickly as their counterparts in electronics, they
had become increasingly dependent on their protected and privi-
leged status as (often) sole suppliers in their national markets.

TABLE 4.1

Main Community RTD programmes (1984–94)

Name	Dates	Budget cost[a] (m ECU)	Objectives
ESPRIT (European Strategic Programme for R&D in IT)	I 1984–8 II 1988–92 III 1990–4	750 1 600 1 350	To promote European capabilities and competitiveness in IT technologies, primarily micro-electronics systems development.
RACE (R&D in Advanced Communications Technologies for Europe)	Definition phase 1985–7 RACE I 1990–4 RACE II 1992–4	21 460 489	To establish European competence in broadband communications by developing the equipment, standards and technology necessary for an Integrated Broadband Communications (IBC) system.
TELEMATICS	1990–4	380	Development of telematic systems in transport, health and public administration
BRITE/EURAM (Basic Research in Technologies/ Advanced Materials for Europe)	BRITE I 1985–8 EURAM I 1986–8 BRITE/EURAM I 1989–92 BRITE/EURAM II	100[b] 450 660	Support for industrial R&D to upgrade technological/ materials base of industrial production.
BAP (Biotechnology Action Programme)	1985–9	75	Support for infrastructure development in biotechnology with particular emphasis on research and training.
BRIDGE (Biotechnological Research for Innovation, Development and Growth in Europe)	1989–93	100	As for BAP, but emphasis put on larger, more comprehensive projects in areas such as advanced cell culture, molecular modelling etc.

TABLE 4.1 (*continued*)

Name	Dates	Budget cost[a] (m ECU)	Objectives
BIOTECH	1992–6	164	Oriented towards basic research and safety assessment; complementary to BRIDGE
ECLAIR (European Collaborative Linkage of Agriculture and Industry through Research)	1989–94	80	Industrial applications of advanced biotechnologies in agro-industrial sector, with emphasis on use of agricultural produce as industrial raw material.
FLAIR (Food Linked Agro-Industrial Research)	1989–94	25	
COMETT (Community Programme in Education and Training for Technology)	Phase I 1987–9 Phase II 1990–4	30 200	Co-operation between university and industry in training programmes for innovation (a) through establishment of university/enterprise partnerships and (b) through transnational exchange of students and staff.

[a] The figures given as 'budget cost' exclude any industrial contribution for the ESPRIT and other programmes which are shared cost programmes. Actual expenditures under the programmes are therefore approximately twice the amount of the budget cost quoted.

[b] BRITE and EURAM were originally single programmes run simultaneously with a joint budget of 100 MECU, or 50 MECU each.

Source: DTI (1991).

Davignon and his advisers, as well as many in the industry, realised that the situation in European telecoms was untenable in the long run. On one hand, technological developments – especially new microwave and satellite transmission systems and cellular networks – were rapidly eroding ideas of natural monopoly, and spurring new competition. On the other, the threats posed by AT&T and IBM, and the rapid emergence of large Japanese multinationals, meant that potential new entrants would challenge existing players. Moreover, the European market was woefully fragmented. In the early 1980s, the Community's (then) 10 member states sported 9 different versions of digital telecommunication switches, while no single national market was, by itself, large enough to support the development of even one. The R&D cost of developing a new generation of digital switches was estimated at between $500 million and $1.2 billion, thus requiring markets of between $14 and 16 billion to be viable. The largest Community markets were West Germany at $11.7 billion, France at $10.9 billion and the UK at $7.2 billion (Von Tulder and Junne 1988: 70). Clearly, if Europe's PTTs (posts, telegraph and telecommunications agencies) and their 'national champion' suppliers did not change of their own volition, they were going to be forced to do so.

Davignon's proposals for RACE formed one arm of a three-pronged strategy designed to pry open the entrenched monopolies of the PTTs. RACE was the supportive arm of the strategy, aimed at coordinating and supporting R&D on the key technologies that underpinned new developments. Alongside RACE, and overlapping with it to a degree, was the push towards standardisation and integration of networks. The final prong was liberalisation – opening up markets and forcing sleeping giants to stand on their own feet and compete with others. To achieve all three objectives, the Commission needed to carry both national governments and the PTTs with them.

The Commission's tactics were similar to those adopted with ESPRIT. Although the first moves were made in 1979, little was accomplished until late 1983, when the Commission set up a joint working group with officials from ministries in member states and their PTT colleagues. They also brought together 80 experts from the telecoms equipment industry and the PTTs to create the Planning Exercise in Telecommunications (PET). Its proposals became the basis of RACE (Commission 1984).

The PET exercise was 'the hook that eventually brought in the telecoms administrations' (Sandholtz 1992: 240). PTT directors could not but be attracted by the vision of an integrated broadband digital network across the Community, while industry was promised a substantive role in its detailed planning. RACE resembled ESPRIT in its methodology, with key decisions left to scientists, engineers and planners in industry and the PTTs. After a two-year definition phase, hopes of launching the programme in early 1987 were thwarted by budgetary wrangles over the second Framework programme. After they were finally settled, funding for RACE was set at 550 million ECU for 1987–92. RACE provoked widespread interest, with projects in this period involving 362 organisations, including 230 companies and over 90 SMEs (Commission 1989).

The Green Paper on telecommunications

As RACE was being developed, the Commission's DG III (industry) launched its Green Paper on telecommunications policy, *Towards a Dynamic European Economy* (Commission 1987). The Paper insisted that the liberalisation of telecommunications in Europe was urgent. It allowed that PTTs might retain monopoly rights over voice telephony, but argued that all other services, and network and terminal equipment markets, should be open to private providers. It also insisted on open network provision (ONP), which effectively meant laying down the structure for a transnational network operating on common standards and interfaces. The Commission's major success, however, was the establishment of ETSI (the European Telecommunications Standards Institute) in 1988. ETSI provided a forum where network operators, equipment manufacturers and telecoms users could meet together to hammer out standards.

The most contentious proposal of the Green Paper proved to be opening up markets for (non-voice) services and terminal equipment, where the Commission had to resort to directives issued under Article 90 of the Treaty. It states that enterprises to which a state grants 'special or exclusive rights' must conform to Treaty provisions on competition. The Commission argued that the PTT monopolies constituted a distortion of competition under Article 86. France challenged this judgement in the European Court of Justice, but the Commission position was upheld.

By the end of the 1980s, the Commission had accomplished

much in the area of telecoms. As with ESPRIT they had played their cards carefully, wooing first equipment manufacturers and then the PTTs on to their side with the sweetener of the RACE programme, finessing the coup with liberalisation through Article 90. Telecoms were not the only arena where the twin tracks of offers of support on one hand, and liberalisation on the other, were the basis for policy.

BRITE-EURAM

If RACE was built in the image of ESPRIT then so too was the BRITE (Basic Research in Industrial Technologies) programme. It was introduced in 1985 as a programme concerned with generic industrial technologies. In this respect it was much broader than ESPRIT or RACE and, in particular, aimed to attract a significant number of SME participants. Like ESPRIT, it was a shared-cost programme, with a budget of 100 million ECU offering programmes of collaborative research across a spectrum ranging from lasers to biological catalysts. The first call for proposals attracted over 500 project bids seeking nine times more funding than was available. Industrial laboratories received 67 per cent of the funding that was allocated, with approximately a third going to SMEs, a far higher proportion than for ESPRIT or RACE.

Early evaluations indicated a very high satisfaction rate from BRITE participants (Farge *et al.* 1988). This result, along with clear evidence of underfunding, acted to spur the combination of BRITE with the EURAM (European Research in Advanced Materials) programme, which had provided some 30 million ECU of funding for areas such as metal alloys and ceramics for engineering. The new BRITE-EURAM programme was funded to the tune of 250 million ECU and ran between 1989 and 1992, concentrating on five main areas: advanced materials; design methods and quality control; applications of production technologies; technologies for production processes (such as CAD/CAM); and aeronautics. These emphases were maintained under BRITE-EURAM II for the period 1992–6.

Biotechnology

The Community's interest in biotechnology derived from the early work of the *Europe Plus 30* group and its successor in the FAST Programme. The FAST report on the biosociety (Commission 1983) took a holistic view of the potential of biotechnology, using a wide definition that encompassed both traditional forms of biotechnology (e.g. beer making), and the narrower US definition that restricted itself to modern techniques of genetic engineering. The wish to find industrial use for agricultural surpluses influenced the design of the Community's first programme, BEP (Biomolecular Engineering Programme), which aimed to develop enzyme chemistry and process plants for this purpose. It was an extremely small programme – 15 million ECU over four years – and involved mostly academic research.

BEP was succeeded by the Biotechnology Action Programme (BAP), which refocused attention on mainstream developments in genetic engineering. The sums involved were still small: 55 million ECU for 1985–9, with 20 million more ECU added in 1987. One notable piece of research funded by the programme achieved a first in gene sequencing of yeast chromosomes, resulting in an article in the British journal *Nature* under the signatures of 147 researchers at 35 European laboratories (Oliver *et al*. 1992). As this project illustrated, most BAP projects were predominantly university- or research-institute-led, and many were organised on the basis of networks with large numbers of participants.

In 1989 a new unit, the Concertation Unit for Biotechnology in Europe (CUBE), was established by the Commission. It tried not only to pull together action by different member states, which tended to pursue highly independent policies, but also to make sure that different Commission services were all singing the same tune. Given that biotechnology overlapped the interests of some seven DGs (research, informatics, agriculture, environment, industry, energy, and development) and entailed tricky issues of risk and regulations, it is perhaps not surprising that the Commission found the CUBE exercise difficult. Biotechnology generally prompted many long and fierce intra-Commission battles (Cantley 1995).

Poor coordination was only one source of criticism of the Community's biotechnology programmes. IRDAC (the Commission's Industrial Research and Development Advisory Committee) complained loudly about the lack of industrial relevance of Community biotechnology programmes in the late 1980s. Their successor – BRIDGE (see Table 4.1) – was more focused. With a budget of 100 million ECU for 1990–4, its funding was divided 40:40:20 between large network projects (mainly basic research), projects targeted at specific industrial or agricultural problems, and other activities such as concertation. Two smaller, more targeted programmes – ECLAIR and FLAIR (see Table 4.1) – retained the focus of BRIDGE on using biotechnology as a weapon against agricultural surpluses. They were succeeded in 1993 by the AIR (Agro-Industrial Research) programme. The EU's biotechnology programmes retained their bias towards academic research well into the 1990s. While the failure to make much impact on industrial R&D was criticised, there were in fact relatively few small European specialist biotechnology firms of the sort common in the US, and developments remained dominated by the large chemical and pharmaceutical companies. The latter's annual research budgets often amounted to more than 500 million ECU. For them, a grant from the Commission of 50 000 ECU was irrelevant. Few saw much advantage in collaborating with other firms of equivalent size; most instead looked to links with small American biotechnology companies (Sharp and Senker 1997).

In short, the EU's biotechnology programmes were not without success stories, such as the 'European Laboratories Without Walls' initiative. It nurtured very large academic networks and pulled together the academic underpinnings of research across Europe. Yet European industrial firms were mostly absent from EU-funded research. When asked why they collaborated with US firms or universities rather than their European counterparts, many large-firm representatives admitted that it was because they were ignorant of scientific capabilities in Europe beyond the science base of their home country (Sharp and Senker 1997).

The Framework programme

By 1985 the Community's new technology policy initiatives, based on shared costs and collaboration between countries and research organisations, were beginning to make their mark. The Single European Act (ratified in 1987) for the first time gave the Community an explicit legal base for these activities. The SEA also specified a new decision-making procedure for agreeing a multi-annual Framework programme, which would be approved unanimously by member states in a package that set out its total budget and main scientific and technological objectives. Its implementation would be through a series of subprogrammes to be adopted by the Council by qualified majority voting. In other words, while providing a firm legal base in the Treaty for research programmes and making it clear that their prime objective was to strengthen international competitiveness, the procedures still required unanimous agreement of member states on overall priorities and spending. Then, the Council would have to endorse specific lines of action in a separate set of votes.

The concept of a Framework programme dated back to Davignon and the early 1980s. Together with DG XII's Director-General, Paolo Fasella, Davignon wanted to pull together the existing work of the JRC with new research and development programmes that the Community was formulating. The result was the Framework I programme, covering 1984–7. Its budget of 3.75 billion ECU represented little more than a relisting of items, such as the JRC budget and ESPRIT, that had already been approved. At a political level, there was considerable dissent, with some member states – especially the UK and West Germany – emphatically opposed to any concept of Community 'management' of R&D activities (Guzzetti 1995: 85).

The background of dissent helps to explain the difficulties encountered in preparing the Framework II programme by Karl-Heinz Narjes, Davignon's successor as Commissioner for Science, Research and IT in 1985. Narjes tabled ambitious proposals to create a 'European Technological Community' (Commission 1985), but met considerable opposition, even from France. In 1986, when he finally put forward proposals for a 10 billion ECU budget for Framework II, the British and West Germans joined forces to oppose (firmly) such a sharp increase in expenditure. Finally, eighteen months later, after the Thatcher government's victory in the British general election of 1987, the Council agreed to a budget of 5.4 billion ECU for Framework II (see Table 4.2). Supporters of EU technology policy who had hoped that the Single European Act would clear the way to a substantial increase in expenditures thought the agreed budget offered a derisory increase in resources.

TABLE 4.2

The Framework II programme (1987–91)

Objectives/areas	Funding	
	MECU	**%**
1. *Quality of life*	*375*	*6.9*
Health	80	
Radiation protection	34	
Environment	261	
2. *Towards a large market and an information and communication society*	*2 275*	*42.2*
Information technologies	1 600	
Telecommunications	550	
New services of common interest (including transport)	125	
3. *Modernisation of industrial sectors*	*845*	*15.7*
Science and technology for the manufacturing industry	400	
Science and technology of advanced materials	220	
Raw materials and recycling	45	
Technical standards, measurement methods and reference materials	180	
4. *Exploitation and optimum use of biological resources*	*280*	*5.2*
Biotechnology	120	
Agro-industrial technologies	105	
Competitiveness of agriculture and management of agricultural resources	55	
5. *Energy*	*1 173*	*21.7*
Fission: nuclear safety	440	
Controlled thermonuclear fusion	611	
Non-nuclear energies and rational use of energy	122	
6. *Science and technology for development*	*80*	*1.5*
7. *Exploitation of the sea bed and use of marine resources*	*80*	*1.5*
Marine science and technology	50	
Fisheries	30	
8. *Improvement of European S/T cooperation*	*288*	*5.3*
Stimulation, enhancement and use of human resources	180	
Use of major installations	30	
Forecasting and assessment and other back-up measures (including statistics)	23	
Dissemination and utilisation of S/T research results	55	
Total	*5 396*	*100.00*

Source: European Commission 1994: Table 8a.2.

It did, however, show a substantial increase in the resources going to ICT (reflecting ESPRIT and RACE) and industrial technologies (BRITE), with energy's share dropping sharply (see also Table 1.2).

Political agreement on the launch of the Framework programme had been underpinned by an understanding that it would be reviewed in its third year of operation. In 1989, a review board led by Pierre Aigrain endorsed the main thrust of the Framework programme, reiterating the commitment to fund only pre-competitive R&D and warning against the drift, as programmes matured, towards funding more competitive elements in R&D (Aigrain *et al.* 1989). Downstream R&D should either be funded by industry itself or through non-EU programmes such as EUREKA. More emphasis, it suggested, should be placed on promoting the 'scientific humus' of the Community – that is, on basic research skills and infrastructure. The report also argued that Framework II, which consisted of 8 broad 'lines' of research and 32 specific programmes, was too complex and needed simplification.

In the light of the review panel's assessment, the Framework III programme (see Table 4.3) was developed for 1990–4, overlapping with the last two years of the previous programme. Funding was originally set at levels similar to the previous programme – 5.7 billion ECU over the five-year period – but was subsequently increased in May 1993 to 6.6 billion ECU. The new Human Capital and Mobility programme encouraged 'mobility' (that is, exchange visits) among both faculty members and graduate students between linked groups of laboratories, and attracted approximately 9 per cent of the budget. Framework III also saw a slight falling off in the resources devoted to IT and telecommunications, and a substantial increase in resources devoted to environmental research. Energy once again dropped in share, from 22 to 16 per cent.

Competition and collaboration – an agenda for the 1990s

By the early 1990s, the pattern of collaboration was well established. The Commission and national governments combined through the Framework programme and EUREKA to offer selective support to companies seeking to undertake collaborative R&D with companies or research institutes in another European country. The sums involved were still not large: less than 4 per cent of total expenditures

TABLE 4.3

The Framework III programme (1990–4)

Objectives/areas	Funding	
	MECU	**%**
ENABLING TECHNOLOGIES		
1. *Information and communications technologies*	*2 491*	*37.7*
Information technologies	1 517	
Communication technologies	548	
Development of telematics systems of general interest	426	
2. *Industrial and materials technologies*	*997*	*15.1*
Industrial and materials technologies	840	
Measurement and testing	157	
MANAGEMENT OF NATURAL RESOURCES		
3. *Environment*	*581*	*8.8*
Environment	464	
Marine sciences and technology	117	
4. *Life sciences and technologies*	*832*	*12.6*
Biotechnology	184	
Agricultural and agro-industrial research (including fisheries)	373	
Biomedical and health research	149	
Life sciences and technologies for developing countries	125	
5. *Energy*	*1 052*	*15.9*
Non-nuclear energies	259	
Nuclear fission safety	231	
Controlled thermonuclear fusion	562	
OPTIMISATION OF INTELLECTUAL RESOURCES	581	8.8
6. *Human capital and mobility*	*581*	
Total[a]	*6 600*	*100.00*

[a] Including 66 MECU for the centralised action of dissemination and exploitation of research results.

Source: European Commission 1994: Table 8a.3.

on R&D within the Union as a whole. Both the Framework and EUREKA programmes became the targets of criticism on the grounds that, on many occasions, collaboration with the US and Japan would have been more appropriate. Given the degree to which European firms lagged behind their competitors in these countries, might more have been gained from strategic alliances with non-European firms?

Yet, intra-European cooperation was not without its own merits. As we have seen, many of the companies involved in EU programmes were traditional 'national champions' in their sector of industry, sustained by government subsidies and given absolute protection by public purchasing guarantees in areas such as defence and telecommunications. Because national champions focused on *national* markets, their production runs were too short, too specialised and too costly to be viable in international markets. Too many firms were content to take their easy profits from their captive national markets rather than risk international competition. It was not easy to wean these companies away from the comfortable lifestyle to which they had become accustomed. One of the achievements of these collaborative programmes was to help them shift towards a more international focus. Mytelka (1991: 207), for example, argued:

> The ESPRIT case nicely sums up the themes of [collaboration and strategic partnership]. It points to the roles that public agencies, in this case the EC, can play in strengthening the system of innovation and the regional technology base by providing financial support and linkage mechanisms for small and medium sized enterprises, facilitating the movement of research results from research organisations into production, promoting transEuropean collaboration and focusing that collaboration in a structured way.

In part the achievement was psychological. By getting the twelve Round Table companies together and discussing common problems, Davignon convinced them, as early as 1983, that there was little future in being a national champion. It is interesting that the members of Davignon's Round Table were prominent supporters of plans to eliminate the remaining national barriers to trade within the common market, which eventually became the Single European Act (see Cowles 1995). The SEA itself added considerably to competitive pressures, and in turn reinforced the search for strategies to cut costs and deflect competition. In this context, collaboration played an important role in identifying opportunities: both for cost cutting (avoiding duplication, exploiting economies of scale) and, more especially, identifying possible partners. After the Davignon initiatives and the SEA came the merger boom of the later 1980s, which led to a considerable increase in concentration in these same high-technology industries through a process of merger, acquisition and rationalisation. In semiconductors, for example, the French producer Thomson married its capabilities with the Italian firm SGS-Ates to form SGS-Thomson. In the UK, GEC took over its smaller rivals Plessey and Ferranti and effectively pulled out of all but the most specialised (defence-related) electronics. In computers, Siemens took over the other major German player, Nixdorf, to form Siemens-Nixdorf. ICL, the erstwhile British champion, was taken over by the Japanese company Fujitsu. In telecommunications, the break-up of the ITT empire and Alcatel's opportunist bid for its European operations in early 1987 acted to parachute Alcatel into the position of Europe's largest telecommunications equipment firm, alongside the well-known names of Siemens and Ericsson. In consumer electronics, the Finnish company Nokia took over (from Alcatel) ITT's interests. Overnight it became a major European player alongside Philips and Thomson (see Sharp and Holmes 1989).

Increasing concentration, and policies that appeared to be encouraging Europe's MNCs to get into bed with each other, all roused fears among Europe's competitors that the real agenda of the single market initiative was protectionist – creating a Fortress Europe. These fears were reinforced by a number of high-profile trade issues that surfaced in the 1980s. The dispute with the Americans over Airbus rumbled on. In spite of strong pressure from user interests (and US suppliers) the Commission refused to cut the extraordinarily high 17 per cent tariff on foreign-made semiconductors (Flamm 1990). Tariffs were actually increased on a number of sensitive consumer electronic items including VCRs and compact disks (Cawson 1990; Tyson 1992). In the period 1985–90, the EC initiated 209 anti-dumping complaints, 80 of which concerned electronics, mostly targeting suppliers in South-East Asia. Unlike the Americans, whose anti-dumping procedures were slow and highly legalistic, the Commission, as both prosecutor and judge, acted decisively. If investigation upheld the complaint, swingeing duties were rapidly imposed (Office of Technology Assessment 1991: 204).

Was the 1992 project really designed to create a Fortress Europe? Consider, for example, this extract from the Cecchini (1988: 73–4) Report:

> A dramatically new environment awaits consumers and producers alike in the integrated Community market post-1992. The removal of a whole range of non-tariff barriers – frontier red tape, closed public procurement, a plethora of different product standards – leads to an immediate downward impact on costs. But this is merely the primary effect . . . Much more substantial gains will be generated by . . . a new and pervasive competitive climate. One in which the players of the European economy – manufacturing and service companies, and consumers of their output – can exploit new opportunities and better use of available resources . . . For firms the era of the national soft option will be over.

Who was deluding whom? Was there not a contradiction at the centre of EC policy towards new technologies? What was the point in seeking to protect and to promote concentration and collaboration among these major European players, while at the same time arguing the benefits of competition?

This double-edged policy naturally puzzled many commentators. However, these twin tracks echoed the longstanding tension that had been implicit in the Community since its foundation – between 'minimalists', who saw competition policy as the only necessary tool of industrial policy, and 'maximalists', who, from the start, argued for more interventionist supply-side powers. With the Single European Act the maximalist stance was legitimised, but the Act itself was liberalising. The tension was not therefore diminished: rather it resurfaced with greater intensity.

Still, it is plausible to suggest that the tension was (and is) creative rather than destructive. The twin tracks amounted to a sort of carrot-and-stick approach, and a necessary dialectic in policy (Sharp 1991a). A clue came perhaps from the anti-dumping arena. While acting tough, the Commission was always ready to negotiate. Of the 209 cases initiated in the five years after 1985, 51 were settled by agreement, usually on the basis of relocation of production facilities from abroad to within the EC, with high levels of local sourcing. Europe's firms faced direct competition on their home ground from these foreign transplants, but the move also brought new jobs, new management styles and role models in the use of new technologies. More generally, the logic behind the push for the single market by 1992 was that a more competitive Europe had to transform its national champions into firms that could compete against all comers in world markets. The result foreseen was firms of a size and influence beyond the control of the nation-state, possibly even beyond the control of European authorities. The Davignon initiative and the Single European Act provided the impetus towards concentration. There were strong pressures to turn them straight into European champions. Doing so, however, risked defeating the whole purpose of the exercise. Control had instead to come from the market, from firms having to compete with each other and with their Japanese and American competitors, in home as well as in foreign markets. Liberalisation and deregulation in this respect became the essential complements to collaboration and concentration – the twin tracks to competitiveness.

It is perhaps appropriate to conclude with a final quotation from the Cecchini (1988: 75) Report:

> In short, strengthening the European competivity [sic] leads, so to speak, to the reconquest of the European market. Failure to meet the demands of competitivity does not mean that the challenges of the (Single) European market will not be mastered. They will. But not by Europeans.

5

EUREKA!

Understanding European technology policy means casting an analytical net that reaches beyond the EU and the Framework programme. The political and economic forces that gave rise to the Single European Action (SEA) did not produce a single-minded effort to expand the EU's remit in technology policy. Consensus did emerge on the virtues of cross-border collaboration as a means to match the scale of American and Asian R&D efforts. However, national differences of view persisted as to how European collaboration should be organised and funded.

The evolution of EUREKA illustrates these points in bold relief. EUREKA was born in 1985 as the 'European Research Coordinating Agency' (although it soon became known by the abbreviation itself): a French-inspired, intergovernmental and decidedly non-EU initiative. From its origins, it included non-EU member states that did not have full access to the Framework programme. By 1997, EUREKA included six new East European democracies and had institutionalised links to many other states in the region. While virtually all of Europe now participates in EUREKA in some manner, its member states continue to maintain very different policies for supporting and funding projects undertaken within it. EUREKA accounts for a significant amount of research in Europe, and a large share of that which is conducted collaboratively. It is an extraordinary initiative in that it seeks to promote a form of collective action – collaborative R&D – with almost no common rules or institutions. EUREKA is a striking case of a programme without policy, or governance without government (see Peterson 1993b: 215–22; Rhodes 1996).

We begin this chapter by providing an overview of EUREKA,

and then sketch its origins and development. In analytical terms, we place EUREKA against the backdrop of the 1992 project, the evolution of European integration and the rise of European technology policy. We try to clarify the meaning of EUREKA, in theory and practice, for the development of European technology policy.

What is EUREKA?

EUREKA is by far the largest of all non-EU collaborative research initiatives in Europe. Although direct comparisons are difficult to make, by the mid-1990s EUREKA represented a total research effort only marginally smaller than the Framework programme. The Framework IV programme was worth about 13–14 billion ECU in Community funding over 5 years, or roughly 2.7 billion ECU per year. An equivalent investment of private funding – which not all EU projects had – would have meant that EU programmes represented a total annual research effort of around 5.4 billion ECU. Meanwhile, the total value (public *and* private funding) of all ongoing EUREKA projects was 11.3 billion ECU, with an average project length of 'slightly above 2.5 years' (EUREKA Secretariat 1996a: 1). Thus, EUREKA represented an annual research effort of close to 4.5 billion ECU.

By 1997, the total value of nearly 1200 ongoing or finished EUREKA projects was estimated at 16.7 billion ECU. The completion of the JESSI project in 1996 – with a total price tag of 3.8 billion ECU – caused the value of EUREKA's project list and its average project size to plummet (see Table 5.1). Nevertheless, EUREKA clearly had blossomed into an important framework for organising and funding projects that, for one reason or another, did not fit within the Framework programme.

Initially, following its launch in 1985, EUREKA brought together 20 participants: the (then) EC 12, the 6 EFTA (European Free Trade Area) states – Austria, Finland, Norway, Sweden, Switzerland and Iceland (which joined in 1986) – plus Turkey and the European Commission. Subsequently, EUREKA was one of the first West European regimes to open its doors to Central and Eastern Europe. Between 1992 and 1997, its membership swelled to 26, including (in order of admittance) Hungary, Slovenia, the Czech Republic, Poland, Russia and Romania.

TABLE 5.1

Evolution of EUREKA's project list – 1985–97

Year	1985	1986	1987	1988	1989	1990	1991	1992	1993	1994	1995	1996	1997
Total Number Ongoing Projects	10	109	165	212	292	369	478	539	675	654	720	718	668
Total Value Ongoing Projects(BECU)	0.4	3.2	4.0	3.8	6.4	7.8	8.4	9.4	15.3	11.7	10.2	11.3	6.2
Average Ongoing Project Size (MECU)	40	29	24	18	22	21	18	17	23	18	14	16	9
Total Number Finished Projects	—	—	—	1	7	18	34	62	129	211	290	360	515

— = nil.

Sources: EUREKA secretariat 1996c; Peterson 1993b; EUREKA secretariat 1997.

EUREKA's founding charter, or Declaration of Principles, is a minimalist and anodyne document. It states that projects may be granted the EUREKA 'label' in virtually any area of civilian technology. All must include partners from at least two member states and feature an 'adequate financial commitment by participant enterprises' (EUREKA Secretariat 1985: 2). EUREKA's coordinating body is its Ministerial Conference, which consists of national research or industry ministers from each member state. It is assisted by a group of 'High Representatives', or senior civil servants. The chairmanship of EUREKA passes between member states each year, with the chair taking responsibility for any new policy initiatives. The initiative's only truly common institution is a 'small and flexible' Secretariat, consisting of civil servants seconded from EUREKA member states, who essentially collect information and have virtually no policy responsibilities (EUREKA Secretariat 1985: 6).

EUREKA is firmly intergovernmental and industry-led. Its member states maintain their own national policies for supporting collaborative projects. The role of public authorities in actually designing projects, while varying somewhat between member states, is generally minimal. Nearly all projects are formed according to a 'bottom-up' methodology: firms and other research organisations design their own collaborative proposals, with research partners entirely responsible for determining a project's membership, management and objectives. According to a set of procedures agreed in 1986, all project proposals must circulate for 45 days on EUREKA's central database to all other member states before they are 'labelled' so that as many potential partners as possible may know of their existence (British EUREKA Chairmanship 1986: 2). However, the original designers of any project proposal are free to accept or reject the overtures of other firms that wish to participate.

Difficult early negotiations took place on precisely what *kind* of project EUREKA should fund. Yet, any genuine restrictions would have been made moot anyway by EUREKA's strict intergovernmentalism, as no government can stop any other from labelling a proposed project that meets the (minimal) criteria set out in the Declaration of Principles. The idea that EUREKA would fund more 'near-market' R&D and avoid the pre-competitive restrictions of EU-funded research was at least implied in the Declaration, which stated EUREKA's aspiration to fund projects aimed at 'worldwide market[s]' (EUREKA secretariat 1985: 1). In practice, however, EUREKA funds a very diverse collection of projects, some of which are clearly pre-competitive. Governments rarely turn down a bona fide collaborative project when the EUREKA label is sought.

EUREKA started out with French-inspired ambitions to fund expensive and complex *grands projets* which could match the scale of large collaborative projects underway in Japan and the US. In the event, it became the favoured framework for ambitious and truly pan-European efforts to develop critical technologies, such as High Definition Television (HDTV) and the next generation of semiconductors (in JESSI), in part because EUREKA allowed the pooling of national *and* EU efforts (see Chapter 8).

However, the long-term trend has been towards more EUREKA projects of a progressively smaller value (see Table 5.1). Most national research budgets first suffered cuts during the recession of the early 1990s and then again in the run-up to EMU, while private R&D stagnated. The knock-on effects for EUREKA were direct.

Any data concerning EUREKA's projects must be treated with caution. In the words of a senior EUREKA official, 'EUREKA is very much a federated structure and a very loose one at that. So there's ample scope for a lot of pretty loose information or simply no information' (quoted in Peterson 1993b: 92). To illustrate the point, participants in EUREKA projects are effectively responsible for estimating the size of their projects, which are often complex and usually combine funding from multiple national and public and private sources.

Nevertheless, as Table 5.2 highlights, EUREKA clearly has facilitated very large collaborative investments in IT. Robotics and environmental technologies have seen the labelling of large numbers of smaller projects. In political terms, EUREKA remains a clearly French (and German) led initiative, although other member states have made much of the running in certain sectors: such as the Dutch in new materials, the UK in lasers, and the Italians in robotics and transport (see Table 5.3).

In short, EUREKA is a strange and amorphous initiative about which it is difficult to generalise. However, it has become an important tool in Europe's technology policy 'arsenal'. Understanding it is essential to gauging the extent to which national technology policy agendas have converged.

TABLE 5.2

EUREKA projects by sector (1997)

	Biotech.	Comm.	Energy	Environ	IT	Laser	Materials	Robotics	Transport	Total
TOTAL number of projects	127	22	29	138	119	14	76	96	47	668
TOTAL project cost[a] (million ECU)	443	665	125	492	3 296	64	182	434	522	6 223

[a] Represents total public and private investment in R&D

Source: Eureka secretariat (1997).

Reagan, Narjes, Mitterrand and the legacy of 1985

The origins of EUREKA are both fascinating and germane to the way it operates. The design of EUREKA was informed directly by the lessons of previous attempts to organise collaborative R&D in Europe (see Chapter 2). One of the clearest was that politics could ruin an initiative regardless of its economic, policy or strategic logic. Joint computer schemes such as Unidata collapsed because of bickering between governments more than between industrial partners. Political criteria mandated a rigid collaborative framework that ensured Concorde's commercial failure. Above all, the European Commission's proposals for new collaborative programmes almost always became bound up in wider political disputes about how much *acquis* the EU should have in technology policy.

The 'technology gap' debate of the early 1980s arose mainly because of European alarm at rapid, previously undreamt of advances by Japanese competitors. The strong role of private firms in organising research consortia in Japan, plus a general desire to avoid politicising research, convinced many European governments that new collaborative programmes should be industry-led. In future, collaboration would be encouraged, but public administrations would demur from choosing how research consortia should be organised or what should be their goals.

A separate set of pressures on Europe stemmed from the Reagan administration's defence build-up, which spurred a 30 per cent increase in US government spending on R&D. In early 1983, after virtually no consultation with European governments, the Americans unveiled the Strategic Defense Initiative (SDI): a plan to spend up to 26 billion ECU to build a space-based nuclear defence system. The Reagan administration's offer of SDI contracts to European firms in spring 1985 set off alarm bells in many European capitals, where it was feared that the invitation was a thinly-veiled attempt to plunder Europe's best researchers and firms.

Karl-Heinz Narjes, the European Commissioner for research, seized on European anxieties by publicly advocating a three-fold increase in EU spending on research in April 1985. At this point, with the Commission's White Paper on the internal market about to be tabled (see Cockfield 1994), the time seemed ripe to relaunch the 'European project' more generally. Increased EU funding for research seemed a logical corollary. Duff (1986: 48) caught the

TABLE 5.3

Total investment[a] by member state in ongoing EUREKA projects by sector (1997)

Member state	Biotechnology	Communications	Energy	Environ	IT	Laser	Materials	Robotics	Transport
Austria	11.6	2.0	0.5	31.1	54.5	1.5	3.5	11.7	10.9
Belgium	14.5	1.3	1.2	18.4	116.7	1.0	14.7	7.1	5.4
Czech Republic	1.4	—	—	4.1	0.8	—	0.2	1.6	1.0
Denmark	28.0	70.4	0.6	24.6	34.7	3.2	6.4	11.2	3.6
Finland	6.0	22.3	10.0	5.1	36.2	0.2	4.8	5.6	4.1
France	99.2	255.5	55.1	112.3	1 033.6	10.3	29.3	75.3	124.1
Germany	57.5	50.4	1.5	80.2	772.9	10.6	11.3	52.5	101.0
Greece	1.9	—	—	1.5	6.4	0.1	—	—	—
Hungary	8.7	—	—	1.7	6.4	0.1	0.2	3.0	—
Iceland	0.9	—	0.1	0.1	5.4	—	0.4	—	—
Ireland	2.8	—	—	1.7	6.7	—	11.6	74.1	146.6
Italy	25.4	13.2	4.0	44.1	392.6	9.6	2.7	—	—
Luxembourg	—	—	—	2.6	—	—	26.9	29.1	21.9
Netherlands	63.0	194.7	2.4	36.8	512.3	1.6	5.0	0.2	13.2
Norway	2.7	1.5	8.5	18.6	31.6	—	2.5	—	1.2
Poland	1.1	—	0.7	3.5	0.2	—	0.1	5.6	1.2
Portugal	8.1	1.2	2.9	1.8	11.9	1.3	0.1	—	—
Romania	2.1	—	0.4	2.2	0.3	—	1.1	4.2	0.4
Russia	0.7	—	—	0.6	0.4	1.0	0.8	2.6	—
Slovenia	0.1	—	—	2.1	6.2	—	—	—	—
Spain	34.7	6.5	2.3	29.0	45.4	2.0	10.0	73.2	15.1
Sweden	20.0	1.0	6.7	10.3	12.2	0.5	4.8	5.4	10.2

TABLE 5.3 (*continued*)

Member state	Biotechnology	Communications	Energy	Environ	IT	Laser	Materials	Robotics	Transport
Switzerland	8.6	2.1	8.9	7.3	12.6	1.8	23.2	29.7	19.3
Turkey	3.5	—	—	3.3	—	—	—	6.4	3.3
UK	37.1	37.6	15.5	34.7	97.0	16.5	19.2	24.3	25.8
EU	0.3	—	—	6.5	1.5	—	0.5	—	—
Others	0.2	—	0.5	1.3	2.1	0.6	0.2	1.1	0.2

— = nil.

[a] Represents total public and private investment in R&D

Source: Eureka secretariat (1997).

mood of the times well: 'Both the Commission and European Parliament have fallen upon high-tech with some relief, arguing confidently that if ever there was a case for European integration, this is it.'

However, only a week after the Commission (1985) unveiled its proposal for a vastly expanded Framework programme, Mitterrand tabled his own proposal for EUREKA. The idea was pitched as an alternative to European participation in SDI, which the French found politically loathsome. Instead of signing on to an American military programme with dubious effects for the arms control process and Europe's technological independence, governments were urged to join in a purely European programme with purely civilian purposes. Coming so closely on the heels of Narjes's call for a huge increase in EU research funding, the EUREKA proposal also reflected French scepticism – shared by the West Germans and British – about a large increase in the EU's R&D *'acquis'*, or its acquired knowledge, attainments and experience.

The domestic context of French political economy in 1985 mattered, too. Mitterrand's EUREKA proposal followed several still-born initiatives to revive France's ailing high-tech industries, particularly the socialists' ambitious *filières*. EUREKA was a new tack: it would fund 'near-market', collaborative research and combine European resources in projects that France could not afford on its own.

Initially, at least, it was unclear whether EUREKA would be truly 'industry-led'. The French proposed that EUREKA should have a centralised secretariat to coordinate 'technical steering committees', which would target topics for collaborative projects. Paris gave strong signals to suggest that EUREKA would require large amounts of funding – up to 8 billion ECU over its first five years – with much of it coming from public sources (Peterson 1993b: 67–8). It took little imagination to suspect that EUREKA was intended, above all, to allow France to channel large dollops of public funds to primarily French projects. Meddlesome scrutiny by the European Commission's competition authorities could be avoided if EURE-KA projects had a nominal 'European' label on them.

The first West German reactions to the French proposal were 'very cold', while initial British responses were 'glacial' (Sandholtz 1992: 273). However, the EUREKA proposal was so vague that outright rejection was almost impossible. For their part, as the crucial

Milan EU summit of June 1985 approached, Delors and Narjes prepared a memorandum that urged that EUREKA be combined or at least closely coordinated with the Framework programme. Mitterrand would have none of it. He secured an endorsement of EUREKA at Milan that was entirely separate from a summit declaration on the Framework programme. In political terms, it clearly mattered that whatever doubts other Community governments and the Commission had about the French agenda, they could not deny France's leadership of Airbus and Ariane, both of which were considered collaborative successes.

In the meantime, industry had begun to take an interest in EUREKA. Promises of public funding, while unspecified, encouraged French national technology champions, such as Matra, Aérospatiale and Thomson, to announce new collaborative agreements with firms from other European states under the auspices of EUREKA. Remarkably, firms began signing up to EUREKA even before political agreement was reached on the initiative's finance, national membership, or rules of participation.

The French managed to convince all of their EU partners plus five EFTA states to send research ministers to discuss EUREKA in Paris about a month after the Milan EU summit. At the summit, Mitterrand announced that France would commit 160 million ECU in new funding to the scheme. Most other governments declined to specify amounts, but hinted that some public funding would be made available. French proposals for a powerful EUREKA secretariat were dropped amid strong opposition from several other member states, notably West Germany. However, disagreements at the political level over this point and others persisted for months, leading European industrialists to complain loudly and publicly about the failure of European governments to put flesh on EUREKA's bones.

At this point, EUREKA might have died a quiet death if its rotating chairmanship had not passed first to West Germany and then to the UK. The period prior to EUREKA's launch had witnessed severe tensions in Franco-German relations. They were exacerbated by the typically agonised reaction of the Kohl government to French demands that West Germany make a clear choice between SDI and EUREKA, Reagan and Mitterrand, America and France. Mitterrand, in his typically uncompromising style, pushed Kohl hard to endorse EUREKA and reject SDI. The French president found an ally in West Germany's fervently pro-European Foreign Minister, Hans-Dietrich Genscher. A key figure in Bonn's coalition government, and the leader of the Free Democratic Party, Genscher cast the EUREKA v. SDI question as a litmus test for Franco-German relations. Eventually, Kohl embraced EUREKA.

After EUREKA's first ministerial conference in July 1985, the West Germans took over the initiative's chairmanship from the French. Officials in Bonn clearly worked hard to mould the initiative to suit the Kohl government's preferences, and brokered difficult negotiations on EUREKA's founding Declaration of Principles (EUREKA Secretariat 1985). The Declaration made it clear that EUREKA would be a decentralised, industry-led, non-bureaucratic initiative that adopted a 'bottom-up' approach, but also could fund large projects (of German interest) in environmental or transport technologies.

The subsequent British chairmanship of 1986 convinced other member states that EUREKA's secretariat should be very small (with seven members initially), which would be restricted to compiling information and managing a central data base of projects. At the same time, the UK gave critical political support to the initiative. EUREKA's list of projects increased in value seven-fold to reach 2 billion ECU by July 1986. Even the UK's reliably Eurosceptic Prime Minister, Margaret Thatcher, endorsed EUREKA as 'a key element in Europe's industrial strategy . . . Through EUREKA, European firms can help us identify the steps to open markets which will most help them' (quoted in Peterson 1993b: 70). With France, West Germany and the UK firmly on board, the momentum behind EUREKA was unstoppable.

In retrospect, it is clear that EUREKA ended up being a decidedly different initiative than was first envisaged by Mitterrand, while still remaining true to the original French blueprint for a non-EU intergovernmental framework. In this context, Mitterrand's efforts to distance Europe from SDI and Reagan's America served a dual purpose: they also ensured that Narjes and the Commission did not achieve a monopoly over new collaborative programmes. More specifically, the French pursued a three-pronged strategy to keep the Commission from hijacking EUREKA. First, they allied with the West Germany and the UK. As larger and more technologically advanced states, all three sought to limit the expansion of the EU's new remit in technology policy.

Second, with a view to the declining fortunes of its own hi-tech firms, the French insisted that EUREKA should give a short, sharp jolt to Europe's research effort. As such, EUREKA needed to fund 'near-market' R&D, which sought to develop marketable products or processes within five years or less. EU control over EUREKA was virtually excluded because of treaty restrictions, which limited the Union's programmes to 'pre-competitive' research.

A third prong in the French strategy was to neglect no potential allies in making the case for EUREKA and against SDI, even if it meant looking beyond the Community's 1985 borders. A few days after the French secured West Germany's initial endorsement of EUREKA in May 1985, Norway declared itself ready to participate as well. All of the EFTA states (and Turkey) followed suit.

In short, the French took considerable pains to distance EURE-KA from the Commission. Not only did 'near market' projects make EU participation problematic. If EFTA states and Turkey were to participate, any notion of incorporating EUREKA into the Framework programme became a dead letter, because the Commission would face the problem of assuring *juste retour* within a programme that included non-contributors to the EC's budget. As a purely intergovernmental initiative, EUREKA's lack of a central budget would 'skirt the problems of fair returns and commercial interests' (Sandholtz 1992: 297).

EUREKA and the politics of a wider Europe

Inviting non-EU member states to join EUREKA was not only a ploy to keep the Commission from hijacking the initiative. The Nordic countries offered top-rank, globally competitive firms, such as Finland's Nokia and Sweden's Volvo, and world-class expertise in robotics. Austria brought strong universities and public laboratories to EUREKA. Switzerland proffered a dynamic coterie of small firms, strong large chemicals or pharmaceutical firms (Ciba Geigy, Sandoz (now Novartis) and Hoffman LaRoche), besides a share of ABB and others, plus large sources of private funding.

Still, it was difficult not to view EUREKA's wide membership as providing disproportionate benefits to non-EU states and firms. As the momentum behind the 1992 project gathered pace, EFTA member states – all of which had domestic markets of 8 million consumers or less – had to exploit every possible opportunity to forge links with the new single market of 340 million consumers. EUREKA offered the EFTANs an important opportunity to link with the Union's research effort. In particular, EUREKA was launched after the signing of the Luxembourg Accord in 1984, which set in motion a series of exchanges with EFTA to create a 'European Economic Area'. Research and science were flagged as areas where cooperation would be deepened.

However, EFTA firms remained excluded for another four years from participation in most industrially oriented initiatives under the Framework programme. Even EU programmes with more decidedly pre-competitive goals, such as promoting scientific exchange or developing economic science, allowed EFTA participation only in projects that included at least two EU organisations to 'protect the Community interest'. Finally, in 1990, the EFTA states asked for full participation rights to the Framework programme, and offered to contribute to its financing on an equal footing with Community states. The Commission (1990: 2) objected, claiming that 'this is a political matter which requires further study in the context of overall relations between these countries and the Community'. In the event, the issue of EFTA participation became highly contentious and slowed full adoption of the Framework III programme in 1991. The full membership of EFTA countries in EUREKA, however, emboldened them in pressing their demands on the EU. By the early 1990s, between a fifth and a quarter of around four hundred EUREKA projects included an EFTA partner.

EUREKA also figured prominently in early discussions between the EU and the former Warsaw Pact states. In February 1990, the EU's Research Council discussed the possibility of opening European collaborative R&D schemes to participants from East European countries. The Commission complained that the idea posed 'considerable conceptual difficulties'. Predictably, it suggested instead that EUREKA and COST should be 'opened up' first (quoted in Peterson 1993b: 120). A few months later, the Conference on Security and Cooperation in Europe (CSCE) met in Bonn and produced proposals for a series of new 'pan-European procedures and institutions', including an enlarged EUREKA that took in all thirty-five CSCE member states, including the US, Canada and virtually all Eastern European countries. The idea was backed both by the Commission and Genscher, the summit's chair.

The proposals generated considerable agitation within EUREKA. Research ministries in most EUREKA member states opposed the use of the initiative as a political tool, particularly by the Commission. As a decentralised initiative with no central budget, which sought to fund 'near market' R&D, EUREKA hardly seemed appropriate as a tool for distributing research aid to the east. Still, the 1990 Dutch chairmanship was forced to take proactive steps to defuse political pressures to expand EUREKA's membership radically and quickly. Clearer criteria were developed for 'third country' participation and joint congresses were organised on EUREKA with the Polish and Hungarian governments.

In 1992, Hungary was admitted formally as a EUREKA member state. After a strong push by Germany overcame the considerable reluctance of other member states, Russia joined in 1993. Slovenia, the Czech Republic, Poland and Romania followed in 1994–7. Demands for membership from seven other eastern countries – Albania, Bulgaria, Estonia, Latvia, Lithuania, Slovakia and Ukraine – were appeased by offering them a form of association through 'National Information Points' (NIPs). Information on EUREKA's evolving project list was circulated to all NIPs. Firms from these countries were welcomed into projects that included participants from at least two EUREKA member states.

By 1997, EUREKA's project database gave details of participation by 44 different countries (see Table 5.4). More than 3000 different organisations participated in EUREKA projects, including more than 25 non-member-state organisations ranging from the US to the Vatican City. The degree to which the Franco-German axis existed at the core of EUREKA was evidenced by the fact that Germany and France continued to provide nearly half of all funding for EUREKA (public and private). Yet, from its origins, EUREKA encouraged the expansion of Europe's 'technological community' further and faster beyond the EU's borders than any other collaborative initiative (see Peterson 1997a).

EUREKA's links to firms and states beyond the EU's borders have complicated its relationship with the European Commission. These links have led to unwelcome demands being made on the Commission, and have made it difficult for the Commission to contribute Community funds to EUREKA projects. One of the most interesting technology policy stories of the 1980s was the way in which EUREKA was created to rival the Framework

TABLE 5.4

National contributions to EUREKA (ongoing projects 1997)

Member State	Participating Organisations (number)	Financial contribution (public + private funds in million ECU)	Total number of projects in which involved
Austria	139	123	91
Belgium	115	180	87
Czech Republic	37	9	27
Denmark	115	183	88
Finland	120	94	55
France	446	1 795	203
Germany	380	1 138	219
Greece	19	10	13
Hungary	44	22	32
Iceland	18	10	9
Ireland	15	12	13
Italy	135	721	76
Luxembourg	2	5	2
Netherlands	248	889	163
Norway	79	81	59
Poland	32	9	22
Portugal	67	34	42
Romania	10	5	6
Russia	35	9	22
Slovenia	31	12	20
Spain	195	218	119
Sweden	134	71	116
Switzerland	269	114	117
Turkey	27	17	15
UK	288	308	149
EU	5	9	6
All others	33	6	25
TOTALS	3 039	[a]6 223	668

[a]   Figures in rows do not add up to this figure because of rounding.

Source: EUREKA secretariat (1993; 1997).

programme, as much as to complement it. The rivalry never disappeared entirely.

In some respects, EUREKA membership became a plausible stepping stone to full participation by the new democracies in the Framework programme. Hungary had become well integrated into

EUREKA within a few years after its accession, in part through the use of EU funds from the PHARE (Poland and Hungary: Aid for the Reconstruction of Economies) programme. Unfortunately, Russia joined in 1993 just as the negative economic effects of the dissolution of the Soviet Union were being felt most. Subsequently, Russian firms usually could not obtain public funding for EUREKA projects, thus producing a relatively low participation rate. More generally, a fierce debate within EUREKA about whether or not Russia really had a market economy and was thus eligible for membership, never really subsided. Officials from several long-time member states continued to complain years later that both Russian officials and firms simply did not understand market forces. They also complained that the only reliable way of communicating with Russia's Ministry for Science and Technology Policy was to send hard copies of documents by courier.

The subsequent accessions of Slovenia, the Czech Republic, Poland and Romania were far less controversial. Both Slovenia and the Czech Republic quickly began generating large numbers of projects, given the size of their economies, after joining in 1994–5. A massive programme of public investment in Poland's transport infrastructure, which promised 2 600 kilometres of highway and rail improvements before the year 2010, plus substantial inward investment from the West, boosted Polish participation in EUREKA. Romania acceded in 1997 on the strength of resolute support from France and a personal appeal by the Romanian Prime Minister, Victor Ciorbea.

Yet, from the point of view of EUREKA's original members, enlargement has not been cost-free. For one thing, it has made the initiative more difficult to manage. All of its decision-making bodies have become large and unwieldy, in a way that perhaps foreshadows the EU of the future. Perhaps above all, it has become more difficult to keep EUREKA focused on the original mission chosen for it: to fund 'near-market' R&D in which private actors take the lead. For the new Eastern member states, the state must often take the lead if they are to participate in EUREKA projects at all. More generally, as one senior EUREKA official put it:

I must say that the new members are quite eager and ambitious and they want to learn, so that's very encouraging, and they are open to criticism more than the old members . . . But enlarge-

ment has diluted the quality of projects in EUREKA, perceptibly.
(Interview, September 1996)

EUREKA grows up: 1985–97

The EU's 1992 project was informed by a powerful and pervasive
new faith in market solutions to economic problems. The conversion
of Mitterrand and the French socialists to slogans such as '*C'est l'en-
treprise qui crée la richesse*' was a key development (quoted in
Humphreys 1991: 119). Another was the emergence of consensus
on the notion that declining European technological competitiveness
required market-led, and not *dirigiste*, solutions. The Commission
managed to convince EU member states – some of them very
grudgingly – to provide more public funding for targeted, pre-competitive research via the Framework programme. However, EURE-
KA was hatched as a decidedly industry-led programme. Firms and
research labs themselves organised and proposed its projects.
Governments promised 'supportive measures' (such as work on common standards) designed to help the results of EUREKA projects
find markets. Nevertheless, the role of governments generally was
confined to deciding which projects to support with what amount of
national public funding.

In important respects, the adoption of this methodology revealed
European states mimicking Japanese methods. In relative terms,
Japanese public spending on research was low as a percentage of the
total spent on R&D in Japan. A high percentage was funded by
industry, instead of the state, which appeared to make Japan's
research effort more productive (see Freeman 1987; Sharp 1993).
EUREKA's industry-led methodology was designed to provide private firms with incentives to fund more of their own R&D, and to
do it collaboratively with other European firms. Public funding was
available – far more from some governments (France) than others
(the UK), with some offering virtually none – but only to projects
that were backed by an 'adequate financial commitment by participating enterprises' (EUREKA Secretariat 1985: 3).

Reliable figures on precisely how much public funding member
states spend on EUREKA projects have simply never existed (but
see Peterson 1993b: 75–90). Note that Table 5.2 contains information on public *and* private funding contributed by each member

state. This level of detail is the most that has emerged from a continuing effort to make EUREKA more 'transparent', although there is
widespread consensus that public funding represents about 35 per
cent of the total value of all ongoing projects.

EUREKA not only has Japanese-style affectations; it also fits with
the ethos of the 1992 project. First, its industry-led approach and
strictly intergovernmental structure means that EUREKA requires
only minimal harmonisation of national policies. Only a minority of
countries (6 of 26, by one count in 1997) have 'dedicated budgets',
or funding earmarked specifically for EUREKA projects, and even
these budgets are small: between 2 and 10 million ECU per year.
Most member states make funds available for EUREKA from a
wide range of national research schemes. The result is a myriad of
different rules, timescales and criteria for funding decisions.

EUREKA also is congruent with the 1992 project in facilitating
an increase in collaborative research, without negotiating detailed
rules to govern it. In its methodology, EUREKA resembles cornerstones of the internal market such as the mutual recognition of standards. The 1992 project was built upon these and other means for
delivering collective goods, while leaving national policy differences
largely intact (see Wallace and Young 1996).

Finally, like the 1992 project, EUREKA was an élite-led initiative,
which had the effect of blurring lines of accountability in the exercise of public policy. Where EUREKA did act to harmonise national policies, the power to determine who received public money often
was effectively transferred to insular and multinational technocra-
cies. The very minimal administrative resources that most member
states invested at the national level in EUREKA – an average of
only four 'man-years' per state (Finnish EUREKA Chairmanship
1992: 3) – was mirrored by its very small and essentially powerless
central secretariat. EUREKA represented an attempt to influence
private sector behaviour with the absolute minimum public power
necessary.

Two categories of EUREKA project in particular tended to
spawn empires within empires: first, its largest and most ambitious
projects (such as JESSI); and, second, its 'umbrella projects'. The latter category were 'stand-alone' frameworks designed to catalyse
R&D in particular sectors by creating dedicated administrations to
generate projects and earmarking money to fund them (Peterson
1993b: 217). In both types of project, responsible national officials

often found themselves with little control over or information about projects. Despite EUREKA's near-market ethos, several of its environmental umbrellas featured minimal participation by industry, thus muddying the initiative's image. Others developed their own information systems and bureaucracies, which acted as barriers to the entry of new potential partners.

EUREKA's most notorious and expensive failure, the HDTV project, was singled out for its lack of transparency during a review by the Dutch presidency of 1991. Although much the same criticism was levelled at the generally far more successful JESSI project, the broader point is that EUREKA, at least in its early years, was not characterised by the sort of accountability and transparency that are considered essential elements of democratic societies.

By the mid-1990s, there was far more information exchanged between national EUREKA offices concerning public funding criteria and amounts than had been the case in the initiative's first few years. Still, accountability and transparency remained problems, which enlargement tended to exacerbate. More experienced member states caucused informally to try to ensure that EUREKA continued to work for their own purposes, which often were quite different from those of the newer member states. In particular, the French agreed to enlarge EUREKA after 1992 with considerable reluctance. In the words of a British official, 'they're not happy about [enlargement] because it means that their grand design is unravelling a bit' (interview, February 1996). One French response in 1995–6 was to argue for new, formal links between EUREKA and two other French-led initiatives, the European Space Agency (ESA) and Audio-Visual EUREKA (the latter an entirely separate initiative for promoting collaborative European film productions). With French encouragement, the Belgian EUREKA chairmanship of the period investigated the ideas of coordinating research underway within EUREKA with efforts undertaken by the ESA and AV-EUREKA, but also pursued a more general and ambitious agenda. It ranged from proposals to try to improve the quality of new EUREKA projects, procedures for the continuous evaluation of existing projects, closer links between EUREKA and the Framework programme, and a stronger role for the EUREKA secretariat. Over time, France had become a crucial backer of ideas for giving more responsibility to the Secretariat, partly as a way to keep EUREKA's mission intact after its enlargement. More generally, the French became concerned that EUREKA's mission was becoming blurred as its membership expanded.

To some extent, EUREKA's enlargement acted to strengthen its links to the Framework programme. Several events organised in Poland and elsewhere to educate eastern research communities about collaborative programmes in the West were organised and funded jointly by the Commission and EUREKA. In October 1993, the EU's Council of Research Ministers agreed that EUREKA projects could be funded without any special dispensation under the Framework IV programme. The 1995 Belgian chairmanship probably expended more time and effort on EU–EUREKA links than any previous chairmanship, even though the issue had preoccupied all EU member states that had ever held EUREKA's chair. Hopes were raised in 1995, when the new Director-General of DG XII was announced as Jorma Routti, the former president of the Finnish research fund, SITRA, which funded much of Finland's participation in EUREKA.

Yet, EUREKA's links to the Framework remained tenuous. Commenting on relations with the Commission, a member of the EUREKA network wryly commented, 'We always have very nice get togethers with them. We always say that we love each other, you know, but we never make love' (interview, September 1996). Between 1994 and 1996, the Commission did not provide funding to a single new EUREKA project.

The UK, which succeeded the Belgians in the EUREKA Chair in 1996–7, finally appeared to achieve a breakthrough on the issue. A declaration on 'synergy' between EUREKA and the EU was accepted at the June 1997 London ministerial conference. It acknowledged that EUREKA might 'need to make changes to its own procedures' to ensure adequate synergy, while proposing that the Commission take measures such as holding back 'a significant part of the budget' for Framework V to be spent in the last few years of its life span (1999–2002). The goal was to allow scope for EU funding of EUREKA projects organised by industry (UK Chairmanship 1997b: 2–4). The London ministerial conference even featured a keynote speech by Edith Cresson (1997) in which she urged a new '*espace européen de la recherche*', particularly through stronger EUREKA–EU links. Routti seemed neutral about synergy with EUREKA: as a national of a small and recent EU member state, he tended to tread lightly in the Commission. Cresson, however, seized on new interest in generating projects of 'strategic interest' by challenging the EUREKA network to come up with three large, ambitious projects – *à la* JESSI – that could be partially funded by the EU under Framework V (UK EUREKA Chairmanship 1997a: 3).

Whatever comes of the synergy initiative, it is clear that EUREKA has 'rounded off the edges' of national European technology policies only very minimally. National policy prerogatives remain jealously guarded, and EUREKA remains purely intergovernmental. At the same time, the trend is towards steps, such as empowering the Secretariat with backing from older and more powerful member states, to try to ensure that EUREKA's purpose is not diluted by its enlargement. More such steps may be on the horizon, particularly further synergy with EU research, which have the effect of harmonising national EUREKA policies. Still, there is far to go before EUREKA and the Framework programme are properly linked, as opposed to working at cross-purposes, as they still sometimes appeared to be doing even in the late 1990s.

Conclusion

We have sketched the historical evolution of EUREKA, and focused mainly on history-making decisions that determined what sort of initiative it would become. In later chapters, we focus on EUREKA's mechanisms for making more day-to-day decisions (Chapter 8), as well as the results of multiple evaluations of the initiative (Chapter 9). For now, it suffices to note that EUREKA provides interesting fodder for competing theories of political integration.

For intergovernmentalists, EUREKA provides the perfect antidote to neofunctionalist theory. EUREKA has been marked by little 'spillover', and seems a case of European cooperation without institutions, or any perceptible, wider political impact beyond its day-to-day, low-key activities. It has resulted in little actual integration or even harmonisation of national technology policies. EUREKA fuels the argument of scholars who insist that European states may cooperate in areas where their preferences converge, but that the resultant regimes remain driven by national preferences, and that they do little to alter the behaviour of national governments (Moravcsik 1993; Grieco 1995).

To illustrate the point, France's powerful preference for European products that could challenge American dominance in industries associated with the new media led the French to back a proposal, originally tabled by the Commission, to create a new EUREKA umbrella for multi-media projects in 1996. Paradoxically, France generally and fiercely opposed the creation of new umbrellas on the grounds that they became unaccountable. However, the French interest in developing European 'cultural products', as a bulwark against ones made in America, overrode any aversion to umbrella projects within EUREKA. For intergovernmentalists, this case illustrates the point that national preferences are 'superior', 'prior' and 'exogenous' to collaboration: they are not conditioned or altered very much by participation in European programmes (Moravcsik 1993).

On the other hand, the EUREKA multi-media initiative lacked much substance when it was agreed that it should be launched under the Belgian 1996 chairmanship. At this point, at the behest of several larger member states, the EUREKA Secretariat took the policy initiative (really for the first time). It organised a three-pronged effort: culling the current EUREKA project list for projects that might be appropriate for the umbrella, surveying national multi-media policies, and asking EU member states what they thought the Commission should be doing in the sector. Run by the single official with the longest experience of EUREKA, Pol Van den Bergen (head of the Dutch EUREKA office from 1986 to 95), the Secretariat was asserting itself as never before. Neofunctionalists could take comfort in the slow but clear trend towards the strengthening of EUREKA's only central institution.

Cutting through the intergovernmentalist–neofunctionalist debate, Sandholtz's (1992) model of inter-state cooperation sheds considerable light on the origins and evolution of EUREKA. Sandholtz (1992: 297) argues that there must first be a demand for collaboration, as there clearly was in 1985: the 'generalised policy crisis in European high technology' seemed rooted in the inadequate scale of Europe's research effort, and manageable only through cooperation. Second, a political agent must provide leadership, as the French clearly did, although important contributions were later made by the (West) Germans and British. Third, and crucially, states must be able to solve the problem of *juste retour*. As Sandholtz (1992: 297) observes, '[b]ecause EUREKA has no central budget, there is no problem of *juste retour*'.

Still, in some respects, EUREKA reflects more than mere 'adaptation' of national policies to suit existing goals. Arguably, it is a manifestation of a 'far-reaching cognitive shift [of] *learning*', involving the actual revaluation of policy goals (Sandholtz 1992: 18). Before the mid-1980s, large European states sought both technological prowess and independence. For example, an explicit goal of the French socialists' *filières electroniques* scheme after 1981 was French independence in the production of semiconductors by 1986 (Sandholtz 1992: 11). By 1985, European governments had found that their policy goal of independence was no longer realisable, and thus they learned to pool (limited) resources at the EU level via the Framework programme. However, they hedged their bets: EUREKA was a new potential route to national technological prowess, even if independence was no longer achievable. EUREKA obviated the need to give up policy prerogatives that remained stubbornly national and jealously guarded.

We have seen that EUREKA's minimal administration, strictly intergovernmental structure, industry-led ethos and civilian emphasis were designed to depoliticise the initiative. EUREKA was created to generate collaborative R&D projects that deserved public support because they were underpinned by economic, strategic or policy logic, not because they met political criteria. Its success may be viewed as proving the wisdom of the strategy of, so far as is possible, keeping politics out of technology policy.

6

Maastricht and Framework IV

In retrospect, the late 1980s were something of a golden era for European integration. The period featured genuine progress towards freeing the internal market, a general economic upturn, and the dramatic collapse of communism in Eastern and Central Europe, as well as the (relatively undramatic) establishment of collaborative research programmes as an accepted feature of Europe's industrial landscape. By the end of the decade, the Framework programme and EUREKA even seemed possible foundation stones for a more general European industrial policy.

However, Euro-optimism faded quickly in the early 1990s. The worst recession in post-war history spurred new populist resistance to closer European integration. In particular, the struggle to ratify the Maastricht Treaty on European Union shocked governments that had become used to 'building Europe' without much reference to the concerns of ordinary citizens. Signed in 1991, the Treaty was first rejected by Danish voters and then approved by the narrowest of margins in France in two referenda held in 1992. The French vote contributed to enormous upheaval in European currency markets, which appeared to derail (at least temporarily) Economic and Monetary Union.

Technology policy became caught up in the general turbulence of one of the most difficult periods in the Community's history. Budgetary negotiations on the Framework IV programme (1994–8) were more politicised and polarised than those on any previous version of the programme. EU technology policy had been given a stronger (if also more tangled) Treaty base at Maastricht, but clearly was not immune to new doubts about European integration.

Yet, after a second Danish referendum produced a 'yes', Maastricht was finally ratified in late 1993. At nearly the same time, a breakthrough was made on Framework IV. The Commission impressed even its most committed critics by adopting a new, hard-headed and self-critical approach to technology policy specifically and industrial policy more generally. Eventually, EU-funded research became more closely linked with and responsive to other technology policy actions, such as the liberalisation of the telecommunications sector, as well as a range of other EU policies. A new initiative to revitalise the post-Maastricht EU, taken at the end of Delors's presidency, further cemented the position of technology policy as a secure part of the EU's policy repertoire.

In this chapter, we examine the development of EU technology policy in the 1990s. We begin by highlighting the importance of the SEA and Maastricht Treaty in legitimising the EU's role. Then, we explain how the Commission managed to secure agreement to Framework IV, with few changes to its proposal, despite resistance to its price tag and a new and more complicated procedure for decision-making. Next, we consider how and why EU technology policy affects and is affected by a range of other policies. We then assess the technology policy implications of Jacques Delors's 1993 White Paper on 'Growth, Competitiveness and Employment'. Our conclusion summarises our central argument: that EU technology policy had become a very different animal by the late 1990s, and an area where the Union's role had been rethought, yet firmly established.

The SEA and Maastricht: legitimising technology policy

Most EU member states were convinced of the need for a new Treaty chapter on research by the late 1980s. The 1992 project promised new benefits for Europe's high-tech industries, but only provided that they could adjust to new challenges and demands. An EU technology policy became viewed as one way to seize on specific effects arising from the creation of the internal market. First, the 1992 project was expected to spur demand for new IT and communications systems to span national borders, as barriers to trade were removed and business networks expanded. Second, financial institutions were expected to invest in new IT products to provide cross-border banking, insurance and other services. Third, increased travel would create demand for new technologies such as laptop computers and mobile phones so that businesspeople could communicate from anywhere in the EU. Fourth, industries would have new incentives to invest in computer-assisted design and manufacturing as a response to both new competitive pressures and new opportunities to sell in 'foreign' EU markets where existing products had to be tailored to suit localised tastes and needs.

Of course, ESPRIT, RACE and BRITE (as well as other initiatives, such as in biotechnology) were all up and running before the SEA was ratified. Yet, the SEA's new Title VI, on research and technological development, was a crucial mandate. It put collaborative EU programmes on a far firmer footing. The SEA also went some way towards giving the Commission licence to badger member states into liberalising telecommunications and ending their cosy alliances with national technology champions. Article 130f explicitly stated that:

> special account shall be taken of the connection between the common research and technological development effort, the establishment of the internal market and the implementation of common policies, particularly as regards competition and trade.

However, in legitimising a Community RTD policy for the first time, the SEA also had the effect of creating high and probably unrealistic expectations about what the Framework programme could accomplish. Arguably, the SEA also failed to secure copper-bottomed national commitments to actions that mattered far more in terms of their impact on European technological competitiveness than any taken within the Framework programme. For example, by far the least faithfully implemented element of the 1992 project was public procurement. By the late 1990s, the Commission was still berating member states about their refusal to open up public markets, worth as much as 13 per cent of EU GDP, to meaningful competition. The implications for technological development were crucial. To illustrate the point, by 1996 public sector IT contracts accounted for about 40 per cent of the British market for outsourcing information systems, or the practice of combining computers, software, and so on, in complex packages to suit specific client needs. Both the total market for 'outsourcing' and the share made up of public sector contracts were growing fast, but most European governments seemed uninterested in subjecting this and other markets to open competition, as opposed to buying from traditional national suppliers.

The competitive situation *was* an improvement on the early 1980s. At that time, governments routinely gave preference to national hardware vendors such as Bull, Olivetti and ICL. EU procurement rules requiring all contracts to be open and competitive were often bent or ignored. By the mid-1990s, EU directives obliged governments to offer major public sector IT contracts based on Open Systems standards. It became more difficult to discriminate in favour of national champions.

Yet, negotiations on the Framework programme itself remained laborious and time-consuming (Peterson 1995b). As net contributors to the Community's general budget, Germany and the UK remained the most frequent critics of the Commission's proposed price tags. Moreover, after its success in linking increased research funding to the implementation of the single market, many of the Commission's ambitions in R&D policy were frustrated at the Maastricht summit in December 1991. The Treaty agreed at the summit contained new provisions giving the EU licence to fund so-called 'demonstration projects' that incorporated innovations developed in EU programmes. It also sanctioned the Commission's right to promote 'all the research activities deemed necessary by virtue of other Chapters' in the Treaty. Above all, the Commission was encouraged by a new Article 130h, which required that 'the Community and the member states shall coordinate their research and technological development activities so as to ensure that national policies and Community policy are mutually consistent'. The Commission was granted the explicit right to take any 'useful initiative' that might promote such consistency.

However, the Commission did not get what it most wanted: majority voting for all Council decisions concerning EU-funded R&D. Research was the very last issue discussed at the Maastricht summit (*not* the Social Chapter, as was widely reported). All member states but one indicated support for the Dutch presidency's proposal to subject all research policy decisions to QMV. During two long and often bitter days of negotiations, the British prime minister, John Major, already had wrung numerous concessions and 'opt-outs' from his colleagues. When he alone resisted the application of QMV to research, the summit's chair, Ruud Lubbers of the Netherlands, exploded and insisted that Major accept the will of the other eleven. Major stubbornly refused and insisted that the European Council only took decisions by consensus, not QMV. On this point at least he was supported by the German Chancellor, Helmut Kohl, who chided Lubbers with the comment, 'Well, he's got you there, Ruud!' The summit then ended.

The Framework programme's overall budget thus remained subject to unanimous voting on the Council. The 'double' legislative procedure was retained whereby separate Council votes (on the basis of QMV) were needed to approve detailed proposals for individual subprogrammes (such as ESPRIT or RACE). The Maastricht Treaty's new 'co-decision' procedure threatened to further complicate negotiations on the budget by giving the EP what amounted to veto power. Thus, although the Maastricht Treaty empowered the Commission in potentially important ways, it threatened to make decision-making on the Framework programme's budget and priorities even more rancorous than in the past.

Research after Maastricht

The Commission's (1992b) response to the RTD provisions agreed at Maastricht was bullish: it argued that Europe's research effort remained both underfunded and poorly integrated. Thus, the Commission's proposal for Framework IV consolidated virtually all EU-funded research activities, including those *not* previously funded through the Framework programme, into a single (and thus larger) budget. At this point, the Maastricht Treaty was still unratified. Yet, the Commission pointed to the Treaty's injunction to 'set out all the activities of the Community' in future versions of the Framework programme. For the first time, the Framework programme's proposed budget included expenditures on items such as support for R&D in third countries (particularly in Central and Eastern Europe).

At first glance, the Commission's proposed 13.1 billion ECU budget for Framework IV seemed to represent a very large increase over Framework III's total of 6.6 billion ECU. The Commission insisted that it was asking for just over 2.7 billion ECU in annual spending for 1994–8, or just slightly more than had been spent in 1992–3. Still, conflicting stories were told about how much of an increase the Commission was seeking. The Commissioner for Research, Antonio Ruberti, told the Research Council on 12 December 1993 that a budget of 12.3 billion ECU represented absolute continuity with Framework III. A member of the EP's Secretariat suggested, with more precision, that 11.726 billion ECU represented 'a *status quo* figure with inflation' (Peterson 1995b: 409). In any event, the Commission's proposal effectively extended the upward trend in the Framework programme's budget.

The Commission's proposal also marked a change in priorities. The thrust of evaluation work through the early 1990s emphasised the need for more effort to be put into the use and diffusion of new technologies. Far from maintaining the Aigrain (1989) review panel's emphasis on pre-competitive R&D, the Commission sought more follow-through of projects to the point where they generated tangible results and demonstration projects.

When the Commission's proposal came to the Council, France joined Germany and the UK in insisting that it was too expensive. Despite being net beneficiaries of the Framework programme, the French had recently become net contributors to the EU's general budget. Before the negotiations on Framework IV began in earnest, Edouard Balladur's centre-right government reluctantly agreed to accept large increases in the EU's structural funds instead of plunging the Union into another internal crisis in the wake of 1992's Danish rejection of the Maastricht Treaty. The new regional funds package was viewed by French negotiators as a *pis-aller* – a makeshift compromise – that considerably stretched the gap between French budgetary contributions and receipts. The Balladur government sought to reduce the gap by cutting the EU's budget elsewhere. In particular, Balladur's firmly Eurosceptic research minister, François Fillon, united with the UK and Germany in insisting that the Commission's proposed budget for R&D was too high.

The 'Big Three' refused to budge in a series of marathon Research Council sessions just prior to the Brussels European summit of December 1993. At this point, the Belgian EU presidency decided to place the Framework IV proposal on the summit's agenda. Apparently, the Belgians hoped that large state leaders would be too preoccupied with more pressing matters to object to a compromise proposal that set the budget at no less than 12 billion ECU, with the possibility of adding a reserve of 1 billion ECU at a later date. In the event, European leaders endorsed the '12 plus 1' proposal without discussion.

Predictably, the EP used its post-Maastricht powers to make Framework IV the first case of co-decision in the EU's history. However, its support eventually was secured in a compromise under which the Parliament's 'pet' items such as non-nuclear energy and third-country (i.e. Eastern Europe) participation received increased funding. The Council adjusted the '12 plus 1' formula agreed at the Brussels summit by accepting that a total of 12.3 billion ECU would be committed immediately to Framework IV (see Table 6.1). A further 700 million ECU was placed in reserve for possible deployment in 1996.

Thus, the RTD policy debate of 1993–4 featured important contributions from the Council and Parliament. However, in important respects, the terms of the debate were set by the Commission's communication of early 1992, *Research after Maastricht*. In it, the Commission chastised member states for retaining the double legislative process and imposing a version of co-decision on R&D which, it predicted, would 'inevitably result in long delays'. Crucially, however, the document was also extraordinarily self-critical. The Commission (1992b: 24) lashed out at 'the proprietary mentality' of its own services, which reinforced 'the tendency of the programs to self-perpetuation'. A major restructuring of the Commission's administrative machinery was promised.

Above all, *Research after Maastricht* was politically astute. Its section on the application of subsidiarity to R&D policy showed the Commission's determination not to repeat the mistakes of 1985, when its extravagant spending plans provoked a political backlash on the Council. Having learned from experience, the Commission (1992b: 17) insisted that:

Now more than ever selectivity is a condition for effectiveness. It would be conceptually inadequate and politically impractical to decide an increase of resources based on mere chance, purely ambitions of expansion, or the simple need of perpetuating existing activities. Opposition to such types of expenditure is absolutely essential.

Research after Maastricht played well with most member states. Yet

TABLE 6.1

The Framework IV programme (1994–8)

Activities/areas	Funding	
	MECU	**%**
Activity 1 – RTD and demonstration programmes	**10 686**	**86.9**
Information and communication technologies	*3 405*	*27.7*
Telematics	843	
Communications technologies	630	
Information technologies	1 932	
Industrial technologies	*1 995*	*16.2*
Industrial and materials technologies	1 707	
Standardisation, measurements and testing	288	
Environment	*1 080*	*8.8*
Environment and climate	852	
Marine sciences and technologies	228	
Life sciences and technologies	*1 572*	*12.8*
Biotechnology	552	
Biomedicine and health	336	
Agriculture and Fisheries	684	
(including agro-industry, food technologies, forestry, aquaculture and rural development)		
Energy	*2 256*	*18.3*
Non-nuclear energy	1 002	
Nuclear fission safety	414	
Controlled thermonuclear fusion	840	
Transport	*240*	*2.0*
Targeted socio-economic research	*138*	*1.1*
Activity 2 – Cooperation with third countries and international orgs.	**540**	**4.4**
Activity 3 – Dissemination and exploitation of results	**330**	**2.7**
Activity 4 – Stimulation of the training and mobility of researchers	**744**	**6.0**
Total	***12 300***	***100.0***

Source: European Commission 1994: Table 8a.4.

the Commission's self-criticism and commitment to subsidiarity were not products of simple altruism. With member states less suspicious of its agenda than in the past, the Commission was better able to control the negotiations on Framework IV. By this point, the Commission had considerable leverage anyway, which sprang from the 'sunk costs' of investments in previous versions of the Framework programme. The basic aims and existence of several programmes, such as ESPRIT or BRITE, were relatively uncontroversial. Essentially, the Commission's proposal for Framework IV was a conservative one that did not rock the boat, and also could be defended on grounds of continuity. However, by undergoing a thorough reappraisal of EU technology policy, and admitting its weaknesses, the Commission endeared itself to the Council, even if it could do little to override the budgetary concerns of the Big Three.

Strikingly, several national delegates involved in the negotiations concurred with a British official that 'about 90 percent of what eventually becomes the Framework programme is determined by the Commission in its proposal' (interview, February 1994). Council Working Groups, which often amend Commission proposals beyond recognition in other policy areas, altered the Framework IV proposal only at the margins. Only one Council Working Group scrutinised the Commission's entire budgetary proposal to spend 13.4 million ECU under Framework IV. Under the terms of the 'double' legislative procedure for R&D (see Table 8.2), Council Working Groups had a second chance later to scrutinise individual programmes under Framework IV. However, with decisions at this second stage taken by QMV, the first crack at amending the Commission's proposal at the first stage was critical from the Council's point of view.

A senior Commission official in DG XII agreed that:

It may be true statistically that 90 percent of what the Commission proposes goes through, but it is erroneous that the Commission swaggers around and gets away with anything . . . We're right to be confident because there's not much within the Framework IV program that is terribly controversial . . . And if the member states are craven and don't know how to lobby, they have only themselves to blame. Anyway, any proposal without very strong Commission backing gives them an excuse to tear it apart (interview, March 1994).

Ultimately, the Framework IV proposal did have very strong backing, but from a somewhat chastened and self-critical Commission. As *Research after Maastricht* made clear, the Commission was prepared to admit that EU-funded research was not the best of all possible worlds. Partly because it took this attitude, the Commission was able to kick its proposal for Framework IV into touch and essentially intact. However, an equally important element in its strategy was to present the Framework programme as a tool that served other, broader EU objectives beyond the realm of technology policy itself.

RTD and 'other policies': towards a strategy?

One of the most revealing passages in *Research after Maastricht* paper asserted that:

> The need for a European industrial policy has reappeared. In the 1970s, industrial policy was characterised by a *dirigiste* and sectoral approach. Today, it is recognised that public interventions in this area must take the form of horizontal activities to achieve the right climate and balance for maximising the productivity and competitiveness of European industry (Commission 1992b: 22).

This plea marked the culmination of a lively debate within the Commission about what the EU could and should do to promote industrial competitiveness. In his insider's account of the Delors Commission, Ross (1995) insists that industrial policy rose to a place of prominence on the EU's agenda mainly because senior representatives of the European electronics industry made direct representations to Delors and his *cabinet* in spring 1990. Within a year, the Commission (1991b) had tabled a broad-ranging communication that represented its first genuine attempt to forge a consensus on a set of principles to underpin an EU industrial policy.

Meanwhile, discussions within the pre-Maastricht IGC about creating a new Treaty article on industrial policy gave licence to DG XIII to issue a plea for Community measures to arrest the declining competitiveness of Europe's electronics industries. It called for five specific lines of action: the modernisation of public infrastructures to create a 'leading-edge' demand for new technologies, the launch of a 'second generation' of EU-funded projects that worked 'more closely to the market', more EU resources for training, a more aggressive EU trade policy, and range of measures to 'create a healthy business environment' (Commission 1991a: 3).

This somewhat *dirigiste* programme for advancing the interests of the European electronics industry died on the vine. The Commissioner for Industry, Martin Bangemann (1992: 20) continued to insist that the 'old, sectoral industrial policy would be replaced by a modern, horizontal approach which would no longer support individual industrial sections [sic] but competitiveness on a large scale'. Meanwhile, the ambitions of the French and others for a new Treaty commitment to industrial policy were appeased by the inclusion of a new Article 130, which merely pledged that the Union and its member states would ensure the 'conditions necessary for the competitiveness' of industry. It did not even contain the phrase 'industrial policy'. Actions under it were made subject to unanimous voting on the Council, thus making it unlikely that the article would be used very often. Moreover, after considerable bureaucratic in-fighting, Bangemann managed to wrest control of ESPRIT away from DG XIII in 1994 and move it to DG III, a directorate with far less of a French accent and which remained far more firmly under his control.

Yet industrial policy considerations were more prominent in Framework IV than in the past. The Commission began to argue that the Maastricht Treaty had 'unified' EU research policy: it specifically had embraced the goal of enhanced technological competitiveness and sanctioned 'all the research activities deemed necessary by virtue of other chapters' of the Treaty. The upshot was that new linkages needed to be constructed between different EU policies, and technology policy itself had to become more strategic and sensitive to the integral objectives of the Union.

To illustrate the point, the Commission (1992b) insisted that EU trade policy had to take into account the relatively low percentage (17 per cent) of EU exports that were high-tech products, especially compared with the US (31 per cent) and Japan (27 per cent). After the Uruguay Round of world trade talks was concluded in late 1993, trade in technologically-intensive products became the primary focus of both the new World Trade Organization (WTO) and EU trade policy. The EU joined the US in trying to push Asian countries to embrace a new free trade agreement in telecoms within the WTO as one element in its strategy for liberalising the sector in

Europe. The Commission also pursued an EU bid to become party to a new international semiconductor trade agreement after the expiry of a bilateral US–Japanese pact in 1996.

Meanwhile, the New Transatlantic Agenda and Action Plan, agreed between the US and the EU in late 1995, created the Transatlantic Business Dialogue (TABD). The TABD brought eminent private sector figures together from both sides of the Atlantic to agree recommendations for public policy measures that could free trade and bring mutual benefits (see Vogel 1997). By 1997, the TABD had laid the groundwork for a deal to eliminate all bilateral tariffs on trade in IT products, thus allowing firms to reap economies of scale in an integrated transatlantic market. More importantly, the TABD was instrumental in agreeing two transatlantic pacts on the mutual recognition of testing and certification standards for a range of high-tech goods, including IT and telecoms. The EU conceded more than the US to get the deals, but was more disadvantaged by the *status quo*, which featured tougher US testing procedures and declining shares for European producers in IT and telecoms markets. The deal also revealed the Commission's increased concern for *users* (as opposed to producers) of new technology.

The 1997 US–EU science and technology agreement was, in some ways, even more ambitious. Negotiations made steady progress despite very different expectations about what the agreement would look like in the end (see Macilwain 1996). The final agreement covered most areas of the natural sciences and engineering and seemed likely to expand jointly funded R&D by a large measure. The broader point is that the Union's trade and technology policies were becoming increasingly interlinked.

Meanwhile, the EU's regional development policy also became linked to RTD policy as never before. When ESPRIT was first created, and then built upon to form the first Framework programme, it was generally accepted that EU research programmes would primarily benefit larger and richer member states, whose firms were more often at the leading edge of technology-intensive industries. In political terms, the Framework programme would compensate wealthier states for their net contribution to funds for regional development and cohesion. In practice, the Framework programme became subject to the principle of *juste retour* to an extent unforeseen at its creation. As such, the Commission took to justifying EU-funded research using rationales such as, 'If it weren't for ESPRIT, we would have no IT or software industry in Greece' (*New Scientist*, 25 January 1992). Such arguments flew in the face of the logic of a *common* EU research effort, which, in theory, should not require each member state to have a presence in each sector of technology. However, given the distributive politics of the Framework programme, the Commission was forced to use them.

The Commission was on perhaps stronger ground in pointing to the long-term benefits of ensuring that EU research funds were spread widely across the Union. Young researchers involved in collaborative projects in the 1990s stood to become the industry leaders of the early twenty-first century, and would know their counterparts in other European countries better because of the Framework programme. In any case, in its annual report on the Framework programme for 1995, the Commission took pains to show that the Union's Objective 1 regions – the least-favoured areas with GDPs less than 75 per cent of the EU average – received a sizeable share of EU-funded research (see Table 6.2).

Of course, relatively large amounts of EU spending on research in poorer regions do not automatically transfer into increased cohesion. On one hand, a 1996 Commission report on RTD policy and cohesion concluded that disparities in income per capita between member states had narrowed significantly in the ten years after 1983, largely because cohesion countries had caught up with their richer EU partners. The contribution of EU-funded research to this

TABLE 6.2

EU research in Objective 1 regions

Share of FW projects with participants from Objective 1 regions	46%
Number of participants from Objective 1 regions as percentage of total	14%
Value of all projects with at least one Objective 1 participant as percentage of total	17%
Objective 1 regions Percentage of EU's total population	26%
Percentage of all EU's researchers	6%

Source: Commission (1996c: 86).

process is difficult to assess, but certainly seems likely to have encouraged the trend.

On the other hand, Fagerberg and Verspagen (1996: 443) insist that the rates at which poorer regions caught up with richer ones declined considerably after 1980. Doubts about the extent to which increased EU research funding can help regions that lack the infrastructure or skills to make effective use of it led them to the dark conclusion that 'for this group, neither R&D efforts nor investment support from the EU seem to matter much' (Fagerberg and Verspagen 1996: 443). Of course, such evidence did not dull the insistence of poorer member states that the EU's research and regional development policies had to be integrated in so far as a 'fair' share of research funding promoted cohesion.

EU technology policy also became linked to new environmental policy imperatives. Spending on environmental research was on the upswing by the mid-1990s. The Commission also embraced new measures to regulate electronic and electrical product waste, particularly under pressure from Germany, where domestic legislation made manufacturers responsible for disposing of old equipment. Computer manufacturers found ways to recycle over 90 per cent of an existing computer, while striving to ensure that recycling did not add extra production costs. Amid estimates that computers would account for 10 per cent of the electricity consumption of most businesses by the year 2000, the Commission considered ways of encouraging the manufacture of personal computers (PCs) that automatically cut their power consumption when not in use.

In short, research became an established weapon in the EU's arsenal of policy instruments. Its focus and priorities were subjects of debate and influences that extended well beyond the relatively closed world of research ministers, officials and project partners who ran and participated in the Framework programme itself. However, it was also one of few policy sectors where a substantial EU policy role was relatively uncontroversial.

Growth, competitiveness and (un)employment

The EU was a considerable weightier organisation by the early 1990s than it had been in the mid-1980s. Regardless of growing Euroscepticism, it continued to invest progressively more resources in its technology policy. However, Europe's economy had fallen into a state of crisis. Its potential growth rate was shrinking, investment was declining, and competitiveness was eroding. Above all, unemployment was increasing at an alarming rate. Employment in the EU actually fell by 1.3 per cent in 1992, and by nearly 1.75 per cent in 1993. The worst unemployment figures in the Union's history undermined its greatest achievement: the creation of the world's largest single market. By itself, the 1992 project was not enough to counter the EU's deep-rooted, structural economic problems, which were exacerbated by high interest rates in the run-up to EMU and the economic shock of German unification.

By this point, Jacques Delors was nearing the end of his long, ten-year reign as president of the Commission. Searching for a legacy, and mindful of the success of the 1985 White Paper on the internal market, Delors surprised European leaders at the 1993 Copenhagen summit by arguing passionately for a new, medium-term strategy, coordinated at the EU level, for pulling Europe out of its economic malaise. Drawing on work done by the Commission's internal think tank, the *cellule de prospectif*, and aided by a sympathetic Belgian Council presidency, Delors tabled a new White Paper on 'Growth, Competitiveness and Employment' at the December 1993 Brussels summit. Its impact was powerful, particularly for technology policy. Its central argument was that innovation was the key to kick-starting Europe out of the recession.

Naturally, the first priority of Delors's 1993 White Paper was unemployment, which stood at a record rate of 12 per cent. However, the White Paper was highly sensitive to hesitations on the part of many member states to do more than just coordinate national policies in search of higher growth rates, as well as the insistence of the British Conservative government that the EU's problems lay in structural inflexibility and over-regulation. Of course, the White Paper's section on RTD policy did not question the wisdom of EMU-driven fiscal austerity. Rather, it emphasised the need to promote more investment in research by the private sector as well as to disseminate and apply RTD results more quickly and widely.

RTD was cast in the White Paper as one element in a wider industrial policy, which it defined in Bangemannesque terms as 'creating as favourable an environment as possible for company competitiveness'. The White Paper also signalled a new determination on the part of the Commission that Europe's research effort should 'take account of the new needs of society' (Commission 1993: 99), particularly by focusing on the environment, health and the media. Not only did this emphasis reflect Delors's concern for preserving the 'European model of society' (see Ross 1995); it also targeted sectors where significant job creation was possible.

The White Paper prominently argued that the EU's research effort was lagging behind those of the US and Japan. It noted that all collaborative programmes accounted for only about 10 per cent of total European spending (although this estimate may be too low; see Ruberti 1997). Surprisingly, however, the White Paper conceded that 'the use made of funds is more important than the amount spent' (Commission 1993: 97). Apparently, the days of haranguing member states *à la* Narjes to expand the Commission's technology policy resources were gone. Instead, the White Paper mostly suggested national actions, such as tax credit schemes for research and lowered social security costs for firms and research bodies, in the context of its more general call for lower taxes on human capital. It asserted that the Commission's proposed RTD actions could have only a 'moderate' impact on employment, although an 'indisputably positive indirect' one (Commission 1993: 101).

The White Paper was Delors's final triumph. It was endorsed with few hesitations at the Brussels summit, where European leaders treated it as far more than just an academic exercise. Even the Conservative British Chancellor, Kenneth Clarke, disavowed his pre-summit criticism and called it 'an impeccable statement' (*Financial Times*, 13 December 1993). The White Paper strongly endorsed the method at the heart of the 1992 project; namely deregulation, especially of labour markets. But it also cleverly combined Delors's vision of a new 'social compact' between employers and labour with the liberalising fervour of the European Round Table of Industrialists' (1993) earlier *cri de coeur*, *Beating the Crisis*, which the White Paper clearly echoed.

Ultimately, the White Paper was tainted by the failure of most of its proposals for new spending on infrastructure projects. Germany, the UK and (eventually) Spain took issue with a proposed 8 billion ECU bond issue on the grounds that it smacked of old-fashioned Keynesian demand management, and constituted a power-grab by the Commission (see Middlemas 1995: 569). However, the White Paper still became a touchstone for EU policy, with virtually all

Commissioners and Councils working on measures to which it gave impetus in 1994.

Perhaps the White Paper's most important legacy for technology policy was its emphasis on background measures such as education, training, risk capital and technology transfer, as opposed to spending on research *per se*. In insisting that the EU had to prepare for the information society, develop communications infrastructures and rethink the very nature of work, the White Paper endorsed the view that Europe had to grasp the nettle of a twenty-first century, post-industrial economy. By this point, white-collar jobs outnumbered production jobs in virtually every EU member state. Between 1981 and the time the White Paper was tabled, the EU (15) had lost over 3 million industrial jobs and nearly 4 million agricultural jobs. However, employment in services had risen by more than 15 million, leaving a shortfall only because of a similar rise in the size of the EU's workforce. The White Paper thus signalled an acceptance of the need to develop Europe's capacity for 'software', or its human capital, as opposed to its capacity to produce physical products.

The new emphasis on software, instead of hardware, made sense given competitive trends in important high-tech industries. For one thing, Europe's software engineering industry – which involves the development of methodologies, technologies and software that make it easier to write computer programmes – was world-class. Europe possessed a range of impressive skills in software and IT services, but lacked many companies with the size, resources and expertise of competitors such as EDS, the computer services arm of General Motors. Moreover, Europe was unable to develop alternatives to major US software packages such as MS-DOS or Windows (developed by Microsoft) or the 1–2–3 spreadsheet (by Lotus). Europe remained a mostly diverse collection of small, quirky markets for software in which packages often could not be sold easily across borders, not least because of language barriers. A more integrated European market and software effort was a logical antidote, even if debates persisted about whether much collaboration was practical or possible in the European software sector.

Meanwhile, the 'European identity' of *hardware* manufacturers in many important sectors became increasingly blurred. For example, while EUREKA's JESSI project into semiconductors generally was perceived as a success (see Chapter 8), the industry became highly globalised in the 1990s. Siemens and Bull both launched memory chip ventures in 1991–2 with IBM. The upshot was that ambitions for forming a strong European manufacturing base through mergers were gradually abandoned. Only Philips – virtually the only diversified European IT company – continued to argue for the maintenance of independent European capabilities across a broad range of electronic technologies. Meanwhile, an increasing percentage of the revenues of most European computer manufacturers derived from services, rather than hardware. The share of total revenues derived from services by some of Europe's leading computer makers in 1992 were estimated at 37 per cent for Siemens-Nixdorf, 27 per cent for Olivetti, and 36 per cent for Bull (*Financial Times*, 17 March 1992).

Computing services remained one of the few areas of growth in an industry generally plagued by recession and market saturation. Even as a record number of PCs were sold in 1995, many manufacturers were struggling to stay in business on wafer-thin profit margins. The largest producers all slashed prices by up to 35 per cent in early 1996, particularly Compaq, the American market leader, but also IBM, which staged a strong comeback (particularly in Europe) and the fast-growing Hewlett Packard. Such 'profitless prosperity' made the industry ripe for a round of often complicated mergers before the year 2000. Indicative was a 1996 deal under which Packard Bell, the US home computer maker, received a cash infusion of nearly $300 million from NEC of Japan in order to purchase Zenith Data Systems from Groupe Bull of France.

The most purely European firms, such as Olivetti and Siemens-Nixdorf, tended to be strong in only one or two national European markets, thus making them highly vulnerable to localised downturns. For example, Olivetti suffered considerably as pre-EMU austerity took hold in its core markets of Spain and Italy. Meanwhile, Compaq, IBM and Apple all had very large manufacturing sites in Scotland or Ireland. Competition in the computer industry was mainly between global oligopolists, making European-level measures to promote the industry problematic.

In contrast, common EU actions were clearly justified in the transition to the grandly labelled, if often ill defined, information society. In this context, the Commission tried to focus member states' minds on the need to push forward the development of new technologies that promised a freer flow of information and wider access to it. For one thing, European markets for IT, broadly defined, were forecast

TABLE 6.3

The Bangemann High-level Group on European information infra-structures [a]

Martin Bangemann (chair)	European Commission
Peter L. Bonfield (UK)	Chairman and Chief Executive, ICL
Eurico Cabral da Fonseca (Portugal)	President, Campanhiua Comunicacaoes Nacionais
M. Etienne Davignon (Belgium)	Président Societé Général de Belgique
Peter J. Davis (UK)	Chairman, Reed Elsevier
M. Carlo de Benedetti (Italy)	President, Olivetti
Brian Ennis (Ireland)	Managing Director, IMS
Pehr G. Gyllenhammer (EFTA)	Former Executive Chairman, AB Volvo
Hans Olaf Henkel ('European Union')	Chairman and Chief Executive Officer, IBM Europe
Lothar Hunsel (Germany)	Chairman-Designate of Geschäftsführung DeTeMobilikfunk
Anders Knutsen (Denmark)	Administrative Director, B&O
Constantin Makropoulous (Greece)	Former Managing Director, Hellenic Information Systems
Pascual Maragall (Spain)	Mayor of Barcelona, Vice President, POLIS
Romano Prodi (Italy)	President Director General, IRI
Andre Rousselet (France)	former Président Director General, Canal Plus
Pierre Suart (France)	Président Alcatel
Gaston Thorn (Luxembourg)	Président du Conseil d'Administration du CLT
Jan D. Timmer (Netherlands)	Voorzitter, Philips Electronics
Candido Velazquez (Spain)	President Telefónica
Heinrich von Pierer (Germany)	Vorsitzender des Vorstandes Siemens AG

[a] Posts held at the time of appointment in 1994.

to continue to grow at a much faster rate – 7 to 8 per cent per year – than the rest of the economy until the end of the decade. While hardware (including computers) accounted for more than 40 per cent of the total market, its annual growth rate (about 6 per cent) lagged behind that of software (9 to 10 per cent) (EITO 1996).

An important legacy of the 1993 White Paper was the formation of the Bangemann Group to study Europe's information infrastructure (see Table 6.3). Its creation was motivated by the European Round Table's earlier pleas and directly informed the Santer

Commission's subsequent embrace of the information society. Chosen jointly by the Commission and Council, the Group's members included representatives of industry, users and consumers of new IT products. Crucially, the Bangemann Group took in individuals with considerable influence in the political world, such as the former Commissioners Gaston Thorn and Etienne Davignon, and Pascual Maragall and Romano Prodi, who subsequently became (respectively) president of the EU's Committee of the Regions and Italy's Prime Minister. The Group even included a representative of EFTA, Pehr Gyllenhammer, the Swedish figurehead of the Gyllenhammer group which was a prime mover behind the 1992 project (see Cowles 1995), as well as the head of IBM Europe, Hans Olaf Henkel.

Buoyed by the support of the Bangemann Group, the Commission adopted several bold directives to liberalise telecoms under Article 90, which gives it the prerogative to promote competition in the 'operation of services of general economic interest'. Access to basic telecoms is a necessity if public access to new information tools such as the Internet and new techniques such as distance learning are to be guaranteed. Moreover, in the words of the head of DG III, Stefano Micossi (1996: 1), access to telecoms is needed to:

> ensure that the Information Society does not lead to exclusion, adding to the divisions that still exist in society. How can we avoid a society in which the computer-illiterate and the non-connected are left on the margins? The Commission's commitment to liberalisation of the information and telecommunications market will be a key factor in ensuring that the products of the information society will be available and accessible to the broadest possible user base.

Thus, a 1996 EU directive ordained that member states would table plans for liberalising markets for most telecommunications services by mid-1997. The directive was cast as part of a wider strategy of orchestrating national actions to ensure that the Union's citizens were not ghettoised in a global information society. The Commission naturally encountered considerable (especially French) resistance: telecoms was the only IT sector in which Europe boasted world-beating hardware producers, many of which became that way

through monopoly procurement relationships with their governments and the high profit margins they guaranteed.

However, by the mid-1990s, as much as 80 per cent of the cost of
many consumer products consisted of information-based added-
value: design, packaging, advertising, distribution, management, and
so on. Increasingly, jobs involving information could be done anywhere where the right skills existed, thus leading to more telework,
or cases in which workers processed electronic information for a
remote client, with results communicated to employers by a telecoms link. The advantage of teleworking for employers was that
contract labour could be bought in relatively cheaply, without the
need to pay non-wage labour costs such as insurance contributions,
equipment and premises. For workers, teleworking offered benefits
such as flexible working hours, more autonomy and the avoidance of
travelling to work. Among EU member states, Sweden and the UK
outpaced others in adopting teleworking, largely because they had
more ISDN (integrated services digital networking) lines, which
could transmit very large amounts of information – including voice,
video and computer data – at high speeds. A Commission (1995c)
report urged member states to accept that increased teleworking was
a natural response to the increased knowledge content of products,
the convergence of computing and telecoms, and economic pressures to outsource work. However, it required substantial modernisation (read liberalisation) of the EU's telecoms sector.

Critics claimed that the 'information society' had potentially
severe social costs. Teleworking introduced cheap labour into
Western labour markets, as some US companies began to use contract teleworkers in India. Many Western workers faced increased
job insecurity, family stress and general anxiety as consequences of
such enormously rapid economic change (Rifkind 1996; Sale 1996).

Still, the Commission took it upon itself to prod member states
into focusing on promising new IT sectors, such as multi-media,
where Europe appeared to be lagging. Markets for products that
brought together full-motion video, sound, animation, still images
and text on a personal computer or workstation were exploding,
quadrupling in one year from 1993 to 1994. Sales of PCs in America
soared in response to demand created by new multi-media PC applications, such as games and video 'books'. Yet European businesses
appeared hesitant to invest in multi-media technologies, even at
the relatively low-cost and low-tech level of CD-ROMs. The

Commission responded with proposals, including one pursued within EUREKA, to put more resources into multi-media research and training.

In short, EU research policy came to be viewed more holistically and strategically after the Delors White Paper. On one hand, as the White Paper insisted, R&D had beneficial long-term effects: it increased demand for products of higher quality, while making the factors of production more productive. On the other, the White Paper and subsequent Commission communications on RTD stated the obvious: 'that the link between R&D and the creation of new markets and jobs is neither simple nor direct and, under no circumstances linear' (Commission 1996e: 11).

Conclusion

Arguably, the 1993 White Paper was an example of the Commission doing what it does best: figuratively, and almost literally in view of Delors's performance at the Copenhagen summit, grabbing member states by the throat and saying, 'You have a *huge* problem. Unemployment is rising inexorably, especially among young people. Across the Union, 15 per cent of people under 25 are out of work, and 28 per cent in Ireland, 30 per cent in Italy, 37 per cent in Spain. You are risking a social explosion. What are you going to *do* with these people?'

Technology policy was cast as an important part of the solution. At the same time, the White Paper acted to lower expectations of what RTD could accomplish by itself. The White Paper presented a convincing case for approaching high unemployment and declining industrial competitiveness as problems rooted in the high costs of labour, energy, transport and telecommunications in Europe. It highlighted how regulation (or deregulation) often affected innovation and job creation far more than research *per se*. For example, the inclusion in the US of unlimited local telephone calls in fixed line rental fees contributed substantially to the development of Internet services in the 1990s, which in turn tended to create jobs and spur technological development (OECD 1996).

While lowering expectations of RTD generally, the White Paper also created a convincing and effective rationale for EU-funded research. Research could not be expected to create lots of jobs quickly, but its indirect effects – skills enhancement, the dissemination of knowledge, and so on – were essential to restoring European competitiveness. Member states' public budgets were under severe pressure in the run-up to EMU, and thus public funds for research were scarce. The Framework programme offered an effective way to 'back up' national research activities (Commission 1993: 102). In particular, EU-funded research would target the 'needs of society', particularly better public health, a cleaner environment and the need to prepare citizens for the information society.

In political terms, the White Paper strengthened the Commission's hand in technology policy in several respects. Insiders to the negotiations on Framework IV cast doubt on whether the tabling of the White Paper at the 1993 Brussels summit had the effect of shaming the European Council into finally agreeing a compromise budget for Framework IV. Nevertheless, Major, Kohl and Mitterrand would have been vulnerable to charges of hypocrisy if any or all of them had held up agreement on Framework IV while endorsing the White Paper, with its balanced and yet urgent plea for unified and immediate action to solve the EU's economic crisis.

Meanwhile, the formation of the Bangemann Group was a shrewd political manoeuvre by the Commission. It acted to consolidate a powerful, high-profile telecoms policy network. When the Group agreed on a course of action, even a radical one, member states on the Council had difficulty resisting its will. While enthusiasm for the Commission's information society campaign was by no means uniform across the EU, it constituted a theme that the Santer Commission could point to both as a boon to European integration and a justification for action at the EU level.

In short, by the late 1990s EU technology policy had a far clearer and more widely accepted rationale than ever before. Its purpose and methods had been considerably rethought in the post-Maastricht period. RTD policy had become far more responsive to the objectives of a range of other EU policies, particularly those for industry, trade and regional development. At the same time, member states (particularly big ones) began to back off on their insistence that the Framework programme should show results, and show them immediately. A strong EU role in technology policy had become accepted as a prerequisite of a modern, dynamic European economy, but it was no longer expected to be a panacea.

7

A European Technological Community?

In 1995, a new Commissioner for R&D, Mme Edith Cresson, arrived in Brussels. A former French prime minister and a political heavyweight, Cresson appeared anxious to make her mark on RTD policy, only to find that her predecessor, Antonio Ruberti, had neatly tied up most loose ends before departing. Framework IV was agreed and waiting for implementation, leaving Cresson with a relatively empty desk. However, criticisms of Framework IV began to emerge even before it started: it was too complex, lacking in focus, and contained too many lines of action. Evaluations of Frameworks II and III stressed the need for closer links between projects and users, more emphasis on application and, above all, on diffusion: getting European industry to worry about using and applying new technologies rather than (the Commission) worrying about who was making the hardware and its components.

These criticisms opened the way to two sets of action that set the EU research policy agenda for the late 1990s. On the one hand, Mme Cresson resurrected the idea of 'Task Forces', originally mooted in the Delors White Paper (Commission 1993). The Task Forces killed a number of birds with one stone. They met the criticism about lack of coordination between Commission activities. They were mechanisms to bring together national, EU and EUREKA activities. They would concentrate on downstream uses and applications.

Another set of actions initiated by Cresson sprang from the same roots, but seemed likely in the long run to have greater impact. A broad 'debate on innovation', again echoing the Delors White Paper but bearing fruit in Cresson's *First Action Plan for Innovation* (Commission 1997b), provoked new thinking about policy goals and coordination. Above all, it raised awkward questions about how best to organise a diffusion-oriented policy, and whether the Commission was better placed than national or regional authorities to lead it.

This chapter offers a snapshot of the state of EU technology policy in the late 1990s (we return to EUREKA in Chapter 8). We begin by examining how much is being spent in which sectors, and highlight a trend towards adding more and more activities to satisfy an increasingly wider array of interests. We then confront the highly politicised distribution of funding between countries and regions, with a view to assessing how much concerns about cohesion have influenced outcomes. Our focus then shifts to linkages between different types of research organisation, and what types of projects tend to be supported by the EU. Finally, we assess the significance of the broader debate about the future of EU research policy that preceded the Commission's proposal for the Framework V programme (1999–2002).

Trends in Framework programme expenditure

We have seen that the Maastricht Treaty's Article 130f committed the EU to strengthening the science and technology base of European industry and bolstering its competitiveness. It also strengthened the Commission's hand by making it clear that it had the right to promote RTD activities necessary to support activities (such as cohesion and environmental protection) covered by other chapters in the Treaty, and to ensure coordination of Community and member state activities. Article 130g of the Maastricht Treaty, which set out the ways in which the Commission might pursue these objectives, reflected the range of activities already being undertaken within the Framework programmes.

Policy was to be implemented mainly through three types of action (see Exhibit 7.1): shared-cost, concerted and direct action through the Community's own research programme in the Joint Research Centre (JRC: see Exhibit 7.2).

EXHIBIT 7.1
Types of EU funding for R&D

There are three main types of funding for projects within the Framework programme:

- *Shared-cost actions*, which apply to most RTD projects, to demonstration (or pilot) projects and to special measures encouraging participation by SMEs. The Community will pay up to 50 per cent of the running costs of shared-cost actions.
- *Concerted actions*, which involve bringing partners together, such as for a meeting or seminar. The Community will pay 100 per cent of the costs of organising such activities (that is, for travel and accommodation) and will also pay for the dissemination of the results;
- *Direct action*, which refers to the in-house research carried out by the Commission through the Joint Research Centre (JRC).

Table 1.2 in the first chapter traces the growth of expenditures under successive Framework programmes. For the period 1994–8, under Framework IV, expenditures averaged just over 3 billion ECU per year.

Table 7.1 shows Framework IV expenditures by programme. The four main heads of action – collaborative RTD (A), cooperation with third countries (B), dissemination (C) and training and mobility (D) – are reflected by the four main lines of activity. From a total of 13.1 billion ECU, 87 per cent was spent on Activity A, with comparatively small sums committed to the other main activities. As Table 7.2 shows, expenditures for third-country cooperation and training and mobility actually fell during the 1990s. With the impending enlargement into Eastern Europe, it might have been expected that international cooperation would take an increasing share of Community resources (see Commission 1995b), but its share sharply declined. In contrast, in spite of tough talk, the JRC budget held up remarkably well.

Framework IV added two new lines of activity: transport and targeted socio-economic research (TSER). Both exemplified the trend towards adding, rather than subtracting, areas of activity. Political compromises inevitably pushed in this direction, particularly as the Framework IV programme still required a unanimous vote of the Council and was subject to co-decision with the European Parliament.

EXHIBIT 7.2
The Joint Research Centre

The Joint Research Centre was originally set up as part of Euratom and split between four sites at Ispra (Italy), Karlsruhe (Germany), Geel (Belgium) and Petten (Netherlands) (see Chapter 2). When Euratom was combined with the other two Communities (the EEC and ECSC) in 1967, the JRC's remit was widened to include issues considered to be trans-frontier – for example, environmental research and standards. Debates have since continued over the role and value of the JRC. A series of reforms were implemented, culminating in moves in the late 1980s to shift more work on to a customer–contractor basis and to make the JRC bid in open competition for funds. Even so, under Framework IV three-quarters of its funds (approximately 1 billion ECU) came directly from the EU's research budget.

Until 1996, the JRC was accountable directly to DG XII. From April 1996 it was established as a separate Directorate-General within the Commission. It is made up of seven institutes at five sites:
• Institute for Reference Materials and Measurement (Geel);
• Institute for Trans-uranium Elements (Karlsruhe);
• Institute for Advanced Materials (Petten);
• Environmental Institute (Ispra);
• Space Applications Institute (Ispra);
• Institute for Systems, Informatics and Safety (Ispra);
• Institute for Prospective Technological Studies (Seville, Spain).

The Institute for Prospective Technological Studies (IPTS) was established in 1994 at Seville in southern Spain. Its main task is to maintain 'technology watch' activities, identifying and mapping developments and trends in new technologies and developing 'Foresight' studies to help identify new trends.

Which member states get how much?

Table 7.3 shows EU expenditures by member states for 1995. It is *not* a very satisfactory table. When examining any programme that lasts for five years, one year's actual receipts by any one country can be distorted by all kinds of factors: the timing of calls for major projects, delays in contract negotiations, periodicity within the programme (more contracts tend to be signed at the beginning rather than at the end of programmes), and so on. For example, while Table 7.3 identifies Germany, France, Italy and the UK as the recipients of most money from the Framework programme, Italy in fact normally appears at the bottom of the four, not the top. Germany, with a population of around 80 million, normally tops the list in terms of the absolute value of monetary receipts. Below the top

TABLE 7.1

Programmes under the Framework IV programme (1994–8)

Specific programme	Acronym	MECU	%
A. *Research, technological development and demonstration programmes*			
1. Information technologies	ESPRIT	2 035	15.4
2. Telematics applications	TELEMATICS	898	6.9
3. Advanced communication technologies and services	ACTS	671	5.1
4. Industrial and materials technologies	IMT	1 722	13.0
5. Standards, measurements and testing	SMT	184	1.4
6. Environment and climate	ENVIRONMENT	566.5	4.3
7. Marine science and technology	MAST	243	1.9
8. Biotechnology	BIOTECHNOLOGY	588	4.5
9. Biomedicine	BIOMEDICINE	358	2.7
10. Agriculture and fisheries	FAIR	646.5	4.9
11. Non-nuclear energy	JOULE/THERMIE	1 030	7.9
12. Nuclear fission safety	FISSION	170.5	1.3
13. Controlled thermonuclear fusion	FUSION	846	6.5
14. Transport	TRANSPORT	256	2.0
15. Targeted socio-economic research	TSER	112	0.9
16. Direct measures (Joint Research Centre)	JRC	1 094.5	8.4
Sub-total		11 421	87.1
B *Cooperation with third countries and international organisations*			
	INCO	575	4.4
C *Dissemination and optimisation of results*			
	INNOVATION	312	2.4
D *Training and mobility of researchers*			
	TMR	792	6.1
Total		13 100	100

Note: This table differs from Tables 1.2 and 6.1 because the 13.1 billion ECU total includes the adjustment agreed in 1995 to take account of the entry that year of Sweden, Finland and Austria into the EU. The total originally agreed for Framework IV was 12.3 billion ECU with the possible addition of 700 million ECU in 1996 if the EU's budget allowed (i.e. a total of 13.8 billion ECU after adjustments for enlargement). After co-decision, agreement was reached on a supplement of only 115 MECU (*Eurotechnology*, no. 87:6, November 1997).

Source: Commission Services (cited in Colombo 1997).

TABLE 7.2

Framework IV commitments compared with expenditures under same heads of activity, 1991–5

Commitments	1991–5		1994–8	FP IV
	MECU	%	MECU	%
Activity A:				
Information technologies and communication	4 192	33.3	3 626	27.7
Industrial and material technologies	1 792	14.2	2 125	16.2
Environment	1 098	8.7	1 150	8.8
Life sciences	1 202	9.6	1 674	12.8
Energy	2 285	18.2	2 403	18.3
Transport	97	0.9	256	2.0
Targeted socio-economic research	52	0.5	147	1.1
Total Activity A	10 749[a]	85.4	11 421	86.9
Activity B:				
Cooperation with third countries and International organisations	717.6	5.7	575	4.4
Activity C:				
Dissemination and exploitation of results	293.8	2.3	352	2.6
Activity D:				
Training and mobility of researchers	820.6	6.5	792	6.1
TOTAL RTD programmes	12 580.6	100.0	13 100	100.0

[a] Including 30 million ECU in JRC support for other EU activities.

Source: Commission (1997b, 1996c).

four, Belgium, the Netherlands and Spain generally form a second grouping, with each receiving approximately 5 to 6 per cent of expenditures, in spite of the fact that Spain has a much larger population than the other two.

Table 7.3 also fails to account for 30 per cent of total expenditure under the Framework programme. This large share cannot all be accounted for by spending on the JRC (line 16) or International Cooperation (line B), as is shown by the figures in Table 7.1. Ideally,

TABLE 7.3

EU RTD payments made to member states – 1995

Country (initials)	Total payments million ECU	As % of total	Contributions to EU budget as % of total
Belgium	158.4	6.24	3.5
Denmark	36.1	1.42	1.7
Germany	273.0	10.76	27.6
Greece	30.7	1.21	1.4
Spain	82.2	3.24	4.5
France	297.5	11.72	15.9
Ireland	23.5	0.93	1.1
Italy	375.2	14.79	9.3
Luxembourg	14.3	0.56	0.2
The Netherlands	111.9	4.41	5.5
Austria	5.4	0.21	2.5
Portugal	16.9	6.67	1.2
Sweden	6.9	0.27	1.2
Finland	11.7	0.46	2.3
UK	318.6	12.56	12.7
Other	775.5	30.35	n.a.
Total	2 537.6	100	100

Source: Court of Auditors (1996: 58).

we would have figures based on receipts across the whole of a Framework programme. However, the Commission will not release these figures. In their absence, Table 7.3 gives a rough guide as to who gets what.

Accepting that Table 7.3 provides some clues on relativities, it is easy to understand why cohesion is such a highly charged issue in debates about the Framework programme. Part of the unwritten Davignon agenda in the early 1980s had been to find some mechanism for channelling Community resources back towards the richer countries, particularly Germany and the UK, who were large net contributors to the Community's general budget. The predictable result was considerable resentment, especially in the early days of ESPRIT, at the degree to which the research programmes were a 'rich man's club' dominated by the big countries and the big firms. This view was reinforced by a report issued in the early 1990s showing that 75 per cent of all public (that is, national and EU government) expenditures on RTD were spent in ten 'islands of innovation' – Greater London, Rotterdam/Amsterdam, Île de France, the Ruhr, Frankfurt, Stuttgart, Munich, Lyon/Grenoble, Turin and Milan. All featured dense networks of enterprises and research laboratories engaged in developing new products and processes. The report was aptly called 'Archipelago Europe' (FAST 1992).

Because EU expenditures on RTD constituted less than 5 per cent of all public expenditures on research in Union as a whole, the degree to which redistribution via the Framework programme could alter this pattern was limited. A deliberate process of redistribution also compromised the principle of peer review and selection according to scientific excellence, which underpinned the shared-cost actions of the Framework programme. Some member states worried that too much attention to the principle of cohesion led to mediocrity in the RTD undertaken (see House of Lords 1997). Germany's submitted comments on the Commission's proposals for Framework V suggested that for some projects it might be better to encourage collaboration that was limited to the more advanced states (Commission 1996d). Nevertheless, the Maastricht Treaty made clear that, as one of the major policies of the Union, cohesion had to sit alongside competitiveness as an objective of the Framework programme.

The crude figures displayed in Table 7.3 show the UK, Germany, France and Italy receiving a combined total of 50 per cent of total EU funding. This result is unsurprising, given that they are the largest countries of the Union and have far greater capacity than other member states to use Framework programme funds, by virtue of having many more scientists and engineers capable of undertaking advanced research and development. Figure 7.1, derived from Commission data on expenditures under Framework programmes II and III, illustrates how the picture changes when looking at the distribution of funding per capita and per R&D employee. In terms of per capita expenditure, Belgium, Denmark, the Netherlands and Ireland are the gainers, with France, Germany and the UK much closer to average levels of funding.

In terms of expenditures per R&D employee, the cohesion countries – Ireland, Greece and Portugal – top the list because they have relatively few trained scientists and engineers. Rates of spending per researcher in Germany, the UK, France and Italy are all much lower. In other words, judged by their capacity to absorb Framework

FIGURE 7.1   Distribution of funding in Framework programmes II and III per capita and per R&D employee (shared-cost actions only)

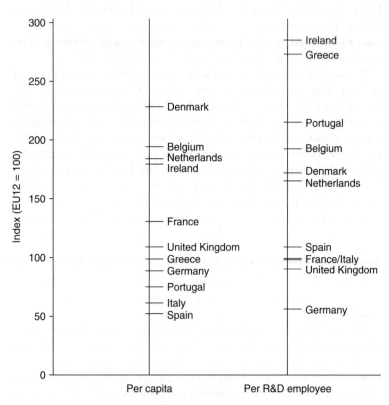

Source: European Commission Services: Eurostat.

programme fund, and contribute to leading-edge R&D collaboration, the poorer countries actually receive a disproportionate share.

The concept of absorptive capacity remains central to much current discussion about the effectiveness of R&D expenditures. The
term refers to the capacity of the economy to absorb new initiatives
promoting R&D. The fewer active researchers in a state, the more
difficult it is for that country to participate in advanced R&D collaborations and to benefit from participation, because relatively few
people capable of understanding state-of-the-art techniques means
opportunities for technology transfer are limited. Participation in
EU-funded projects offers a chance for scientists and engineers from

outside 'Archipelago Europe' to learn what sort of infrastructures are needed and how to conduct and manage leading-edge research.

The argument about absorptive capacity suggests that there should be an accepted division of function between the funds disbursed by the EU under the structural funds and under the Framework programme. The structural funds were consolidated in 1987, after the Single European Act recognised that some regions could be disadvantaged by the 1992 project, particularly less industrialised regions (Objective I) and older industrialised regions suffering from long-term industrial decline (Objective 2). A slice of these funds was earmarked for RTD actions, precisely to help establish the institutional and training facilities necessary to build up science and technology capabilities.

Between 1994 and 1999, total RTD commitments under the structural funds amounted to over 25 per cent of the *total* budget of Framework programme IV, with the sums allocated to Greece, Spain, Ireland and Portugal far exceeding any sums these countries received from the Framework programme (see Commission 1996a). For example, according to Table 7.3, Greece received about 30 million ECU in 1995 in RTD funds from the Framework programme, whereas it received an average of 133 million ECU a year earmarked for RTD from the structural funds during this period (Commission 1996a). In other words, the structural funds were a much more important source of funding for the cohesion countries than the Framework programme. The structural funds are also administered by national and regional governments, not by the Commission, which sometimes brings advantages. The example of Ireland, where the national government deliberately geared its programmes to make the most of Community initiatives, illustrates how effectively national governments can use EU programmes to maximise growth benefits (CIRCA 1993).

In short, the largest countries with the most advanced RTD facilities receive the largest amounts of funding under the Framework programmes. Nevertheless, there are many different ways of cutting the cake. Absorptive capacity emerges as the most sensible criterion by which to judge the appropriateness of the distribution of Framework programme funds. It should be for the structural funds to provide the necessary resources to build up infrastructures and capabilities in cohesion countries, whereas the Framework programme should concentrate on providing 'new avenues for institutional learning and institutional innovation' (Lundvall 1992: 316).

EXHIBIT 7.3
Regional disparities and EU programmes

Regional analysis allows a sharper geographical focus on the areas benefiting most from the RTD programmes. The 'Archipelago Europe' study (FAST 1992) suggested that 75 per cent of public R&D expenditures were concentrated in 10 prosperous (and largely northern) industrial regions. Calculations based on Commission (1996a) figures show that those same regions received 51 per cent of funding under Framework II and 47 per cent under Framework III.

These same 'Archipelago' regions contained 28 per cent of the EU's population and 47 per cent of its total R&D personnel (Commission 1996a). There was a considerable concentration of *national* RTD capacities in these regions. The Île de France region around Paris contained 18 per cent of the French population, generated 28 per cent of GDP, housed 39 per cent of R&D personnel, undertook 44 per cent of government-funded R&D and 53 per cent of business R&D. The same regional concentration is seen in cohesion countries. In Portugal, the area around Lisbon was home to 61 per cent of the country's R&D personnel, and undertook 51 per cent of business R&D. In Greece, the Athens region contained 50 per cent of R&D personnel and performed 62 per cent of business R&D. Thus, the question of disparities in absorptive capacity is just as germane at the national level as within the EU as a whole.

Linkages and participants

The Framework II programme involved over 12 000 participants, Framework III over 18 000. Figure 7.2 shows that Germany, France, and the UK had the largest number of participants, with France and the UK the most active players. To put the total number of participants into perspective, the Commission received over 24 000 proposals in 1995 (the first year of Framework IV) involving 100 000 applicants. With approximately one bid in five successful, the Framework IV programme in its first two years involved some 3 000 projects and 20 000 participants, many more than in earlier years (Commission 1997f : 516).

Figure 7.3 shows participation by type of institution in the Framework programme. Figure 7.3(a) shows Framework II (in which ESPRIT and the telecommunications initiatives played a large part). Large firms accounted for over 40 per cent of 'collaborations' (in

FIGURE 7.2   Number of participants in Framework programmes II, III and IV

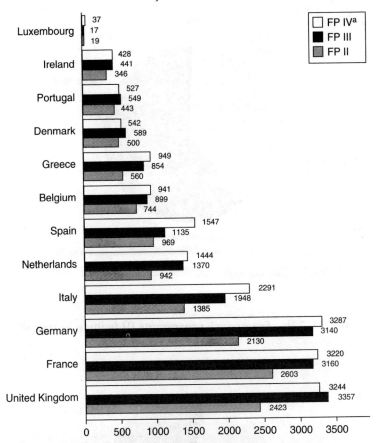

a   Shared cost actions only. For Framework programmes II and III, number of participants in EU 12. For Framework programme (1997f) IV, number of participants in EU 15 for 1994–6 only and shared cost actions only.

Source: Commission 1994a: 240; 1997f: 549.

the EU's own jargon), research centres for 21 per cent, higher education institutions (HEIs) and small firms each 19 per cent. In Framework III (Figure 7.3(b)), the share of large firms had shrunk to 30 per cent and that of small firms had risen to 21 per cent. This shift was very much in line with Commission policy. Note that the higher education and research centre sector also gained.

FIGURE 7.3a   Framework programme II funding by type of participant

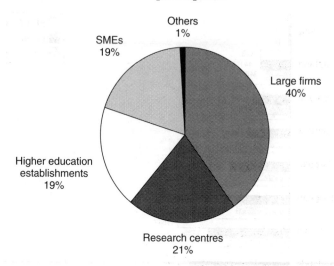

Source: Commission 1994:243.

FIGURE 7.3b   Framework programme III funding by type of participant

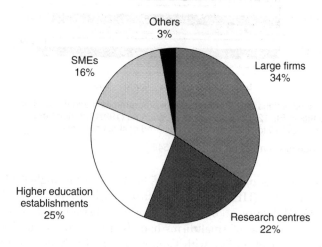

Source: Commission 1997f: 521.

Figure 7.4 breaks these figures down by country and programme. A number of interesting features emerge. First, large-firm participation came predominantly from the larger, more advanced countries and smaller-firm participation disproportionately from the cohesion countries. This finding is not surprising, because the poorer member states are home to very few large firms. Second, in relation to their numbers in the Union as a whole, SME participation remained poor. Even for those few SMEs that fell into the high-tech category, there were many barriers to participating in EU programmes, not least the resources necessary for preparing proposals, the low

FIGURE 7.4   Distribution of Framework programmes funding (shared-cost actions only) by research performers in Framework programmes II and III

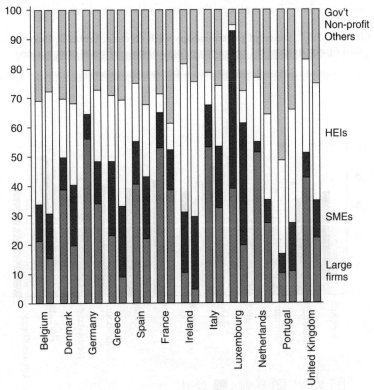

Note: For each country the first column is for FPII and the second for FPIII.

Source: European Commission Services.

chances of success and slow contract and payment procedures (see Exhibit 7.4).

Figure 7.4 shows how important the HEI and research institutes sector were in the 'mix' of institutions under the earlier Framework programmes. Sharp inter-country differences are clear in the organisation of research. In the UK, for example, HEIs play a major role in research. In France, universities are primarily teaching institutions, and most research is conducted in specialist institutes. Both sets of institutions dominated the more academic programmes such as biotechnology, but also played a surprisingly large role in both the ESPRIT and telecommunications programmes, especially for the cohesion countries. The implication was that the Framework programme was creating new opportunities for these institutions to learn by enabling participation in collaborative projects, despite some evidence of a tendency for élite, northern institutions to group

FIGURE 7.5   Share of partnerships with Greece, Ireland, Portugal and Spain in general research programmes (shared cost actions only)

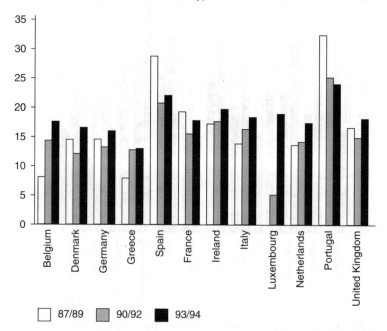

Source: European Commission Services.

EXHIBIT 7.4
The problems of SMEs

Small and medium-sized enterprises (SMEs) present a particularly difficult problem for the Framework programme. By the late 1990s, only 10 per cent of SMEs could be termed 'high-technology' or 'leading-technology users'. Yet, the SME sector was enormous, amounting to 15 million firms, 99 per cent of all enterprises, 66 per cent of employment and 65 per cent of business turnover in the European Union. Between 1988 and 1995, enterprises with fewer than 100 employees accounted for almost all new job creation in the EU (Commission 1995a: 17).

A small proportion of SMEs has always been in the forefront of new technologies. Witness the development of the computer industry and its software suppliers, or the new biotechnology sector that emerged after the 1970s. Europe, whose industries have traditionally been dominated by large firms, must be concerned at its lack of highly innovative SMEs. With large enterprises down-sizing and delayering, increasingly global multinational companies (MNCs) are dependent upon supply chains of local enterprises. Having a lively, flexible small-firm sector capable of using modern, computer-controlled techniques is essential to participating in these supply chains.

SMEs therefore are important players, not only in the *development* of new technologies but also, and even more crucially, as *users* of new technologies. Diffusion as a policy goal essentially involves stimulating SMEs to acquire skills and capabilities to use new technologies. As we have seen, SMEs have not so far been major players in the Framework programme.

The low participation rate of SMEs is hardly surprising. In the first place, the RTD programmes deliberately aim at pre-competitive research. The time to market is, for most SMEs, too long to contemplate. Second, it requires time and energy to negotiate with potential partners. Large companies have specialists who concentrate on such tasks. For small companies, collaboration often means crucial time taken away from key players such as research directors. Finally, even if successful, projects frequently take months of negotiation and payment can be delayed for months.

The Commission has begun to address these issues. In 1996, an Action Plan for SMEs (Commission 1996b) was introduced. It beefed up the earlier CRAFT initiatives aimed at making applications quicker, and introduced new initiatives providing seed-corn capital and loan guarantee schemes for start-up firms. The Action Plan also established a series of Innovation Relay Centres aimed at promoting technology transfer. Nevertheless, there is increasing recognition that these top-down measures have had limited effects. Umberto Scapagnini, president of the European Parliament's Energy, Research and Technology Committee, and a key player in the Framework V debate, called for a reassessment of the role of SMEs within Community programmes, suggesting that the Structural Funds should play a more important role in supporting SMEs in research projects (*EuroTechnology* 1996:14).

themselves together while spurning their southern counterparts (Gambardella and Garcia 1995). More recent data, set out in Figure 7.5, show trends in partnerships between 1987 and 1994. They indicate an increase in partnerships between cohesion countries and the more advanced industrial countries of northern Europe. Note also the reverse of this trend – namely the sharp drop in collaboration between Spain and Portugal, as these long-time partners became more integrated into wider European networks.

Linkages are not, of course, limited to the shared-cost programmes. One of the areas that (rightly) received increasing attention in the late 1990s was the exchange programmes that enabled researchers and postgraduate students to gain experience by working in universities and research institutes in other European countries. Under Framework IV, these programmes were grouped under 'Training and Mobility of Researchers' (TMR), taking 6.1 per cent of the total Framework IV budget (see Table 7.2), which was slightly down on earlier programmes. Still, the EU has fostered a very considerable expansion in mobility, with considerable flows of students from, particularly, Greece, Spain and Italy (but also Germany and France) towards other countries, with the UK topping the list of recipients, followed by France, Germany, the Netherlands and Belgium (in that order). Given the need to train a cadre of researchers from the poorer member states and regions to help upgrade facilities and capabilities, such exchanges are vital. All sides often benefit from the cross-fertilisation of ideas that occurs.

Collaboration between establishments across national frontiers is, of course, an essential requirement of the Framework programme. By the late 1990s, substantial evidence existed to suggest that EU-funded collaboration had encouraged subsequent involvement in further collaborations. Universities and research institutes appeared more likely to continue collaborations than industrial participants, but industrial rates of continuation were not negligible. Collaboration between research organisations from the technologically stronger countries (Germany, France and the UK) was more likely to continue than collaboration between firms and labs in less advanced member states (Commission 1994: 254–5). The explanation may be that southern countries are more often subcontractors rather than full partners in projects, and therefore play a lesser role in formulating and implementing project ideas, a factor that may be expected to change as these countries develop their capabilities.

The 'new' innovation debate: towards Framework V

These patterns of collaboration were generally well established by 1995, and they clearly informed the Commission's thinking in the (1995a) Green Paper on Innovation. The Green Paper also drew inspiration from Delors's 1993 White Paper on 'Growth, Competitiveness, and Employment'. The White Paper presented a holistic view of innovation. It called for action to create jobs, but simultaneously emphasised the need for education, training and job flexibility as well as more and better coordinated spending on research and development. On the latter point, the Commission (1993: ch. 4) was explicit:

> In the Commission's opinion Europe's research and industrial base suffers from a series of weaknesses. The first of these weaknesses is financial. The Community invests proportionately less than its competitors in research and technological development . . . A second weakness is the lack of coordination at various levels of RTD activities, programmes and strategies in Europe . . . The greatest weakness, however, is the comparatively limited capacity to convert scientific breakthroughs and technological achievements into industrial and commercial successes.

The Green Paper was an attempt to respond to these criticisms by initiating consultations with a view to developing a 'genuine European strategy for the promotion of R&D' (Commission 1995a: 2). It concentrated especially on the innovation problem: '[t]he context of innovation has changed profoundly over the past twenty years. The increasingly rapid dissemination of new technologies, and the constant changes which require ongoing adaptation are a challenge to society as a whole' (Commission 1995a: 5). With this admission, the debate of the 1980s – about how Europe could become competitive in the *making* of new technologies – was finally over. The new debate was concerned with *using* new technologies: it recognised that the EU's problems stemmed basically from the low take-up and use of new technologies. The key issues were therefore diffusion and application.

Much of the Green Paper was devoted to an extended diagnosis of European barriers to innovation. The EU's problem was one of 'innovation in a straitjacket'. Europe had too small and too frag-

---

EXHIBIT 7.5
The Task Forces

The idea of Task Forces, after first appearing in the Delors White Paper (Commission 1993), was resurrected in 1995 by Edith Cresson, the newly appointed Commissioner for RTD, and Martin Bangemann, who was reappointed as Industry Commissioner. Both wished to respond to repeated criticisms of a lack of focus in the Framework IV programme. The Task Forces were designed to mobilise resources at both Community and national levels in order to focus more closely on innovation problems that were featured in the 1993 White Paper and directly touched on areas of public/industrial interest. Neil Kinnock, the new Commissioner for transport, also threw his weight behind the initiative, as was reflected in the first eight subjects chosen for Task Forces:

- new-generation aircraft;
- the car of tomorrow;
- multimedia educational software;
- vaccines and viral illnesses;
- the train and railway systems of the future;
- inter-modality in transport;
- the ship of the future;
- environment-friendly water technologies.

The initial tasks assigned to the Task Forces were to define research priorities in their respective areas, and to identify obstacles to innovation and options that might speed the effective application of EU research by industry. They were asked to work with industry, users, researchers and public authorities in the member states, and explore ways of coordinating research efforts between different authorities. The Commission (1996c: 4) insisted that: 'The Task Forces are an essential part of the Commission's strategy to improve the impact and reduce the fragmentation of research across the EU.'

---

mented an R&D effort. In particular, its record on industrial R&D was poor, and it failed to anticipate new trends and technologies. Its education and training systems were too academic, and lacked practical technical and experimental content. There was little mobility of researchers (and therefore cross-fertilisation of ideas), either between countries or between occupations. There was far too much regulation and red tape. Intellectual property rights were more difficult and more expensive to enforce than in the US. Both financial institutions and tax systems vitiated against enterprise.

To answer these criticisms, the Green Paper proposed measures aimed at mobilising resources across both the national and Community levels. Coordination between different levels of government activity was one theme, while unlocking the potential of people (via better training, mobility, and so on) and small businesses, was another. Thirteen separate 'Routes of Action' were identified. Most were highly generalised (such as streamlining administrative procedures), but each was broken down into more specific 'actions' to be pursued either at Community, national or regional level. Among the more specific proposals was an extension of the Task Forces (see Exhibit 7.5).

The Green Paper and the responses to it formed part of the wider debate initiated by the Commission in 1996 about the shape of the Framework V programme, which was due for launch in 1999. The innovation agenda, however, had acquired its own momentum, as revealed in the Commission's (1997b) sequel to the Green Paper, *The First Action Plan for Innovation*. It identified three main areas for action:

(1) *Fostering an innovation climate.*   The aim was to stimulate people to think more innovatively. The proposed measures concentrated on education and training opportunities and encouraging exchanges between countries and jobs. Management training was highlighted as a priority.

(2) *Establishing a framework conducive to innovation.*   The emphases were on patenting, finance and regulation. Finance for SMEs was particularly important with a need for more 'business angels' – entrepreneurs willing to back new companies – and seed-corn capital to fund high-tech start-ups.

(3) *Gearing research to innovation.*   The key issues were technology transfer and awareness. The Commission proposed to encourage 'technology watch' activities, 'campus companies' (university-based SMEs), demonstration projects, and other ways of encouraging companies, large and small, to strengthen their research activities.

Implementation of the Action Plan was the responsibility of both the Commission and EU member states. For the Commission, it was a matter of using instruments and procedures already set up, largely within the Framework programme, and cajoling and persuading member states to follow suit. The Commission's discretion was limited by the tendency of the Council to shift resources between heads and to initiate entirely new programmes. Much of the discussion, partly for these reasons, shifted to the development of the Framework V programme and the ways in which it could be shaped to promote the diffusion and application of new technologies.

In July 1996 the Commission tabled its first working paper on Framework V, which carried the title *Inventing Tomorrow – Europe's Research At The Service Of Its People* (Commission 1996b). It formally opened the debate on the size and shape of Framework V. Subsequently, every member state submitted comments on the working paper, as did many organisations, all of which were published by DG XII and posted on the Internet (see ESF 1996; House of Lords 1997; Commission 1996d; 1997a; 1997d.) The Commission pledged to take these comments into account in the proposals it put forward.

After a year of consultation, a number of clear lines of criticism emerged from the numerous reports and comments. The main criticisms were as follows:

(1) *The Framework programme was too diverse and lacked focus.* The eighteen separate 'lines of action' agreed for Framework IV, let alone the specific sets of programmes agreed under each line, spread Community resources too widely in a 'scatter-gun' approach. Given that EU expenditures amounted to only a small share of total expenditures on RTD in the Union, it was better to concentrate resources on fewer areas where expenditures could have more impact.

(2) *Procedures were too inflexible.* The Maastricht procedures were themselves seen as one of the main causes of fragmentation, because unanimous Council voting plus co-decision with the Parliament meant that every special interest had to be accommodated. Negotiations on the Framework programme involved eleven different Directorates-General of the Commission in Brussels, as well as a plethora of ministries and interest groups in member states. The result was that, once agreement was reached, no one wished to disturb it even when priorities changed.

(3) *Too much money was spent on the big programmes.* Given the shift in emphasis away from producing 'hardware' to diffusing 'software', ESPRIT and the telecommunications programmes still consumed too much of the budget.

(4) *'Pre-competitive' research meant RTD without any obvious use.* This

criticism echoed the old complaint about spending EU funds on pre-competitive R&D that had no practical application. By way of response, increasing emphasis was already being put on methods such as demonstration projects (designed to 'demonstrate' how an innovation could be applied) and the Task Forces.

(5) *Not enough attention (or money) was paid to SMEs.* In spite of the Commission's attempts to increase the share of SMEs in the Framework programme, their slice of total resources remained too low. Most SMEs were technology followers, not technology leaders. Thus, what was required were more programmes to help encourage and stimulate these companies to improve their innovation performance: more help with proposal writing and finding partners; 'one-stop shops' providing advice on finance, business and technical issues; demonstration projects; virtual networks through the Internet, and so on. This sort of help required close contact with the SME concerned and knowledge of its particular circumstances. It was often best provided by national or even subnational governments.

(6) *The conflict between cohesion and competitiveness remained unresolved.* Sir William Stewart, in his evidence to the House of Lords Select Committee, put it bluntly: 'Cohesion has been used to justify mediocrity' (House of Lords 1997: para. 2.32). The same view was reflected in the German position paper on Framework V.

(7) *Poor administration – long decision times, poor management, late payments – deterred many research organisations from even applying for EU funds.* The most prevalent and longstanding criticisms of the Framework programme were that it was over-bureaucratic and slow. As suggested by Luc Georghiou, a leading technology policy analyst from the University of Manchester, the only solution was 'root and branch' reform of DG XII (House of Lords 1997: 2.69).

The Commission's (1997e) response to these criticisms was to table proposals for a much simplified Framework V programme. They envisaged a limited number of 'thematic programmes' to be promoted under the first activity covering collaborative R&D activities, and three 'horizontal actions', namely international linkage, innovation and participation by SMEs, and improving human potential.

The Amsterdam Treaty, agreed in mid-1997, contained new provisions for majority voting on the Framework programme which meant that the next Framework programme (VI) would be mercifully free of the need for a unanimous Council vote). However, lengthy negotiations took place after the Commission tabled a proposal to spend 16.3 billion ECU on Framework V, with the Parliament insisting on 16.7 billion and the Council anxious to limit expenditures. Framework V still required a unanimous Council vote.

The Council finally opted for a budget of 14 billion ECU in its common position of early 1998, thus triggering once again co-decision with the Parliament. The Commission was keen to see expenditures rise in real terms, justifying the increase by referring to *Agenda 2000*, its medium-term plans for the EU's future (also adopted in summer 1997), which urged increased funding for Community level actions promoting high-value-added activities. The Council and EP did agree on the shape of the new programme. It simplified the existing sixteen lines of action of Framework IV (see Table 7.1) to only four: Quality of Life and Management of Living Resources; the User-Friendly Information Society; Promoting Competitive and Sustainable Growth, and Preserving the Eco-System. Each of the thematic programmes comprised three further sets of actions: key actions (seen as being suitable vehicles for Task Forces), generic research objectives, and infrastructure support. Figures 7.6(a) and (b) demonstrate how the Commission saw them fitting together.

Separate lines were retained for the Euratom programmes (fission and fusion) and for direct action measures (essentially, the costs of the JRC). Table 7.4 sets out Framework IV and V proposals under similar heads. Overall, the distribution was remarkably little changed. The only sharply reduced share was for the Information Society programmes, while the Quality of Life and Living Resources and the environmental programmes all gained a little. The JRC also lost in relative terms, but the training and mobility programmes gained. Once again, given the pressures of enlargement, the sums devoted to international cooperation were surprisingly low. Meanwhile, for all the talk about small firms and diffusion-oriented programmes, the allocation for dissemination was ludicrously small. Moreover, as the full description of the Quality of Life and Living Resources thematic programme in Figure 7.6(b) illustrates, the programme detail proposed was as complex as ever.

It was clear that the Amsterdam Treaty was not going to be ratified by the time Framework V was due to be agreed (in spring 1998), and thus a smooth passage to approval by the Council and EP via co-decision was highly unlikely. Even before the Commission put a

FIGURE 7.6a Thematic programmes and horizontal actions suggested for Framework V

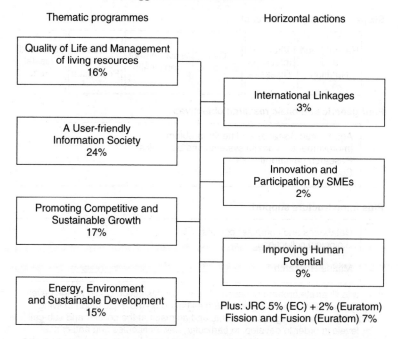

Thematic programmes   Horizontal actions

Quality of Life and Management of living resources 16%	
	International Linkages 3%
A User-friendly Information Society 24%	
	Innovation and Participation by SMEs 2%
Promoting Competitive and Sustainable Growth 17%	
	Improving Human Potential 9%
Energy, Environment and Sustainable Development 15%	Plus: JRC 5% (EC) + 2% (Euratom) Fission and Fusion (Euratom) 7%

Source: European Commission (1997c), updated by Commission Press Release 12 February 1998.

proposed price tag on Framework V, Spain refused to endorse the Commission's general approach to Framework V (1997e), insisting that an explicit link be made between its budget and the continued existence of the cohesion fund, which awarded aid for transport and environmental projects to poorer EU member states. Cresson fiercely and publicly attacked the Spanish for holding the Framework V programme 'hostage', and putting at risk its agreed timetable (*European Report*, 16 May 1997). Commission officials wearily admitted that the Spanish and EP were likely to fight a pitched battle, especially over increased funding for Central and Eastern Europe.

In sum, Cresson succeeded in changing considerably the parameters of the debate about EU-funded research. The Amsterdam Treaty promised less tortuous future negotiations. There remained

FIGURE 7.6b   Unpacking thematic programme I: Quality of Life and Management of Living Resources

Six key actions (Task Forces)

Health, Food and Nutrition	Viral and Infectious Diseases	Cell Factories	Environment and Health	The Ageing Population	Rural and Coastal Areas

Four generic and basic research objectives

Age-related diseases and health problems
Improvements in health systems and bio-ethics
Research on natural risks
Socioeconomic aspects of life sciences

Plus infrastructure support

Databases and computer centres
Biological collections
Clinical Testing
Marine Research

[a] Text to illustrate breadth of action: 'The aim of this action would be the development of multidisciplinary technologies based on the exploitation of living organisms (micro-organisms, plants and animals) at the cellular and sub-cellular levels in order to develop, in particular, new antibodies and anti-cancer agents, bio-treatment methods for waste, and new biological processes in the agri-food industry.'

Note: This diagram is illustrative of the state of play in the Framework V negotiations as of early 1998. The proposals are not exhaustive. Different headings and subprogrammes could well emerge after negotiations.

Source: European Commission (1997c), updated by Commission Press Release 12 February 1998.

little evidence, however, of a true 'European Technological Community'.

Conclusion

We have seen that an extensive EU research 'empire' had emerged by 1997, fifteen years after the Davignon ESPRIT initiatives had

TABLE 7.4

Framework IV compared with Framework V proposals[a]

	FP IV 1994–8		FP V 1999–2002	
	MECU	%	MECU	%
Improving the quality of life and Management of Living resources	1 835	14.0	2 239	15.9
Creating a User-friendly Information Society	3 604	27.4	3 363	24.0
Promoting Competitive and Sustainable Growth	1 722	17.2	2 389	17.0
Energy and Environment	1 597	12.2	2 048	14.7
Nuclear Fission and Fusion	1 017	7.7	979	7
Direct Measures - the JRC	1 095	8.3	969	7
International Cooperation	575	4.4	458	3.2
Dissemination/SMEs	312	2.6	350	2.6
Training and Mobility/Human Potential	792	6.1	1 205	8.6
Total	13 100	100	14 000	100

[a] Based on Council's Common Position agreed in February 1998

Source: Table 7.1 and Commission Press Release, 12 February 1998.

catalysed the programmes of the early 1980s. While still accounting for less than 5 per cent of the Union's budget, technology policy became the third largest item in that budget and impinged on the activities of a large number of Commission services. The EU's range of programmes grew to embrace not only the pre-competitive generic research that was the focus of ESPRIT but also, increasingly, activities focused on the dissemination of new ideas, the use of new technologies and the cross-fertilisation of ideas through the exchange and mobility programmes. An increasing number of firms, large and small, universities and research institutes were drawn into the EU's web, and an increasing number of researchers participated in its programmes.

Something of a watershed in the evolution of EU technology policy was reached in 1997. In her two years as Commissioner, Cresson had succeeded in initiating a broad debate about the purpose and focus of the EU's programmes. The debate had two main axes. The first was the Framework V programme itself, which highlighted the problems of fragmentation, coordination and administration. The second was the wider debate about innovation and competitiveness, which brought to the fore the Union's relative failures in high technology, in spite of fifteen years of EU technology programmes. This debate, however, also emphasised the broader context of innovation and the importance of not just making new technologies, but also using and diffusing them. It was seminal in shifting the thrust of EU technology policy in that direction.

The great unanswered question remained: precisely what had been achieved by fifteen years of European technology policies? How far did the existing range of programmes deserve to be continued much as they were? Did the EU's programmes need to shift more towards the EUREKA 'bottom-up' approach? Or was an even more radical shake-up of policy required? A close look at RTD policy decision-making, to which we turn in Chapter 8, helps us frame, focus and ultimately answer these questions.

8

Decision-Making: Who Gets What and Why?

After the experiments of the early 1980s, European collaborative RTD programmes expanded quite rapidly. By the late 1990s, both the Framework programme and EUREKA were characterised by complicated and often hermetic systems of decision-making. In 1995, Edith Cresson admitted that 'our procedures are too bureaucratic and our delays are too long' (quoted in Commission 1995b). The Belgian EUREKA Chairmanship (1995: 3) acknowledged that the initiative continued to be plagued by problems of insufficient transparency.

In this chapter, we try to untangle and clarify decision-making within the EU's technology programmes and EUREKA. We are interested in 'big decisions' concerning the broad scope and focus of European technology policy, as well as big, strategic projects into high-definition television (HDTV) and semiconductors. However, we also examine how more mundane, day-to-day choices are made about which projects and technologies are funded (and which are not). The EU is viewed by most political scientists as a system of 'multi-level governance', in which different types of decision are taken at different levels, which are dominated by different actors. Our framework for analysis assumes that EU decision-making generally takes place at three different levels of analysis (see Table 8.1), which are more or less distinct in different policy sectors.

Our central argument here is that the high politics of research policy – played out at what might be called a 'super-systemic' level of analysis – are often surprisingly dramatic and hard-fought. However, the gap between this level of analysis and the operational,

TABLE 8.1

Levels of analysis in EU decision-making

Level	Decision Type	Dominant Actors	Rationality	'Best' model(s)
Super-systemic	'History-making'	European Council; governments in IGCs	Political	Liberal intergovernmentalism; neofunctionalism
Systemic	Policy-setting	Council; COREPER	Political; technocratic	New institutionalism
Sub-systemic	Policy-shaping	Commission committees; Council groups	Technocratic; consensual	Policy networks

Source: Adapted from Peterson (1995a).

or 'sub-systemic' level of individual collaborative programmes is very wide. Criteria for determining what are 'good' decisions at these two levels, or the rationalities which govern decision-making, are very distinct and different from one another. In research policy, compared with other areas of EU policy, there is simply not much action at the intermediate, or systemic, level, where EU institutions bargain and legislate according to the 'Community method' of decision-making.

The high politics of RTD policy

The mid-1980s marked a watershed in the development of European collaborative programmes. EUREKA was transformed from a vague French vision to an actual programme. Meanwhile, the declaration of the 1985 Milan European summit committed the EU to increase spending on research to 6 per cent of the Union's total budget by the end of the decade. At this point, it appeared that 'history-making' decisions to shift substantial RTD policy resources to the European level had been taken. In EU decision-making, such particularly weighty decisions may 'alter the Union's legislative procedures, rebalance the relative power of EU institutions, or change the EU's remit'. They usually are taken at the highest political levels, or at a 'super-systemic' level of analysis that transcends the Union's day-to-day policy process (Peterson 1995a: 72).

Armed with the Milan declaration, the Commission badgered member states to deliver on their commitment to EU research. However, starting with the proposal for Framework II in 1985, battles over research budgets were long and bloody. Germany and (especially) the UK refused to endorse the Commission's ambitions. Meanwhile, France tended to lead a coalition that generally favoured the expansion of collaborative programmes. France remained a net beneficiary of Community-funded R&D, while also pouring considerable national funding into EUREKA (see Ministére de la Recherche 1992). Negotiations on a budget for Framework III (1990–4) were long, but concluded under the resourceful chairmanship of France's research minister, Hubert Curien, during the 1989 French EU presidency.

The political equation in France had changed radically by the time that debates began on Framework IV (1994–8). By this point, France had become a net contributor to the EU's general budget, and was governed by a right-wing, semi-Gaullist coalition. It thus became another budgetary sceptic, along with the UK and Germany, on EU research questions. The Union remained far from its goal – now almost ten years old and barely remembered – of spending 6 per cent of its budget on research.

The political reality was that the Framework programme no longer served its original (unspoken) purpose: to compensate large, richer member states for their net contributions to the EU's budget. By the early 1990s, the Framework programme had become an essential element in the research efforts of Greece, Portugal and Ireland, where it accounted for between 10 and 35 per cent of all civil R&D spending. Mostly owing to skilful Spanish diplomacy, cohesion was presented in the Maastricht Treaty's Article 130a as an all-pervasive value to inform the making of all EU policies (including research). A cohesion-oriented R&D policy became viewed, at least in some circles within the EU's institutions, as a boon to European unity. For Germany and the UK (and to a lesser extent, France), the idea that RTD policy should promote cohesion, as opposed to European excellence, was an anathema. The intergovernmental politics of research policy thus pitted the 'Big Three' against a broad coalition of most other member states and the

Commission. The latter camp was led, in some respects, by Italy, whose somewhat chaotic national research policy had produced few success stories. Italy benefited disproportionately from the JRC, and DG XII became something of an Italian *domaine réservé*, particularly under the reign of two consecutive Italian Commissioners for Research, Fillipo Pandolfi (1988–92) and Ruberti (1993–4). The consequence was that Italy supported larger Framework programme budgets instinctively (Peterson 1996: 239–40).

Meanwhile, with an eye on the (generally) declining fortunes of Philips, the Dutch position tended to lament the cooling of political enthusiasm for large projects driven by large technology producers. It was exemplified by the Dutch MEP, Almam Metten, who warned in a debate on the Framework IV programme that 'Europe's electronics industry will be decimated by the year 2000' if drastic action was not taken immediately (*European Voice*, 2 February 1994). However, as funding generally declined for 'hardware' programmes such as ESPRIT, the Dutch became less enamoured of more funding for EU research.

More generally, northern enlargement and pre-EMU austerity made it more difficult to lever money out of the Council for anything, RTD included. Attempts by the Commission to activate the 700 MECU 'reserve', agreed as part of the Framework IV budgetary compromise, hit a brick wall in 1996. The addition of three new net contributors to the EU's central budget – Austria, Finland and Sweden – landed the Commission with an unenviable sales job. The Commission made its pitch on the basis of the work of the Task Forces, one of whose purposes was to mobilise support for spending the reserve. Cresson ensured that their proposals appealed directly to the 'Big Three'. She stressed the French interest in developing new educational software, observing repeatedly that three computers existed in France for every 100 students, compared with 11 for every 100 American students. A German official conceded that, 'we basically support these proposals because they are more market-oriented and focused, although we want to know more about the specifics. It's interesting that smaller countries are reluctant: they are not the winners from the proposals' (interview, October 1995).

In the event, the content of the proposal mattered little, given the overwhelming tide of fiscal austerity sweeping the Union. The support of many research ministers and officials for the proposals was brushed aside by their counterparts in national finance ministries. In the event, the UK and Germany were joined by Austria and Sweden (as well as France and Netherlands) in a coalition that blocked Cresson's proposals, but agreed to a (weak) compromise to spend 100 million ECU of the reserve. Later, they were joined by Spain – which increasingly linked its agreement on RTD to assurances about continued cohesion funding – in a bruising dispute with the EP, which insisted on mobilising at least 200 million ECU from the reserve. The eventual compromise, struck in late 1997, was to allocate 115 million ECU for research into land-mine detection, renewable energy and BSE ('mad cow disease').

Apparently undeterred, Cresson made the work of the Task Forces the 'cornerstones' of the Commission's proposal for Framework V (1999–2002). The Task Forces were a clever response to criticisms that the EU's programmes were not well coordinated, either with each other or with national programmes, nor 'relevant' enough to the EU's competitive decline. Still, with the Amsterdam Treaty – which finally applied QMV to RTD policy – unable to be ratified before Framework V was due to be launched, the input of the Task Forces did not change very much. The generally rather grim high politics of fiscal austerity in the late 1990s meant that the negotiations on Framework V were no less hard-fought than those on any previous version of the programme.

No politics please, we're EUREKA

EUREKA was always meant to be free of intergovernmental wrangling. In practice, EUREKA has been largely depoliticised, leaving aside decision-making concerning enlargement and its *grands projets*. In the latter context, EUREKA has been touched by 'high politics' most often when decisions have been needed on the contribution of the EU to strategic projects such as JESSI and HDTV.

High-Definition Television　The HDTV project was funded primarily through EUREKA, but supported in a variety of ways by the Commission. Launched in 1986, this EUREKA project ploughed more than 600 million ECU into the development of a new-generation TV system based on a technical standard developed in Europe. At one point, its total cost made it the second largest capital investment project in Europe after the Channel Tunnel (Cawson 1992). Its primary participants – Philips, Thomson and Nokia – lobbied their governments and the Commission hard to support the project. Even the British government under Margaret Thatcher stumped up a considerable sum in subsidies (Cawson *et al.* 1990).

The project's advocates insisted that the alternative to a massive, rapid and unified European effort in HDTV was the imposition of a Japanese standard that would make all existing TVs obsolete, and give Japan's producers a lead in spin-off markets worth as much as 100 billion ECU. Community governments thus agreed a directive in 1986 to promote the use of the so-called MAC ('multiplexed analogue components') packet of HDTV standards for satellite broadcasting in Europe, while EUREKA aimed to develop hardware that employed the standards. Originally developed in the UK, the MAC standards offered the potential to upgrade gradually the quality of TV pictures and sound, initially using existing equipment before eventually – quite far in the future, it was assumed – yielding a full-blown, next-generation, digital system.

The EU directive promoting the MAC standard was to expire in 1991. The Commission thus began to prepare a fresh directive with the intention of actually banning all broadcasts in Europe that did not use the EUREKA standard. Battle lines were quickly drawn between states with 'hardware champions' and those without indigenous TV manufacturers. France and the Netherlands, as the homes of Thomson and Philips, pushed hard for a tough directive that would force satellite broadcasters to use the MAC standard. Germany was at least sympathetic to the hardware champion position, given Nokia's recent purchase of all ITT's German TV manufacturing interests.

The UK took an entirely different view. It had no indigenous TV manufacturer but was home to Rupert Murdoch's Sky TV, a pioneering satellite broadcaster, which had already invested heavily in alternative, non-MAC standards. Under mostly British pressure, the new HDTV directive was watered down to the point where it required only satellite services launched after 1995 to use the MAC standard. In practice, the directive allowed existing broadcasters such as SKY to use non-MAC standards, thus provoking fury at Philips and Thomson. At the same time, it imposed significant costs on prospective new broadcasters, most of whom had little confidence in the commercial viability of the MAC standard. The directive pleased almost nobody.

The Commission's response was predictable. First, it claimed that the directive was a step forward in terms of developing an integrated EU industrial policy, even if it was riddled with flaws. In the words of a senior DG XIII adviser, Joan Majó Cruzate, 'The most important point is that it exists' (*Financial Times*, 17 March 1992). Second, the Commission proposed a budgetary fix: Pandolfi promised that he would seek nearly 1 billion ECU in Union funding to give broadcasters and programme-makers incentives to use the MAC standard.

Pandolfi's bid for a large dollop of funding was pitched as part of the Commission's HDTV 'Action Plan'. It was backed enthusiastically by EU states with hardware champions, but firmly rejected by the UK. The fervently Eurosceptic British telecoms minister, Edward Leigh, complained that over 90 per cent of European households that already had satellite TV (and nearly all in the UK) would have to scrap their systems if the MAC standards were imposed.

The HDTV Action Plan thus was kicked upstairs to the European Council, and became a bargaining chip at the difficult 1992 Edinburgh summit. John Major, the summit's chairman, apparently gave discreet assurances to Ruud Lubbers, the Dutch Prime Minister, that the British veto on the HDTV Action Plan would be lifted if the Netherlands supported a British plan for the siting of new EU institutions. After the summit, however, the UK refused to withdraw its reserve on the Action Plan. Lubbers launched a furious and public attack accusing Major of bad faith (Peterson 1993c: 509).

Within a few months, the row was made redundant by technological developments in the US. Rapid and unanticipated advances towards a fully digital system made the EUREKA HDTV system obsolete anyway. As he took over the telecoms portfolio in early 1993, Martin Bangemann announced that the Commission would no longer seek either funds or political backing for the MAC standard. At this point, the EUREKA HDTV project was effectively dead.

A variety of lessons might be culled from the HDTV experience (see Peterson 1993c; Cawson and Holmes 1995). Perhaps the most salient is that when technology policy enters the realm of high politics, the Commission almost naturally finds itself caught in a no-win situation between competing industrial and national interests. Its longstanding effort to create an integrated EU industrial policy makes it difficult for the Commission to act as an honest broker, and there is often no imaginable policy that does not alienate powerful firms and governments.

JESSI   The JESSI project into advanced semiconductors was no less tricky for the Commission. JESSI was the successor to the so-called Megaproject, which was launched at the same time as ESPRIT in 1983–4 and primarily linked Philips and Siemens (not Thomson) with funding from both the Dutch and West German governments to the tune of 140 million ECU. JESSI followed in its path in 1989. It brought together virtually all of Europe's producers in the sector, including Philips, ICL, Siemens, Thomson-SGS and Plessey, to develop the next generation of memory chips. Total funding for JESSI during its seven-year life-span was more than 3 billion ECU, with public funding amounting to about half. By most accounts, the project helped European producers make tangible progress in closing the technology gap separating them from their non-European competitors (see EUREKA secretariat 1995a; Hobday 1995).

Yet, JESSI became caught up first in internal Commission bickering about the EU's relationship with EUREKA and then in the budget cutting that followed German unification. The Commission initially signalled that it could provide as much as half of all public funding for JESSI. However, after an obtuse fight over legal rights to research results, the Commission ended up contributing only around a quarter (EUREKA secretariat 1995a: 10). The European IT Round Table vented its frustration publicly and strong mutual recriminations ensued between Pandolfi and heads of European IT multinationals (see *The European*, 1 November 1991).

Another complication was the German decision to slash its public funding commitment to JESSI under the budgetary strains of unification. Some participating firms pulled out as JESSI's total budget for 1992 was cut by a quarter. With the project's future hanging on a knife-edge, the Germans were pressed hard, by Siemens as well as other EU member states, to resume their contribution. Eventually, Germany came back on board and the project was seen through to conclusion in 1996. The main lesson of JESSI, in the eyes of one senior EUREKA official, was that, 'the Germans always eventually come up with the money. They kick and scream and then they do it' (interview, EUREKA Secretariat, October 1995).

Still, Germany – along with the UK – remains the most instinctively sceptical member state on most questions related to collaborative R&D. A general perception persists in Germany that the most
important research projects should be funded domestically (Peterson
1996: 234–5). Compared with their counterparts in other member
states, German firms have tended to be slow and late in establishing
themselves as active political players in Brussels decision-making
(Cowles 1996). To some extent, post-unification cuts in public funding at home have pushed Germany's research community to look
harder at European opportunities. Regardless, as one German official insisted, 'the Commission cannot justify the low German return'
from the Framework programme (interview, March 1994).

EUREKA's wider impact   Scepticism about EU-funded research has
been fuelled by EUREKA's existence as an alternative framework.
Ultimately, EUREKA has had three important effects on EU decision-making. First, it has provided a handy rationale for resisting
higher budgets for the EU's programmes. The rapid eastern
enlargement of EUREKA, for example, helped EU member states
to justify a 'substantially reduced' and generally stingy (4.4 per cent)
share of Framework IV funding for 'international cooperation'
(Commission 1995b: 1e).

Second, the dominance of EUREKA by France, Germany and
(to a lesser extent) the UK has acted to harden political divisions in
debates about EU research policy. The 'Big Three' have frequently
concurred that new initiatives should be organised within EURE-
KA, and not by the EU, so as not to increase their net budgetary
contributions to the Union. Meanwhile, the Commission and poorer
member states have tended to see EUREKA, and the dominance of
rich states within it, as one justification for trying to ensure that the
Framework programme embraces cohesion objectives.

Third, EUREKA has blunted the Commission's industrial policy
ambitions. Ultimately, it has been EUREKA that has spawned the
most ambitious, strategic projects, such as JESSI and HDTV. These
projects have genuinely combined all (or nearly all) European efforts
and capabilities. As such, the Commission has had, in practical
terms, little choice but to support them with funds and other supportive measures. Yet, after hopes were raised by the Milan
Declaration of 1985, the organisation of most *grands projets* within
EUREKA, and the persistence of high politics more generally in

EU technology policy, have been sources of profound disappointment to the Commission.

The systemic level: why RTD policy is different

The budgetary politics of the Framework programme clearly invoke
the highest political levels. At a stretch, budgetary choices on the
Framework programme might even be considered history-making
decisions, because they go far towards determining the EU's
research activities for as many as five years at a time. It is plausible
to view bargaining on the Framework programme's budget as essentially intergovernmental between self-interested EU member states.

In contrast, most EU policies are 'set' after bargaining that in
nature is at least as inter-institutional as it is intergovernmental, if
not more so. 'Policy-setting' decisions are taken according to one of
several versions of the Community method of decision-making: the
Commission proposes, the EP amends, the Council disposes, and so
on (see Table 8.1). The 'new institutionalism' – with its broad con-
ception of institutions, and its concern with the 'beliefs, paradigms,
codes, cultures and knowledge' embedded within them – offers a
valuable set of analytical tools at this level of analysis (March and
Olsen 1989: 26; Armstrong and Bulmer 1998: 51–3).

EUREKA was created as a non-EU initiative without supranational institutions. Leaving aside questions concerning JESSI,
HDTV and the enlargement of EUREKA, the initiative has rarely
been the subject of attention from ministers more senior than junior
industry, trade or research ministers. Decisions which made history
in 1985–6 concerning EUREKA's institutions and industry-led
methodology *did* implicate foreign ministries and senior research
ministers. Afterwards, EUREKA's Ministerial Conference became a
progressively more mundane affair. It retained formal powers to give
any proposed project the EUREKA label. However, the Conference
gradually became a rubber stamp body for decisions taken by
EUREKA's High Level Group (HLG) of civil servants to 'notify' –
essentially, to approve – projects.

Otherwise, EUREKA has very minimal rules to govern decision-
making. Individual member states may fund any project with any
technological goal with any amount of public funding. Providing a
proposed project involves cross-border collaboration, no member

state can block any other from giving it the EUREKA label (see British EUREKA Chairmanship 1986: 3). Virtually all decisions, which determine how projects are labelled and funds are distributed, are *national* decisions. In short, a systemic level of decision-making, in the sense of procedures for making *collective* decisions about the thrust and content of EUREKA's activities, simply does not exist.

In contrast, despite the Commission's protests, the Framework programme remained subject to a 'double' legislative procedure in the post-Maastricht period (see Table 8.2). The procedure originated in the Single European Act, according to which initial decisions on five-year budgets and the broad objectives of the Framework programme required a unanimous Council vote. After these decisions were taken, the Commission had to secure Council approval for individual research programmes in a separate set of votes (by QMV).

According to the SEA, the Council was required only to consult the European Parliament during the first phase of decision-making. However, the second phase was subject to the cooperation procedure, which gave the EP considerable amendment prerogatives. Framework III thus featured pitched institutional wars over the content of individual programmes and the launch of actual research was delayed for periods ranging from 13 months to 2 years. A series of 'theatrical inter-institutional meetings' were needed in 1991 to solve the disputes, including one involving all three presidents, of the Commission, the EP and the Council, to discuss *only* RTD (Elizalde 1992: 320).

The Maastricht Treaty made agreement on a five-year budget and set of priorities for the Framework programme subject to the new co-decision procedure, which gave the EP actual veto power. However, the Council continued to act by *unanimity* under a quirky version of co-decision, with RTD the only area in the Maastricht Treaty (besides culture) subject to it. The procedure became a pet peeve of Jacques Santer's:

> The Union has a huge budget for research, which is vital for the single market and for competitiveness. But we now have to decide on this through unanimity and co-decision with the European Parliament. This makes it almost impossible to reach conclusions. Majority voting here is not a matter of principle, simply of better functioning. (Quoted in *The Observer*, 29 October 1995)

TABLE 8.2

The post-Maastricht decision-making process for RTD policy

1. Commission agrees proposal for the Framework programme's budget and general priorities (for four to five years).
2. Submission of proposal to Council and EP.
3. 'First reading' of EP (amendments proposed).
3. Development of Council's 'common position' (in light of EP's proposed amendments) by unanimous vote.
4. 'Second reading' by EP on Council common position (with amendments raised and voted upon).
5. Convening of 'conciliation committee' (unless Council accepts proposed EP amendments).
6. Council–EP agreement on overall proposal (with Council acting by unanimity).
7. Submission of Commission proposals for individual programmes (i.e., ESPRIT, RACE).
8. Council adopts individual programmes (by qualified majority after 'consulting' EP).
9. Commission develops 'work plans' for individual programmes
10. Commission submits 'calls for tender'.
11. Proposed projects scrutinised by independent experts and management committees.
12. Lists of projects to be funded approved by the Commission.

Equally, supporters of the EP's new post-Maastricht powers considered this strange version of co-decision to be a travesty:

> Since the essence of the co-decision procedure is the negotiation of compromises between Parliament and Council, and whereas it will be extremely difficult for Council to modify its position where unanimity is required and where it may well have reached that position only with great internal difficulties, this particular requirement, again at the insistence of the UK, effectively neuters the co-decision procedure. (Corbett 1994: 208)

The second stage of RTD decision-making, when individual research programmes are approved, remained subject to QMV but Maastricht downgraded the EP's role to consultation. The Council was able (and often willing) to ignore proposed EP amendments. The Parliament had new incentives to fight hard to defend its position at five-year intervals when general budgets and priorities were set, knowing that its influence over research policy was likely to be minimal between them. Meanwhile, the Commission was empowered at the second stage, as qualified majorities for its proposals were relatively easy to construct on the Council.

Thus, decisions on the budget and priorities of each Framework programme became highly politicised, in that they defined the scope of the EU's remit in RTD policy for relatively long (four to five year) periods of time and implicated the highest political levels. Moreover, the application of co-decision made them prone to institutional wars. The Commission, together with its allies in the industrial and research communities, fought hard to defend its proposal for Framework IV. The Council, needing to act unanimously, was uncharacteristically single-minded under the 1994 Greek presidency, but only after very hard and long bargaining between budgetary sceptics (France, Germany and the UK) and more spendthrift member states. In its very first opportunity under the co-decision procedure, the EP tried hard to make its mark and, in the words of a British official, 'to be on the frontiers of institutional procedure' (quoted in Peterson 1995b: 397).

Ultimately, a decision on Framework IV was expedited by the looming 1994 EP election, which limited the Parliament's appetite for argument and delay. Subsequent decisions were taken relatively quickly on individual RTD programmes. It helped that the Commission tabled proposals for twenty specific programmes in early March 1994, even before agreement was reached on a final budget for Framework IV. In Commissioner Ruberti's words, the intent was to send a 'political signal' to the Council and EP emphasising the Commission's strong will to get programmes up and running by the end of 1994 (quoted in *Agence Europe*, 11 March 1994).

In any case, the Commission became increasingly able to control the decision-making process effectively once 'big' budgetary decisions, taken every five years, were out of the way (Peterson 1995b). However, its control was extenuated by factors both external and internal to the Commission itself. For example, the Parliament continued to hound the Commission for more funding for one of its pet programmes, the JOULE programme into non-nuclear energy, even after the Framework IV negotiations were finished. In a particularly nasty exchange, the Commission was accused by several MEPs of manipulating scientific evaluations of proposals submitted under JOULE in a 1995 call for tender (see *Agence Europe*, 16 September 1995; *European Report*, 20 September 1995).

Moreover, the Commission was a powerful but far from united actor in RTD policy (see Cram 1994; 1997). The point was illustrated by very public differences between Pandolfi and Bangemann over the extent to which EU research should move closer to the market in the late 1980s. Rivalries between Commissioners often cross-cut with those between DGs III (industry), XII (science and research) and XIII (telecommunications). The shift of the ESPRIT programme from XIII to III in 1994 marked a significant victory for Bangemann, who insisted that the industry portfolio should include control of any programme with such broad implications for industrial competitiveness. DG XIII, which previously controlled a full 50 per cent of information and communications technology (ICT) spending, was hardly a winner from the division of funding agreed under Framework IV (see Table 8.3).

Meanwhile, the principle of *juste retour* remains entrenched even within the Commission. Members of Commission *cabinets* often take it upon themselves to defend their own member states' interests when EU research funds are actually allocated to projects. Within the Commission, DGs must submit lists of projects that they propose to fund under programmes such as ESPRIT or BRITE to the college of commissioners. At this point, members of *cabinets* scrutinise them carefully to ensure that a sufficient percentage of funding within individual programmes is devoted to projects involving their own member states. As few members of *cabinets* have the expertise or inclination to vet proposed projects for their strategic or technological value, *juste retour* tends to inform decision-making even at this stage of the policy process. Sometimes, the Commission's services have to construct special actions that will benefit a particular member state in order to redress alleged imbalances.

Above all, the Commission's competition policy responsibilities

TABLE 8.3

Division of ICT activities under Framework IV

DG XIII (telecommunications)	16%
DG III (industry)	21%
DG VII (transport)	3%
DG XII (science & research)	60%

Source: European Commission services.

continue to sit uneasily with its RTD policy ambitions. The push to encourage the more rapid dissemination of technology led to an unholy row in 1995 over a proposed block exemption (from scrutiny by DG IV) of licensing agreements on patents and know-how. Cresson argued, in the face of opposition from the Commissioner for Competition, Karel van Miert, for a sweeping exemption on the grounds that information on technology licences was often inherently confidential and thus inappropriate for DG IV investigation. She was outvoted when a decision was taken by the college of Commissioners.

The point is that RTD policy outcomes are determined more by internal debates within the Commission than the EU's 'Community method' of inter-institutional decision-making. Few very important decisions are taken at the systemic level once the Commission has secured agreement on a five-year budget and overall strategy for the Framework programme. After this point, the Commission has considerable autonomy to decide who gets what in fora that are not independent of political considerations, but generally removed from close political scrutiny.

The 'sub-systemic' level: incest and corporatism?

It is easy to understand why the Commission's RTD policy role, although substantial, has attracted relatively little academic or popular attention. The EU's labyrinth of committees and procedures, as well as the technical complexity of RTD policy, are powerful deterrents to scrutiny by all but a small group of specialists. RTD policies often are shaped in important ways at a 'sub-systemic' level of decision-making, especially as proposals are formulated at the beginning of the policy process and implemented at its end. At both stages, the Commission works closely with Europe's industrial and scientific communities. It has gone to great lengths to nurture, even to manufacture, unified policy networks in order to strengthen its hand *vis-à-vis* the Council.

Ruberti's brainchild, the European Science and Technology Assembly (ESTA), is a good example. Created in 1994, ESTA brought together 96 eminent academics and industrialists to give the Commission advice on broad strategy as it prepared for Framework V. ESTA held plenary sessions twice a year, and had a small elected bureau and numerous working parties. Complaints from its delegates that the forum was a 'waste of time', and that its purpose was to rubber stamp the Commission's pre-existing plans, were not unknown (see Krige and Guzzetti 1997: 474). However, the Commission (1996e: 50–6) persisted with ESTA, with Cresson pledging to get Framework programme managers and service units to interact with it more systematically. With more budgetary wars ahead on Framework V, the Commission clearly hoped that the Assembly could help legitimise its RTD agenda.

In some respects, ESTA seemed to rival the longstanding Comité de la Recherche Scientifique et Technique (CREST), which had been created as a joint committee of the Council and Commission in 1974. Ostensibly, the Commission could argue that CREST's purpose had always been to coordinate national research policies, and thus it needed ESTA specifically to help it develop strategies for the Framework programme. In practice, CREST had always provided general advice to both the Council and Commission on RTD policy.

Another important body in the mare's nest of expert committees was the Industrial R&D Advisory Committee (IRDAC), which was crucial in setting priorities for industrially targeted EU research. In late 1995, the Commission expanded the membership of IRDAC, particularly to include more senior industrialists serving in a personal capacity (and appointed by the Commission), as well as five representatives of European 'peak-level' associations, such as the European employers' federation (UNICE) and the European Trades Union Congress. In future, IRDAC's mandate would extend to broader strategy, and not just RTD narrowly defined, in a reflection of both the Framework programme's new 'service ethos' *vis-à-vis* other EU policies and Cresson's penchant for big thinking.

More generally, the Commission practises a unique brand of corporatism to legitimise its RTD policy. Panels of 'the great and the good', such as ESTA and IRDAC, are primarily involved in policy formulation, while panels of experts are important players in policy implementation. Their memberships often overlap, with the Commission acting as the link between them. Procedures for allocating EU funding to specific activities and projects, and thus determining who gets what, assign a powerful role to nominally independent experts. Outcomes then may be justified on technical or scientific grounds. Of the more than a thousand specialised committees that advise the Commission generally, over 70 per cent consist mainly of scientific or technical experts (Elizalde 1992: 324).

For each individual programme such as ESPRIT or BRITE, the Commission develops a work plan, which elaborates upon the broad lines agreed in the Research Council and sets out specific strategies to be pursued by each individual programme. At this stage, important decisions are taken that determine which technologies and firms will benefit most from EU-funded research. Work plans are developed in close consultation with working groups and panels of researchers and experts.

A management committee of national experts monitors the implementation of each work plan. Management committees can express an unfavourable opinion, by a qualified majority vote, on the lists of projects the Commission proposes to fund, thus requiring a vote by the Council to unlock funding. However, the procedure still gives the Commission considerable autonomy (see Docksey and Williams 1995: 127–8). Many delegates to management committees are national 'experts', instead of civil servants. As such, they defend national interests less aggressively if Commission choices can be justified on technical grounds.

Still, the vexed issue of 'comitology' is a live one in RTD as much as any other policy sector. In practice, committees are concerned mostly with ensuring a 'fair' distribution of projects and funding between member states. As a DG XIII official puts it, 'in management committees, you wouldn't hear a line such as "we put 18 per cent of the Community budget in, we want 18 per cent back". But that type of argument lurks in the background when people claim "this share of funding is too low for us"' (interview, October 1994).

Even at the sub-systemic level, the Commission must respect *juste retour*, which even appears to operate at the level of individual programmes. Spain, for example, gets a remarkably similar share of receipts – usually not far from 6 per cent – from each and every individual EU programme (see Table 8.4). Still, the Commission's services enjoy considerable discretion in sub-systemic decision-making. For example, the Commission generally may switch as much as 15 per cent of funding between broad areas without the blessing of the Council (Gaster 1991: 249).

Meanwhile, the Commission frequently defends its proposals on the grounds of 'Community interest'. When it does, it often is seek-

TABLE 8.4

National receipts from EU RTD: Spain (results to 10 October 1996)

Programme	Total no. of projects	projects with Spanish participants	% of projects with Spanish participants	Total Budget MECU[a]	Finance allocated to date MECU	Finance allocated to Spain MECU	Return %
Telematic applications	341	146	42.8	898	544.1	33.2	6.1
Communications technologies(ACTS)	203	71	35	671	563.2	29.9	5.3
Information technology (ESPRIT)	438	127	29	2 035	924.8	60.3	6.5
Industrial technology (BRITE/EURAM)	211	67	31.7	1 722	453	23.5	5.2
Standards, means and testing (SMT)	44	10	22.7	185	38	2.4	6.3
Environment and climate	285	88	30.9	566	201.5	11.7	4.1
Marine science and technology (MAST)	47	17	36.2	243	92.2	9	9.8
Biotechnology	210	73	34.8	588	282.8	14.7	5.2
Biomedicine and health	319	115	36.1	358	146.8	8	5.4
Agriculture and fishing (FAIR)	314	113	36	646	267.1	20	6.4
Non-nuclear energy (JOULE-THERMIE)	425	101	23.8	1 030	310.3	17.6	5.7
Nuclear fission security	180	66	36.7	170	129.6	8.5	6.6
Thermonuclear fusion (1995)	b	b	b	846	100.3	5.4	5.4

TABLE 8.4 (*continued*)

Programme	Total no. of projects	Projects with Spanish participants	% of projects with Spanish participants	Total Budget MECU[a]	Finance allocated to date MECU	Finance allocated to Spain MECU	Return %
Transport	109	45	41.3	256	117.3	5.8	5.0
Socio-economic research (TSER)	38	24	63.2	112	20.8	1.4	6.7
International cooperation (INCO)	439	54	12.3	575	131.6	3.1	2.4
Innovation	149	31	20.8	312	77	7.9	10.3
Training and mobility of researchers (TMR)	1 560	346	22.2	792	335.8	30.7	9.1
Total	3 558	1 081	30.4	12 005	4 736.2	293.1	6.2

[a] This figure does not include funding given to Direct Actions and support to the community policies carried out by the Centro Común de Investgación 1095 MECU).

[b] In this programme research projects are not, strictly speaking, financed. The funds allocated to Spain were dedicated solely to the construction TJ2 in the CIEMAT.

Source: Spanish Ministry of Foreign Affairs.

ing to foster or consolidate networks of actors that support the Commission's agenda in a given sector. The practice can provoke charges that the Commission is 'buying its own political constituency' at the expense of funding excellence. For example, a proposed list of agricultural R&D projects was rejected by a management committee in October 1995, amid accusations that the Commission had approved many projects with low scientific marks and rejected ones with higher marks.

Generally, however, the Commission has managed over time to foster identifiable policy networks in most sectors. A generally closed circle of actors tends to be involved repeatedly in decisions that determine which projects and technologies receive funding in given sectors. The process is highly incestuous: evaluators of proposals often are recipients of large grants from EU programmes, and mutual back scratching inevitably occurs. Of course, some networks are more single-minded and insular than others. For example, in its early days ESPRIT could fairly be described as an insular policy community dominated by the Round Table of 'Big 12' European IT firms (see van Tulder and Junne 1988). Yet, as a Commission official in DG XIII argued:

> That's only one type of charge against the Framework programme. The Round Table has many, many times complained – even in writing – that they don't get a big enough share of the programme. So the truth is somewhere in between . . . But it is much easier for the Commission if it wants an 'industry opinion' to go to the Round Table for it. (Interview, October 1994)

The early dominance of the Community's IT policy network by Big 12 firms was largely replicated in EUREKA. Both the HDTV and JESSI projects were propelled by Europe's largest multinationals. Originally geared to suit large microchip producers, JESSI underwent 'a great deal of change in objectives', owing to Philips's ostensible withdrawal from the project in 1992 (EUREKA secretariat 1995a: 3).

More generally, not only EUREKA's *grand projets* but also its 'umbrella projects' tended to develop their own administrations, funding rules, reporting systems and decision-making mechanisms. The original purpose of umbrella projects, such as EUROTRAC for atmospheric research and FAMOS for robotics, was to catalyse projects in these sectors by earmarking funding and granting limited autonomy to their organisers. However, several became exclusive empires within empires, which resisted the entry of outsiders. By the late 1990s, EUREKA member states were studiously avoiding the creation of new umbrellas. The lesson was that, once constructed, policy networks could quickly take on minds of their own.

Industry structure is an important determinant of the cohesiveness of sectoral policy networks. Until recently it was plausible to argue that 'there are no European networks in the area of biotechnology worth speaking of, because the European chemical and pharmaceutical companies have not yet perceived this as an approach that would best suit their individual interests' (Esser 1994: 6–7). Trying to construct an EU biotechnology policy network, resembling those in IT or telecoms, seemed inappropriate and even counterproductive.

However, in the face of shrinking profit margins and mounting R&D costs, Europe's largest chemical companies met repeatedly at the level of research directors in 1994. One result was the collective submission of proposals for new EU-funded projects to the Commission (*Financial Times*, 29 March 1994). Subsequently, the participation of industry in EU biotechnology programmes doubled between Frameworks III and IV, with the Commission clustering proposals together into 'integrated projects' in several priority areas. Virtually all of the major players in the European industry – including Rhône-Poulenc-Rorer, Unilever, Roche and Hoechst – were involved in at least one project. The clear intent was 'to fund not just a ragbag of projects done by a haphazardly self-selected group, but projects that draw together as many as possible of the key players' (Herman 1995: 12). Somewhat triumphantly, the Commission claimed that 'a European approach comes almost naturally in the field of biotechnology today' (*European Report*, 4 October 1995).

As the Framework programme grew, many RTD policy networks expanded their memberships and became less insular. For example, the influence of the Big 12 Round Table waned as Bangemann became more involved in IT policy. The Round Table's 1991 proposals for temporary protective measures to force open foreign markets, preferential treatment for EU producers in projects to stimulate demand, and relaxed competition rules were nowhere to be seen in the Commission's (1991a) White Paper on IT. The Round Table gradually became a less cohesive unit as Philips underwent a severe internal crisis in 1990–2 and ICL was booted out after Japan's Fijitsu took a controlling share in the firm, and its members began to lobby on broader issues – trade, competition and industrial policy – which were more divisive than RTD policy.

Meanwhile, the Commission began to focus on measures to assist the computer software and service industries. Round Table firms continued to be represented in the Bangemann Group, which worked on general IT policy issues, as well as on Industrial Working Groups which developed work programmes. However, the Commission kept them out of its Industry Advisory Panels of IT *users* on the grounds that Big 12 firms were primarily producers whose interests were not the same as those of most IT users. More generally, by the mid-1990s the Commission was taking new steps to rotate project evaluators and ensure that work programmes were not designed each year by the same set of individuals. It claimed that nearly 4500 experts sat on its various evaluation panels set up before the launch of Framework IV (Commission 1996e: 7).

Ultimately, however, most calls for tender, or Commission requests for proposed projects, are vastly oversubscribed. One consequence is that the Commission and its advisers have considerable latitude to choose beneficiaries. To take one example, a 1996 call under the EU's IT programme into Multimedia Systems – a relatively uncrowded and new industrial sector – produced 461 proposals, of which only 110 were funded.

The wide discretion that the Commission enjoys has encouraged member states to press for tighter quality controls yet simpler management procedures. The Commission is constantly criticised by participants in EU programmes for being too bureaucratic and slow in concluding contracts and (especially) paying out subsidies. Often, however, just two or three officials are given responsibility for handling thousands of applications for funding. Member states want tighter procedures, but they are rarely willing to fund more Commission posts to apply them.

Particularly under Cresson, the Commission (1996e: 1b) acknowledged that the management of EU programmes left much to be desired. It took steps in 1995 to simplify and shorten the project contracts, with a view to clarifying technological transfer rules, giving participants stronger intellectual property rights, and requiring a 'technology implementation plan' at the end of each project. The changes were greeted enthusiastically by most member states.

However, none of them diluted the Commission's power to determine outcomes of sub-systemic decision-making, and many of them actually enhanced it. Put simply, the Commission has become the ringleader of most RTD policy networks, many of which now act with considerable autonomy.

Conclusions

European technology policy has not broken free from the exigencies of high politics. National sovereignty, interests and financial returns from the EU's budget still concern policy-makers, far more than the architects of the Framework programme would have hoped. EUREKA is largely depoliticised, but only because it poses little threat to national sovereignty or prerogatives. EUREKA's 'bottom-up' mode of decision-making means that it lacks much capacity for collective action. *Juste retour* is not an issue.

EUREKA is paradoxical in several respects. If there was ever a European initiative to exonerate the assumptions of intergovernmentalism – that national preferences are supreme, policies result from intergovernmental bargains, and common institutions simply enforce their terms – then EUREKA might seem to be it. However, EUREKA trundles on, and, in a number of sectors such as HDTV and computer chips, it has pushed national policies towards embracing common goals, and has even brought the Commission on board. If political spillover seems absent from EUREKA, the initiative certainly has acted as a framework for functional spillover in that it has facilitated a significant joining up of previously independent national research efforts.

As for the EU's Framework programme, one view would hold that the politics of budget-setting are clearly intergovernmental: witness the need for the Brussels European summit to break the logjam on Framework IV in 1993. Neofunctionalists could counter that the Commission controlled the negotiations for the most part, with help from allies such as the Belgian Council presidency. This view also would highlight the roles played by transnational élites from Europe's industrial and science communities, along with the EP, in pushing for a larger budget for EU research (Peterson 1995b: 405), as well as the eventual sanction of QMV for all research decisions by the Amsterdam Treaty

Moreover, it is clear that member states retain relatively weak means for controlling EU research policy after they agree a budget and general priorities every five years. The systemic level of decision-making, which is crucial to understanding outcomes in most other EU policy sectors (Hayes-Renshaw and Wallace 1997: 244–73), seems hardly to matter. To explain why, a new-institutionalist analysis would highlight three factors: the organic (unplanned) evolution of institutions, path dependency, and relationships between experts and policy-makers in EU governance (see March and Olsen 1989).

The often unpredictable manner in which political institutions develop, especially in the EU, is well illustrated by the (literally) last-minute decision at the Maastricht summit to apply a rogue version of co-decision to the Framework programme. With the Council needing to act unanimously, and the EP wielding effective powers *only* on 'big' decisions, it is hardly surprising that institutional wars are fought at a higher political level than is normally the case in EU policy-making. The systemic level features decision-making by majority votes on the Council, with the EP only consulted (or ignored). It is *not* where the action is.

The new-institutionalist notion of path dependency highlights the power of the argument, often used effectively by the Commission, for continuity in R&D. Most EU programmes are the outcomes of complex political bargains based on issue linkage. Once agreed, member states are usually reluctant to unstitch such bargains because to do so is to invite the unstitching of related bargains and invite a frenzy of unravelling (Scharpf 1988). The consequence is that EU programmes tend to be tinkered with only at the margins.

Finally, new institutionalists highlight an increasingly fundamental problem of modern governance: 'a sharp division of labour between specialists and policymakers is impossible to sustain, either conceptually or behaviorally' (March and Olsen 1989: 30). Most Commission officials who work on RTD policy are scientifically trained, and usually act according to technocratic rationality. Moreover, the Commission has assembled dense networks of experts to provide advice that is 'objective' and technical, as opposed to national and political. RTD policy tends to validate Pierson's (1996: 137) new-institutionalist treatment of EU decision-making, according to which 'time constraints, scarcities of information, and the need to delegate decisions to experts may promote unanticipated consequences and lead to considerable gaps in member-state control'.

Still, the Commission's continuing need to play politics with research policy is a source of considerable frustration to its officials. Most share the view of a senior DG XII official that 'with a completely egalitarian peer review, Framework would be better than it is now and we would have more completely European R&D activities' (interview, March 1994). However, national demands for a bigger slice of RTD funding are rarely expressed blatantly in formal bargaining. Far more often, they are pursued in informal bargaining in more discreet settings. Thus, the concept of policy networks offers a model for understanding how decisions are taken that determine who gets what in EU research policy (as well as within EUREKA). Policy networks tend to form around specific technological sectors. Actors with valued resources – expertise, ideas, and political *nous* – get access to these networks, while others are excluded. Usually, actors have incentives to share their resources, and they engage in bargaining designed to maximise both their collective benefits, as well as their individual share of the loot.

The Commission tends to play the role of ringleader within most networks, because it retains the crucial resource of power to set the agenda at every level of decision-making. Even when the Commission's proposals get caught up in high politics, and it ostensibly loses in bargaining with member states, it still often manages to set the agenda for future decision-making episodes by mobilising allied networks. For example, even though Cresson was unable to secure agreement from the Council on her plans for spending the 700 MECU reserve under Framework IV, the work of the Task Forces clearly was intended to get the prior backing of key research constituencies for the Commission's proposal for Framework V.

Of course, in advance of the ratification of the Amsterdam Treaty, negotiations on the Framework V programme were likely to be laborious and complicated. The Commission despised them as 'clearly *incompatible with the fast-changing needs of scientific research and technological development* . . . Research will thus keep waiting . . . for a federal Europe!' (Elizalde 1992: 320; emphasis in original). By the late 1990s, the EU remained far from a 'federal Europe', but the Commission acted with considerable autonomy and power in RTD. It probably enjoyed more of both than it did in any other EU policy sector.

9

What Has Been Achieved?

This chapter poses a straightforward question to which there is no simple answer. Political economists must be modest and acknowledge the 'yawning gap in our knowledge' of what really determines innovation, and concede that 'we still have no satisfactory theory to explain [say] the higher rate of innovation in Germany than in the UK' (Pavitt and Patel 1991: 368). Yet, technology policies must be judged by their success in promoting innovation. After more than twenty years of European-level measures to promote innovation – and with strong caveats about causes and effects – we may begin, at least, to answer the question: what has been achieved?

'Results' can only be judged against objectives. *Competitiveness* has always been a core objective of European technology policy, particularly in light of profound concerns about the 'technology gap' of the 1980s. The Single European Act gave the EU 'the objective of strengthening the science and technology basis of European industry' to make it 'more competitive at an international level'. Implicitly, by laying down mechanisms that required collaboration between countries and institutions and promoted the mobility of researchers, the EU's programmes were given objectives that related to economic and social cohesion. By extension, promoting inter-country and inter-institutional cooperation meant that Community programmes contributed to the education and training of European scientists. Of course, the Maastricht Treaty reinforced the cohesion objective.

Meanwhile, EUREKA appeared to focus more narrowly on promoting competitiveness through near-market research. Yet, its Declaration of Principles was somewhat vague:

> The objective of EUREKA is to raise, through closer cooperation among enterprises and research institutes in the field of advanced technologies, the productivity of Europe's industries and national economies on the world market, and hence strengthen the basis for lasting prosperity and employment . . . EUREKA projects will . . . be directed both at private and public sector markets. (EUREKA Secretariat 1985: 1)

We end up, therefore, with a rather mixed bag of objectives by which to evaluate European collaborative programmes:

- promoting competitiveness, particularly industrial competitiveness at an international level;
- strengthening Europe's science and technology base;
- promoting economic and social cohesion;
- encouraging collaboration between industry, academia and research institutions in different countries;
- stimulating the education and training of young scientists.

With these objectives as our criteria, we offer a general assessment of the Framework programme and EUREKA. We begin by examining studies that have assessed the impact of collaborative programmes on national research activities. Our analysis then shifts to evaluations of the effects of these programmes on European industries in specific sectors. Next, we turn to findings from studies that have offered broad, 'macro-judgements' on the performance of EUREKA and the Framework programmes, before we assess Europe's general technological performance from a variety of perspectives. Our conclusion offers our own perspective on what has been achieved.

National impact studies

If EU programmes account for less than 5 per cent of total EU member state spending on research then the most significant potential effects of collaborative programmes are their role as catalysts for technology transfer, skills enhancement, new linkages between research organisations, and so on at the national level. Between 1992 and 1994 the Commission oversaw a series of impact studies in EU member states, conducted by independent experts, to assess the impact of the EU's Framework II research programmes in each country. Table 9.1 presents some findings from these studies.

The data suggest that the two most important benefits of EU-funded research were, first, the transfer of knowledge and skills, and second, the stimulation of transnational collaborations. Many participants reported previous links with some of their current partners. Still, a high value was placed on the Framework programme's linkage effects, as large numbers of research organisations built upon and expanded earlier linkages (Commission 1994: 254–6).

Large companies and SMEs tended to collaborate mostly with other (large) firms, while universities and research institutes most often teamed up with each other. Surprisingly, few university–industry linkages appeared to have been fostered by the EU's programmes. Industrial participants tended not to choose direct

TABLE 9.1

Major benefits from involvement in EU R&D contracts (Framework II impact studies)(%)

Country	New scientific skills	Research skills	Training content	Link with other R&D organisations	Initiation of joint projects
Belgium[a]	52	37	21	46	41
Denmark	37	19	11	16	15
France	82	29	39	62[b]	68
Germany[a]	91	92	n.a.	93	64
Greece	26	22	13	20	17
Ireland[a]	75	62	31	68	48
Italy	28	34	1	29	6
Portugal[a]	87	56	61	64	44
Spain	17	23	18	25	15
UK[c]	n.a.	72	n.a.	n.a.	n.a.

[a] Multiple answers allowed.
[b] Refers to 'new and durable' collaborations.
[c] The UK used a different classification; results not really comparable.

Source: Commission 1994 (table 8c.2).

competitors as partners but instead formed vertical linkages up or down the supply chain (to suppliers or users) or cooperated with indirect competitors.

EXHIBIT 9.1
The UK impact study

The UK Impact Study (Georghiou *et al.*:1993) was widely acknowledged to be the most comprehensive and in-depth of all those conducted. Its conclusions were largely positive. For example, the UK had the most collaborative links of any member state (17,853). Its researchers were most likely to collaborate with their fellow nationals (as 13 per cent did). Participation was biased towards academic labs and research institutions, and academic views about participation were very positive: 84 per cent claimed substantial benefits and 93 per cent intended to reapply for funds. Industry was more cautious in its response, but 76 per cent of firms still said they were intending to reapply. Table 9.2 sums up expected outcomes from the research.

TABLE 9.2

Expected outcomes from EU supported projects

	Academic	Industry	Research organisations
	← Percentage reporting outcome →		
Further EU funding	87	76	65
Other funding	83	60	43
Enhanced skills	71	68	75
New processes	36	43	55
Commercial links	35	38	55
Funding from own org	34	56	52
Improved processes	20	32	42
New products	18	25	51
Prototypes	18	18	49
Improved products	16	26	48
Patents	9	14	21
Standards	8	14	30
Licences	5	9	25

Source: Georghiou *et al.* 1993.

The study concluded that 'probably the most important and sustainable effect has been to reorientate the research community to the point where it regards itself as a part of an emergent scientific community'. The response of the *Economist* (1993) was 'Big Deal!', casting doubt about whether making researchers 'feel European' really represented value for money.

Exhibit 9.1 describes the UK impact study in more detail. Other country studies, such as Germany's, placed more emphasis on identifying the factors that contributed to a successful collaboration. The German survey found that the key factors were technically attainable and appropriate goals, as well as good project management (Reger and Kuhlmann 1995: 130–1). All the national impact studies found that the EU's programmes created a more stable collaborative environment, encouraging partners to go on working together even after Community funding was exhausted.

To illustrate the point, Figure 9.1 compares collaboration between British researchers in engineering and materials with their EU and US counterparts between 1981 and 1994. Before the mid–1980s, collaboration was more common with US researchers. Afterwards, there was a marked increase in EU collaborations to the point where they far exceeded those with American researchers.

Looking across all the member states surveyed, the most important factors that motivated participation in the EU's programmes were: first, obtaining EU funding; second, gaining access to complementary expertise; and, third, strengthening collaborative linkages. EU funding appeared to be a more important motivator for SMEs than large firms, and crucially important for consortia made up of universities and research institutes.

FIGURE 9.1   Comparison of British collaborations with US and other EU researchers 1981–94

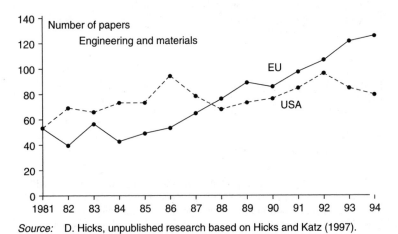

Source: D. Hicks, unpublished research based on Hicks and Katz (1997).

The average EU contribution to the total R&D budget of participating organisations varied between countries, but was generally significant, particularly in less-favoured regions. In Greece, the average EU contribution to industrial organisations amounted to 47 per cent of their R&D budgets in 1990. In the UK, by contrast, the EU provided about 10 per cent of all funding spent on university research (POST 1996: 50). Most participants reported that it would have been impossible to launch their projects without EU funding. Of course, there is always a tendency for participants to answer such questions positively in order to encourage continued funding. It was clear, however, that the opportunity of applying for Community funds had been an important catalyst to the formation of many consortia (Commission 1994: 253).

Many technology policy analysts were surprised at how positive participants were about the returns they expected from projects. Most industrial participants reported that new products or processes would be commercially applicable within 3 to 5 years. There was also broad agreement among firms that the Community RTD programmes had made an important contribution to their structural competitiveness, largely through improved scientific knowledge, research skills and strengthened innovative capacity (Commission 1994a: 257–8).

On the negative side, participants complained that the administrative burden of preparing and submitting a proposal was too great, especially given the relatively low (one in five) chance of success; non-participants made the same complaint, more strongly. Complaints about over-bureaucratic procedures, especially slow decision-taking procedures and delays in receiving payments from the Commission, were reported frequently in all member states. Part of the problem, foreseen in the late 1980s by the chair of the EP's Energy, Research and Technology Committee, Antonio La Pergola, was that programmes such as ESPRIT became popular to the point where new mechanisms had to be built in to filter out an increasingly larger share of an expanding pool of applicants (see Watts 1989). One effect was to make EU programmes progressively more unwieldy and unworkable. The American journal, *Science* (November 1991), went as far as to claim that 'the [EU's] programmes are not well run, and their value is debatable'. One Commission response was a simplified, two-stage application procedure that was introduced to the CRAFT programme, an industrial and materials programme designed specifically to assist SMEs under Framework III (see Exhibit 7.4), and then extended to other EU programmes. Still, much discontent remained about the over-bureaucratic methods of the Commission.

EUREKA was designed to be an antidote to the bureaucratisation of collaborative R&D. Small national administrations working on their own initiative, as well as declining national public budgets for research, help explain why relatively few evaluations of EURE-KA have been conducted at the national level. Most have tended to produce the same, rather predictable conclusion: that member states get out of EUREKA what they put in. For example, a 1989 French survey concluded that the initiative was a '*succès indéniable*' for France, where relatively large amounts of public funding were earmarked for it (IDS Consultants 1989). A later French survey found that EUREKA had promoted the creation of collaborative networks in areas *not* covered by the Framework programme, and had encouraged French firms to become far more globalised (see Larédo and Breitenstein 1993).

In contrast, several early surveys of British EUREKA participants revealed that relatively few were keen to participate in the initiative again (Hinder 1987; IFT Marketing Research 1989; SEPSU 1989). The low levels of public funding available in the UK for the scheme, combined with onerous reporting requirements, meant that 'a lot of time delays and bureaucracy [were] encountered' (IFT Marketing Research 1989: 32). British research organisations generally viewed the EU's programmes more favourably than EUREKA, and placed a high value on their experience of collaboration, but a relatively low value on EUREKA *per se*.

To summarise, national impact studies generally have positively endorsed the Framework programme, while criticising its tendency to bureaucracy. National evaluations of EUREKA have produced results that mirror quite directly the extent to which member state technology policies have made EUREKA a national priority. Nearly all studies have highlighted the value placed by participants on developing the European science and technology base. EUREKA or Community funding was welcomed as making a worthwhile contribution, with the high quality of the research funded by the Framework programme (and to a lesser extent, EUREKA) generally acknowledged. As might be expected, participants ranked access to funding as a major benefit, but opportunities for networking often seemed to be valued even more highly. Finding partners from other European countries, being exposed to new market opportunities, and having opportunities for the cross-fertilisation of ideas were what really counted.

Industry-based evaluations

The national impact studies offer an across-the-board look at the overall impact of collaborative initiatives in one country. They tell us little about how far the programmes have helped promote industrial competitiveness across European industries. Of course, the criterion of enhanced competitiveness is problematic. The Framework programme is deliberately restricted to pre-competitive R&D. In other words, it funds R&D aimed at improving general techniques rather than work associated with getting specific products to the market. Strictly speaking, this restriction means that EU-funded projects should not be judged in terms of new products and processes launched onto the market. Even though EUREKA projects often perform 'near market' R&D, they too have to respect EU competition rules. In any event, EUREKA has always included quite a lot of projects that are clearly not 'near market' projects. Moreover, the effects of collaborative R&D programmes on competitiveness are difficult to isolate from other factors. They are only likely to be clearly discernible after programmes have been in existence for several years.

The paradox of EU programmes that operate under pre-competitive restrictions, but are judged according to their contribution to competitiveness, was confronted in an influential 1991 study (Metcalf *et al.* 1991). Its authors pointed out that technology was a key factor in the competitive process because technological change, and the ability to sustain its momentum, had been shown, time and again, to be crucial in creating and maintaining competitive advantage. Evaluation studies needed therefore to concentrate on how far EU programmes had succeeded in stimulating firms to undertake and maintain innovative activities.

The study emboldened critics of the EU's pre-competitive restrictions, such as Jacques Stern, the former chairman of Groupe Bull:

ESPRIT is not at fault, neither are the people managing the programmes, who are doing a good job in Brussels. But governments can question spending large amounts of money from one pre-competitive program to another if there is no industrial application. The final goal of ESPRIT must be to bring . . . innovative and competitive products to the markets that serve real needs. (*Financial Times*, 17 March 1992)

Stern and representatives of many other European MNCs urged a merger of ESPRIT with EUREKA, or at least stronger links between them. One possible model was the JESSI project on semiconductors, which attracted substantial public funding from both the EU and national governments. A panel of independent experts described the project's results as 'positive and impressive' (EUREKA Secretariat 1995a: 1). It also found discontent about the project's slow decision-making procedures, its lack of accessibility by SMEs, and its general unwieldiness. Still, no less than a quarter of participants reported that their competitive situation had improved as a consequence of JESSI.

In a somewhat back-handed way, the JESSI model – particularly its focus on generating tangible results – found an unlikely supporter in the EU's Court of Auditors, which is responsible for vetting all EU expenditure. Beginning in the early 1990s, the Court issued a series of stinging critiques of the EU's research programmes. Despite billions of ECU in expenditure, it claimed, only a small fraction of EU-funded research had produced concrete results: research activities funded by the Commission between 1986 and 1990 had created only about 50 tangible inventions and 280 jobs (Court of Auditors 1991). It wanted more funds to be put into the practical application of research. A later report (Court of Auditors 1994) specifically on ESPRIT criticised the slowness of its procedures and the minimal exploitation of findings. The Court asserted that, as projects neared completion, partners became less and less motivated to exploit their results, and each partner often executed the final stages individually.

The Court's pronouncements on research were attacked by the Commission as speculative and amateurish. Yet, the Court's lack of expertise in research and technology assessment appeared not to deter it from passing fiercely critical judgements on the Framework programme. They reflected the new self-assertiveness of the Court, which became a far more politicised body after the

Maastricht Treaty made it an official EU institution (see Peterson 1997b).

The Court of Auditors' judgements also mirrored the widespread assumption that the EU's programmes should aim to produce commercial results and enhance European competitiveness quickly and tangibly. This contrasted with the Metcalf *et al.* study, which emphasised the contribution of knowledge, skills and learning (the software) as well as new artefacts (the hardware) to the process of technological change. They pointed out that many of the benefits derived from collaborative programmes were often naturally 'software'-oriented and, by their nature, more difficult to measure.

An evaluation of one of the EU's biotechnology programmes, the Biotechnology Action Programme (BAP) illustrated these points well. BAP was mostly geared to scientific research and the majority of its participants were academic or non-profit research teams. Measuring 'output' in such circumstances was difficult. By definition, pre-competitive research is not immediately commercialisable and does not lead to patents. However, the evaluators found that BAP-supported research papers had a 25 per cent higher citation rate than those for a control group, and that 20 per cent of the researchers who had worked in BAP consortia were employed in industry five years later. This indicated that BAP had engendered a sizeable technology transfer between academia and industry (Magnien and de Nettancourt 1993; GTS 1993).

A completely different approach was adopted in an evaluation of BRITE-EURAM, which has always had more industrial and SME participants than most other EU programmes (Ledoux *et al.* 1993). This study assessed both *direct* effects – new products, new knowledge or lower costs – as well as *indirect* effects – or longer-term gains in terms of technology, organisation or commercial advantage and attempted to put numbers on them. The results are summarised in Table 9.3. It shows that, on average, the benefits secured from an EU grant were of the order of 13:1 for the direct effects and 4:1 for the indirect effects. Putting the two (direct and indirect) together, the study concluded that for every ECU invested in the scheme, there was a payback worth 7 ECU within five years (Ledoux *et al.* 1993: 20–25).

Specific details of the study are particularly interesting. They showed, for example, that consortia that included an academic research institution were more successful than those without acade-

TABLE 9.3

Benefits from participation in BRITE-EURAM: direct and indirect payoffs

Parameters

Number of projects	50
Number of participants	176
Number of measured economic effects	611
EC funding – MECU[a] received, 1987–91	39.4

		Direct Effects	Indirect Effects
Benefits Estimated MECU[a]	Before January 1994	413.3	132.2
	Before January 1996	522.5	160.8
Ratios[b] Benefits: Original EC Funding	Before January 1994	10.5:1	3.4:1
	Before January 1996	13.3:1	4.1:1

[a] MECU adjusted in all instances to 1991 price levels.
[b] It is important to recognise that these figures are *not* rates of return, but an attempt to put a value on the benefits gained by the firm measured against funds received by the EU. The firm itself will have put at least an equivalent sum, and often far more towards the project. The project need not make a profit to register a positive return. In some cases, firms making losses reported a positive return. For details of methodology see Ledoux *et al.* (1993).

Source: Ledoux *et al.* (1993: 20).

mic partners (Ledoux *et al.* 1993: 39). It also appeared that SMEs gained less from participation than large firms, and that indirect benefits were greater than direct benefits for many SMEs (Ledoux *et al.*: 28). Considerable variation also existed between sectors. For example, SMEs gained substantial benefits from participation in the initial BRITE textiles programme, which had been geared to encouraging traditional firms in the textile sector, many in less-favoured regions, to switch to modern design and manufacturing processes (Ledoux *et al.* 1993: 48–9).

Taking the broad run of industry-based evaluations, three main findings feature prominently (see Commission 1994: 257–62):

(1) *Different types of research organisation react differently to Framework programme opportunities.* Firms in traditional industries use EU pro-

grammes as a means of trying out new technologies. The effect is to encourage more internal R&D within these companies, and EU funding is a critical factor for such firms. In contrast, many larger high-technology firms factor the EU's programmes into their business plans and are often willing to alter the direction of their development work in response to funding opportunities. Corporate laboratories in large firms typically seek EU funding when internal funds are blocked. Public research institutions most often cooperate with each other, but high rates of project success (broadly defined) seem to result most often when they collaborate with private firms.

(2) *'Learning benefits' are considerable for both individual researchers and firms.* Individuals gain from knowledge acquisition and technical know-how derived from work on research contracts. Firms gain in areas such as the handling of regulations and standards. For many the gain is simply in learning how to collaborate. Building up trust with partners and learning about how to organise large consortia are important benefits.

(3) *There is no straightforward relationship between collaborative research programmes and competitiveness.* Any attempt to measure the impact of the EU's programmes in this way inevitably leads to distortions. The same applies to EUREKA, even if distortions would tend to be less severe because it encompasses more near-market research. Collaborative R&D programmes are not an end in themselves, but a catalyst to other activities. As such, they should be viewed as an investment in the health of the economy.

Evaluating EUREKA

In the history of RTD collaboration, EUREKA is one of the programmes most often evaluated. Two particularly broad-ranging evaluations were conducted in the early 1990s: one by the Dutch EUREKA chairmanship (1991) and one independently of any EUREKA government or institution (Peterson 1993b: 128–60). Both confirmed that EUREKA had built upon established patterns of collaboration more than it had prompted the creation of new ones. However, participants generally expressed a high level of satisfaction with EUREKA, and many were keen to participate again. About 40 per cent of all EUREKA projects appeared to be truly additional, or unlikely to have been launched without EUREKA.

Both surveys found that partners were motivated to participate in EUREKA more to secure the cross-fertilisation of ideas than public funding *per se*.

Both evaluations found a large firm–SME dichotomy. SMEs were far more likely to be engaged in genuinely 'near-market' projects, but also were far less satisfied with the initiative or the assistance they had received from public bodies. The Dutch chairmanship's survey did not break down their large survey sample by nationality of participant (apparently for political reasons). However, the independent survey found that 'national rates of satisfaction' with EUREKA varied considerably, and correlated closely with how much public funding and general support for the initiative was available in particular member states.

The early 1990s saw Western Europe revert to a familiar pattern of responding to economic recession by slashing public R&D budgets. Falling public funding for EUREKA was an important factor compelling the French chairmanship of 1993 to launch an evaluation of the initiative's 'industrial and economic effects'. It shed particular light on two features of EUREKA. First, more than 30 per cent of all projects were *not* 'clearly product-oriented'. Many of these projects appeared to bring together large firms who were direct competitors in projects that were clearly pre-competitive – a pattern no longer prevalent within the EU's programmes. Second, while confirming that most EUREKA consortia were based on pre-existing groupings, the French survey found that a majority of projects were structured on vertical market relationships and featured collaboration between, say, knowledge suppliers, component manufacturers, system assemblers and users. This pattern of vertical networks characterised many European research consortia, including those funded by the EU (see Von Hippel 1988; Larédo 1996).

Most respondents to the French survey considered EUREKA to be less bureaucratic than the Framework programme, but also complained about the lack of synchronisation between national funding policies, delays in receiving funds and a general lack of transparency. Unusually, the 1993 evaluation *did* break the data down by nationality of participant (apparently at French insistence). It thus highlighted the different 'additionality effects' of very divergent national funding policies (see Table 9.4).

Two years later, under the results-oriented chairmanship of Switzerland (which traditionally has offered *no* public funding to

Swiss industrial participants), an independent study was launched to evaluate EUREKA's actual results after 10 years of its operation (EUREKA Secretariat 1995b). Respondents aired familiar complaints about the need for synchronisation of EUREKA funding policies and inadequate quality control. Its authors flagged the very sharp decline in average project size, and bemoaned the fact that 'large strategic projects have practically disappeared' (EUREKA Secretariat 1995b: 8).

Yet, the study's broad conclusion was that half of all completed EUREKA projects could be considered successful, while only 20 per cent were outright failures (EUREKA Secretariat 1995b: 35). A majority of firms reported commercial developments of products and/or processes. An even larger share (about two-thirds) of participants of all types reported some type of 'positive results' from participation in EUREKA, thus providing evidence of learning benefits, sometimes even when projects themselves failed. Still, the obsession of governments with competitiveness and concrete results

TABLE 9.4

**Effects of public funding by country in EUREKA
(% of industrial responses)**

Country	Did not have public funding	Would not have done project without public funding	Would have done project anyway	Would have done project differently
Austria	16	20	0	64
Belgium	12	45	4	37
Denmark	5	26	21	47
Finland	13	35	17	35
France	7	56	19	18
Germany	21	43	1	35
Italy	14	27	28	31
Norway	25	53	8	14
Netherlands	14	23	26	37
Spain	25	13	22	40
Sweden	43	16	19	16
United Kingdom	16	47	20	17

Source: EUREKA Secretariat (1993: 66).

was reflected in the report's very broad (and wildly speculative) estimate that EUREKA would produce 'an overall turnover in the
region of billions of ECU within the next 2–3 years' (EUREKA
Secretariat 1995b: 7).

As if all of this evaluation were not enough, the 1996 Belgian
chairmanship of EUREKA secured agreement on new moves
towards 'Continuous and Systematic Evaluation of EUREKA', with
annual impact reports on the results of finished projects. Results
published in 1997 highlighted two points. First, about 40 per cent of
finished EUREKA projects had already achieved some type of commercial impact before completion. Second, the 1997 study was the
first to try to measure the job creation effects of EUREKA. Its
authors concluded that 'the principal effect of EUREKA on
employment appears to have been to safeguard jobs'. Still, they
insisted, the ability of EUREKA or any other collaborative initiative
to generate employment was not great, and 'the numbers [are] not
on average large' (British EUREKA chairmanship 1997: 2).

Towards the Davignon assessments

The fetish of governments to know precisely what they were getting
for their investment in collaborative programmes – clearly reflected
in EUREKA – also was highlighted in the Maastricht Treaty, which
mandated regular monitoring and assessment of both the
Framework programme generally and specific EU programmes.
Monitoring in this context was seen as a management process to be
undertaken by the Commission. Assessment meant a retrospective
review of a programme to evaluate its goals, achievements and
problems.

Every five years an independent panel of experts was to be set up
to assess the management and activities of Community RTD programmes. These five-year assessments of the Framework programme were intended to feed into discussion of the next version of
the programme. In February 1997, the first such assessment under
these procedures – led by the venerable Etienne Davignon – was
presented to the Commission (1997c). Less than a year earlier,
Davignon had chaired a similar panel convened by the Belgian
chairmanship of EUREKA to assess *The Role and Medium Term Future
of Eureka* (Davignon Group 1996). Together, the two Davignon

assessments provided a relatively comprehensive snapshot of the state of European collaborative programmes at the end of the 1990s, as well as a rather muscular set of recommendations for making them more effective in the twenty-first century.

The Davignon assessment of the Framework IV programme was intended both to contribute to the debate about its successor, Framework V, and to judge the existing programme under three headings – relevance, efficiency and effectiveness. The report's main criticism was that the Framework programme was not focused or strategic enough, mostly because decision-making still required unanimity every five years on the Council. The upshot was 'too many multinational shopping lists' (Commission 1997c: 17). Qualified majority voting (QMV), as was applied subsequently to the Framework programme by the Amsterdam Treaty, would allow a greater strategic focus.

The Davignon panel also urged that more resources be targeted on areas where there could be genuine European added value, such as where science needed a 'critical mass' of research, or where work could contribute to establishing EU-wide norms and standards. In terms of efficiency, the panel condemned the Commission for over-bureaucracy and delays, calling for quicker decisions, more feedback and more staff to cope with the workload. Finally, in terms of effectiveness, the panel called for a switch of emphasis away from shared cost projects towards more diffusion-oriented projects. In particular, the Davignon panel wanted project managers to be given direct responsibility for ensuring dissemination and more SMEs to be incorporated into projects. The panel's overall conclusion was that '[t]he Fifth Framework programme needs to make a qualitative leap forward; it should not be a straight forward prolongation of the Fourth Framework programme' (Commission 1997c: 9).

The 1996 Davignon report on EUREKA contained many of the same recommendations, even offering the broad assertion: 'It is quite clear that the European response [to declining competitiveness], whether by the European Union programmes or EUREKA, has not reached the level required by the global challenge' (Davignon Group 1996: 1). The report bemoaned EUREKA's general lack of large, strategic projects and condemned cuts in national funding for the initiative as well as the stubborn refusal of governments to synchronise public funding commitments. New and stronger links between the Framework programme and EUREKA were viewed as an urgent necessity, while a clearer division of labour between them was recommended. Perhaps most controversially, the Davignon Group (1996: 1) urged EUREKA's member states to give the initiative more focus: 'Europe needs to identify additional strengths and build on them, rather than to concentrate primarily on trying to correct weaknesses.'

The Davignon Group's bold and strongly opinionated evaluation of EUREKA highlighted for many outside observers fundamental flaws in the dominant approach to the evaluation of European collaborative initiatives. High-level panels such as the Davignon Groups were usually made up of 'the great and the good': individuals who either helped set up the programmes in the past or whose firms benefited from them now. Critics asked: how could such panels be objective? A separate but related criticism was that too much monitoring and evaluation was done internally in the Commission, instead of by outside agencies. Experts employed on such evaluations were paid by the Commission (and often employed on other contracts), and thus likely to be relatively friendly to its agenda.

In defence of the Commission, it could be argued that it simply lacked the resources – as well as the objectivity – to evaluate EU research programmes. One independent study (although published by the Commission – 1990a: 3) found that 'the Commission's practice of performing evaluations was highly regarded'. In any case, limited political will existed among member states to ensure that EU funds were well spent: it remained a much higher priority on the Council generally to ensure that *juste retour* was achieved.

Meanwhile, in the context of a pervasive, new, 'value-for-money' culture that infused the post-1995 Santer Commission, the Framework programmes came under increasingly closer scrutiny by the Court of Auditors (1995). While estimating that about 7 per cent of the EU's total annual budget (or 5.3 BECU – more than proposed for Framework V) had been misspent through fraud or improper accounting, the Court gave no estimate for how much was wasted out of the Framework programme's budget, ostensibly a good sign. However, the Court lambasted the Commission for failing to spend a single ECU out of a 50 000 ECU fund within Framework III earmarked specifically for 'measures against fraud'. The Human Capital and Mobility programme, in particular, was singled out as highly bureaucratic and open to nepotism: the Court found a very high success rate among applicants from institutions with scientists on the programme's selection panels. Some member states, particularly Germany and the UK, applauded the Court of Auditor's diligence, while downplaying the Court's conclusion that the Commission needed more resources to monitor the research spending properly. The point is that even the apparently technical task of evaluating the EU's research programmes, a difficult and complicated business in the best of circumstances, became caught up in inter-institutional and intergovernmental political games in the late 1990s.

Europe's technological performance

A final, if indirect, way of getting a grip on the effectiveness of European collaborative research programmes is to shift attention away from the programmes themselves and look to macro-economic indicators of performance, especially those relating to high-technology industries. Table 1.5 in the first chapter presents a broad overview of the EU's position *vis-à-vis* its main competitors. On all counts, it presents a depressing picture. R&D expenditures as a percentage of GDP is not only lower than for either the US or Japan, but has fallen during the 1990s. Expenditures per inhabitant are less than half the levels in Japan. Business-funded R&D as a percentage of total R&D, a good indicator of the commitment of industry to innovation, is again lower than the levels achieved in the US and Japan.

When we look at industry performance, trade and patenting performance provide a good indication of competitiveness and innovation. The Commission, following the OECD, ranks industries by their R&D intensity (R&D to sales ratios). The high-technology sectors are aerospace, chemicals, pharmaceuticals, electrical equipment, electronics, data processing, office equipment, motor vehicles and scientific instruments. As Table 1.4 shows, Europe leads only in pharmaceuticals and chemicals, with a significant second place in aerospace. In areas such as computers, electronics and scientific instruments, the EU lags behind both the US and Japan.

Table 9.5 uses this categorisation to look at trends specialisation and it shows that, if anything, the EU has tended to become more specialised (as compared with Japan and the US) in low-tech sectors. A plausible, if rather depressing, conclusion is that the competitiveness of European industry has, if anything, deteriorated during the

TABLE 9.5

Specialisation[a] **in high-, medium- and low-tech industries**
(OECD = 100)

	Japan		US		EU	
	1970	**1992**	**1970**	**1992**	**1970**	**1992**
High-tech	124	144	159	151	86	82
Medium-tech	78	114	110	90	103	100
Low-tech	113	46	67	74	103	113

[a]   The index is based on the share of a country's (region's) total exports of manufactured products in that category, divided by ratio for all OECD countries. An index of over 100 indicates a greater degree of specialisation than the OECD average; one of less than 100 indicates less than average.

Source: OECD STAN Database (cited in Commission 1995a).

life spans of the Framework programme and EUREKA. Notably, the EU lags badly in most sectors associated with electronics (but not telecommunications), in spite of the considerable focus on these sectors in ESPRIT and EUREKA.

A similar picture emerges when patent statistics (regarded as a good indicator of innovation) are compared: the EU emerges consistently at the bottom of the league tables. Only in terms of scientific publications does it hold its own, which is why the Commission (1995a) Green Paper on Innovation makes much of the excellence of the EU's science base, but also the deterioration of its technological performance. The problem lies, according to the Green Paper, in the processes that help to translate science into technology.

All these statistics have to be treated with caution. As Keith Pavitt (1997:18–9) has pointed out, in retrospect, fears about Europe's technology gap in the 1960s were misplaced – sales, productivity and R&D expenditures in European firms were all growing faster at that time than in US firms. By the 1980s Germany, Sweden and Switzerland had caught up and indeed overtaken the US in terms of aggregate business funding of R&D. All had increased their world export shares in automobiles, machinery and chemicals, largely at the expense of the US.

In the late 1990s with countries such as Portugal and Greece being joined by Sweden and Finland, and the eastern *Länder* united with West Germany, the Union was a very different grouping from the Community of the early 1980s. Statements about aggregate trends could be very misleading. Trying to compare the EU, with 370 million citizens and 15 separate national governments, with the single-nation figures for Japan or the US was not comparing like with like. By many measures of R&D performance, Germany (population 80 million) did just as well as Japan (population 124 million). Pavitt (1997:13) summed up as follows:

> Given the comparative resurgence of US technological performance since the late 1980s, it is fashionable today to criticise more broadly European institutions, practices and cultures – in management, education and corporate governance – as inferior to their US counterparts. This is debatable. In some areas (e.g. workforce education), Europe is probably not behind. And for every explanation of US success in terms of flexibility, private initiative and entrepreneurship, there is a plausible explanation in terms of macro-economic policy or massive government funding. The subject therefore deserves further study, but not hasty action.

Conclusion: multiple objectives = mixed results

We began this chapter with the question, what has been achieved? and suggested that success needed to be judged against objectives. A rather complex set of objectives was set for the Framework programme and EUREKA. Competitiveness was a prime objective, but it had to be set beside the strengthening of the science and technology base, the stimulation of collaboration, the training of young scientists and engineers, and the promotion of economic and social cohesion.

Of these five objectives, the evidence presented in this chapter leaves no doubt about the achievement of these programmes in *stimulating collaboration*. The conclusions of numerous evaluations make it clear that not only have the programmes yielded a complex web of links between firms and researchers that stretch across the Union, but that this effect is very highly valued by participants. Many European firms have become members of complex *global* alliances, or 'techno-economic networks', which have become such important sources of innovation in the late twentieth century (see Larédo and Mustar 1996). A crucial question is whether, given the importance of these worldwide networks, there is any point in seeking to promote specifically *European* collaborations. Does this emphasis now divert from more outward-looking alliances?

In stimulating collaboration, the programmes have helped further two other objectives – *strengthening the science base* and *promoting the education and training of young scientists and engineers*. There is no shortage of data to suggest that European science still outperforms its competitors in most areas in terms of scientific publications and citations (see Commission 1994: 29–40). Collaboration that brings together centres of excellence across Europe serves two purposes. It promotes the cross-fertilisation of ideas and the transfer of knowledge and skills between research institutes and, of prime importance for innovation, between the academic and industrial research sectors. Programmes that promote the exchange of postgraduate students and young researchers under the HCM and TMR schemes have created new routes for technology transfer. Together, the exchanges stimulated by the EU's shared cost programmes and EUREKA have been an area of considerable success, despite evidence of rather loose controls over spending, and some nepotism.

Likewise, as Chapter 7 stressed, the Framework programmes (and for that matter EUREKA) clearly provide valued opportunities for scientists and engineers from the less-favoured regions to participate in consortia that bring them into contact with leading-edge technologies and institutions, thus promoting *cohesion*. At the same time, there are some worrying signs of a North–South divide, with the South as junior partners. The programmes do provide opportunities for what Lundvall (1992: 316) has called 'avenues to institutional learning and institutional innovation', but doubts remain as to how far these opportunities are fully exploited.

We are left therefore with the problem of *competitiveness*. It is easy to conclude that the achievements of collaboration have here been modest. European programmes may have helped to bring firms and research groups together across Europe, and thus reinforced the science base and promoted cohesion. Still, the EU's actual performance in high-technology sectors has deteriorated.

Broad statements of this kind about the EU's competitiveness tell us very little unless particular sectors or member states – whose national economies remain quite different – are specified. For example, many German firms have imported large quantities of leading-edge technologies in electronics and have thus provoked a deterioration in Germany's high-tech trade surplus, but they have applied them with good competitive effect in middle-tech industries, such as machine tools. Meanwhile, the UK's mechanical engineering sector – a large middle-tech industry – suffers from low quality standards, spends less on R&D than its competitors elsewhere, and tends to 'neglect innovation' (IFO Institute 1997). Yet because it imports so little technology, its trade balance looks healthier.

In evaluating their impact, we must concede that collaborative R&D programmes remain relatively small, if still important, policy instruments. They have become 'an integral part of the national research system' in virtually all European states, 'since they mobilize almost all major R&D players' (Larédo 1996: 2). However, their impact clearly is limited and should not be overstated. For example, in the early 1990s, Siemens employed nearly 20 000 researchers, of whom perhaps 75 were paid through funds obtained from ESPRIT (Gaster 1991: 254).

Another caveat is that European collaboration may make sense in many sectors, but may still be very difficult to pull off, even with subsidies, where national industries remain strictly 'un-Europeanised'. A good example is software technologies, where the EU has considerable excellence but for which the Commission admits high-quality proposals are hard to attract. UK companies, many of which are world-class, rarely submit proposals for EU-funded projects which account for a relatively small percentage of the total research effort of large companies in the sector (DTI 1997: 4).

In other sectors, collaboration is both routine and essential, and European programmes have facilitated it. However, that does not necessarily mean that European collaborative programmes remain the right public policy. For example, Hobday (1995) concludes that ESPRIT has made a significant contribution to improving the 'technical competence of European semiconductor producers'. However, he casts profound doubt on the wisdom of subsidies for closer-to-the-market collaboration, as has been advocated for years by many in the European chip industry. Even starker is Hobday's (1995: 14) insistence that 'European-owned firms are now sufficiently large and competent to make their own decisions without subsidy or direction.' If the prescription to ban all subsidies to European chip producers seems a radical one, it might be noted that Sematech – the US government-backed semiconductor industry research consortium – decided to stop accepting direct US government funding after 1996. In the somewhat high-flown words of Craig Barrett, CEO of Intel (the world's largest chipmaker) and a director of Sematech, 'It is a matter of principle. The industry can now afford to support the consortium and we should. We are setting an example for other US industries and for the world' (*Financial Times*, 10 June 1994). The broader point, perhaps, is that the mere act of convincing European firms to form consortia, as their US counterparts have done, has been a worthwhile policy goal, but it may no longer need to be subsidised with public money.

In short, European collaborative programmes may not have achieved 'competitiveness', but may have actually achieved quite a lot of other equally important objectives. Broadly speaking, around half of all firms who participate in collaborative research state that the 'acquisition of new competencies' is the most important legacy of participation in projects (Larédo 1996: 7). It could be argued that collaborative research programmes are best judged by their success in sharpening the EU's research skills, and not its competitiveness (see Strange 1998).

Ultimately, the most important evaluators are Europe's industrial and research communities. They have certainly endorsed collaboration and the major programmes that promote it. EUREKA participants are not without complaints, but most seem broadly pleased with the initiative, are keen to participate in it again, and EUREKA's project list remains large. Despite all of their failings, most EU programmes have a ratio of approved to rejected proposals of between 1:5 and 1:7. By the end of 1995, more than 10 000 individual projects were under way within the Framework programme, with an average Community budgetary contribution of 1 million ECU per project. An average of four member states and 6.5 participants were involved in each (Commission 1996e: 6). It behoves the policy analyst to be sceptical of claims about EUREKA and the Framework programme's success. Still, there is good evidence to suggest that collaborative research funds 'are not merely industrial subsidies, but rather premiums towards RTD excellence' (Elizalde 1992: 333).

10

Conclusion

As we have seen, there is no straightforward answer to the question: how much have European technology policies actually achieved? Nor could we or anyone else offer a set of incontestable policy prescriptions. However, in this chapter we present both an assessment of past achievements and suggestions for the future.

We begin by examining the question of how European technology policy can promote economic growth, given recent and radical changes in the political economy of RTD. We then confront a central dilemma: can a 'European Technological Community' cohere or survive in a climate of new doubts about European political unity? Next, we consider the related question of whether European solidarity is practical, let alone sensible, in an increasingly globalised economy. Finally, we conclude with a critique of European technology policy in the late 1990s and some prescriptions for its future.

Technology policy – an engine for growth?

The main motivation for the introduction of ESPRIT and the other schemes that became the Framework programme was competitiveness. European companies, it was argued, were losing market share to their American and Japanese counterparts because they were falling behind in both the production and use of new technologies. Even worse, the very act of falling behind had increasingly dire consequences because learning curve advantages were so great. Companies that had gone down learning curves associated with microchip production, video recorders and parallel processing computers had almost unassailable advantages over those that hung back. ESPRIT and EUREKA offered subsidies to help take European companies down future learning curves associated with these and other strategic technologies.

As we have seen, Davignon's motives were complex when he set up ESPRIT and then the Framework programme in the early 1980s. He was confronted with a European industrial landscape in which most high-tech capabilities were tied up in large firms that were not globally competitive. Most were cocooned as national champions within their own national markets, fed on a diet of cost-plus defence and government contracts, sustained by incestuous relationships with the major publicly owned utilities, and protected from competition by a variety of trade barriers. Davignon knew that the roots of Europe's declining competitiveness lay as much in the lazy ways of national champions as in the disadvantages they faced from being slower to develop their interests in new technologies. His strategy was to encourage European firms, via subsidised collaboration, to recognise the benefits that the single market could offer. At the same time, he would force them, via the liberalising and deregulating measures of the 1992 project, to become more competitive initially in Europe, and then globally.

Fifteen years on, the landscape seemed to have changed beyond all recognition. By a process of restructuring involving mergers, acquisitions and demergers, the national champions of the early 1980s either had become global players in markets characterised by global oligopoly (that is, dominated by relatively few large MNCs), or had been swallowed up by competitors. The Davignon agenda – with its twin tracks of increased collaboration and stiffer competition – contributed to this process. However, other, stronger forces drove the trend toward global oligopoly. Primary among them was technological change itself, which opened up competition in telecommunications, linked capital markets worldwide and provided the tools for hands-on management of distance operations. The end of the Cold War and the declining importance of the defence sector, along with privatisation and deregulation (especially of capital markets), added momentum, but also an extra element of uncertainty and turbulence to markets. The outcome was a concentration of power among (mainly) older players. Europe saw the demise of firms such as Plessey, Grundig and France's CGCT (Compagnie Générale des Communications Téléphoniques), concentration around firms such as ABB, Philips, Siemens and Thomson, as well as the emergence of new players including Nokia and Alcatel. Globally, firms such as Microsoft, Sun, Samsung and Lucky Goldstar became major competitors alongside older giants including IBM, Ford, Hitachi or Mitsubishi.

In increasingly globalised markets, competitiveness acquires new meaning. For all his eccentricities, it is impossible to deny the force of Krugman's argument that competition between firms is what really matters. Competition between states is clearly no longer a zero sum game: 'If the European economy does well, it need not be at US expense; indeed, if anything a successful European economy is likely to help the US economy by providing it with larger markets' (Krugman 1994: 34; see also Strange 1998).

Equally, a successful European economy requires competitive European firms. As the Commission's (1993: 57) White Paper on 'Growth, Competitiveness and Employment' argues:

> The globalisation of economies and markets [means] . . . we must think increasingly in terms of competitive rather than compara-tive advantages. Comparative advantages traditionally relate to endowment in factors such as national resources and are therefore fairly rigid. *Competitive advantages are based more on qualitative factors and can thus be influenced to a large degree by corporate strategies and by public policies.* (Emphasis added)

This logic underpins the policy shift away from the *grands projets* of ESPRIT to new concerns with intellectual property rights, deregula-tion, venture capital and small business. If competitive advantage is the policy goal, then new questions arise: does it make sense to use resources to establish a strong capacity in chip manufacture, given the high barriers to entry and lack of pervasiveness of chip-making technology, rather than in the highly pervasive *chip-using* technology? (see Pavitt 1997). The logical route to competitive advantage is not subsidising the production of high-technology goods but rather ensuring the use of such goods and their associated process tech-nologies. What matters are high-productivity jobs and the associated (high) value that diffusion of new technologies adds to gross domes-tic products.

In the competitive advantage stakes of the 1990s, two key issues have emerged. One is attracting investment from multinationals who remain the major players and drivers of an increasingly globalised system. The second is the ability to supply and service these firms, many of whom have downsized or de-layered, thus shifting jobs from within their company structures to associated networks of outside companies.

The degree to which MNCs have shifted to outsourcing has tended to be exaggerated. For example, most motor car manufacturers retain control over their major assembly operations. As such, when these firms make choices about where to invest and produce, states and regions compete fiercely to influence these choices. Firms such as Toyota, with its huge assembly works at Derby in the UK, assemble vehicles for the European market with parts manufactured throughout Europe, as well as in Japan and South-East Asia. Yet, with increasing use of 'just-in-time' systems, relationships between local suppliers and assemblers have become closer: parts have to be delivered on time and to specification, with zero tolerance for faults or defects. Tight networks or clusters of firms thus have emerged around large assembly plants. It is within these networks, as much as large MNCs themselves, that good jobs and wealth are created. They help shield small firms from the turbulence of the market and stimulate the use of new technologies. Firms that service or supply major multinationals often must be able to use and master modern computer-controlled production techniques that can deliver to the (high) standards required. Thus, large MNCs invest – and so induce the creation of high-value-added jobs – in regions that can offer the necessary high levels of skills.

In other words, technology policy becomes an engine for growth if it encourages the use and diffusion of modern production methods, nurtures skills that attract investments by MNCs, and maximises the value of jobs they create. In contrast with the recent past, technology policy promotes economic growth above all when it stimulates firms, large and small, to go down learning curves associated with *using* (as opposed to *producing*) new technologies. In the context of this overarching objective, specific policy goals become those that encourage firms to develop demonstration models or to apply new process technologies. A simple, if useful, policy goal is to encourage the formation of consortia in which some firms act as role models, showing others how to use new technologies.

In the late 1990s, an equally important policy goal has become training scientists and engineers to develop the skills and capabilities to use new technologies. Companies must undertake R&D to have the knowledge in-house that is needed to understand and use state-of-the-art technologies. In this context, many American firms benefit from high levels of government support for basic research. Researchers trained to high (doctoral) levels of competence in leading-edge technologies are an essential element in the thriving American sector of high-technology small firms in electronics and biotechnology.

To summarise, technology policy came to the fore in the early 1980s, ostensibly to help Europe's large electronics companies hold their own as producers in the face of stiff American and Japanese competition. By the late 1990s, many European companies still lacked a competitive edge, and worries grew about unemployment, but the focus of policy changed. Most large companies fought for shares of intensely competitive global markets in which uncertainty and innovation had become a way of life. While retaining a home base, they operated around the world. Crucially, from a policy point of view, these multinationals collaborated at the regional and local level with a large number of firms, big and small, as well as at the global level with other MNCs. There seemed little logic any longer in technology policies that 'paid' these MNCs to collaborate (least of all with other EU firms) or to undertake R&D activities. To maximise job creation and growth, it seemed far more sensible to encourage the diffusion of new technologies and to promote the health of smaller companies.

Technology policy: an engine for integration?

In important respects, the economic effects of technological collaboration are clearer than their political effects. By the late 1990s, it was relatively easy to show that EUREKA and the Framework programme had encouraged firms to think in European terms, to work with firms beyond their national borders as a matter of routine, and to seek new market opportunities beyond their traditional home markets. In some cases, it was possible to attribute tangible economic benefits to collaborative programmes, such as the (admittedly speculative) estimate that EUREKA would produce an increase in turnover of 2 to 3 billion ECU for its participants (EUREKA Secretariat: 1995b: 7).

The political effects of European technology policies were more ambiguous. As Williams (1989: 175–6) argues:

> European technological collaboration must be weighed above all in terms of what substantively it produces . . . But for the student of politics it also has another, and ultimately more fundamental, aspect. This is its contribution to integration. Judged in terms of this aspiration, even collaboration that is relatively unsuccessful in a formal sense may provide a positive thrust. For collaboration involves the creation of links between scientists, businessmen [sic] and officials in participating countries, with politicians too being called upon to pronounce a blessing in the major instances. And links once formed will have a tendency to survive the particular circumstances of their formation.

It is thus worth asking: to what extent have European collaborative programmes had the effect of cementing the EU together politically?

We have seen that the high politics of agreeing budgets for the Framework programme have been hard-fought and rancorous. Clearly, governments continue to respond to domestic economic interests when they engage in debates about which sectors should benefit from EU-funded research and how much money each should receive. In a world of increasingly globalised companies, it has become more difficult to define domestic economic interests clearly, as oligopolistic MNCs invest beyond their home borders, bringing jobs and growth to far-flung regions. Nevertheless, governments remain advocates of the interests of firms who employ their citizens and fill their public coffers with tax revenue, sometimes regardless of their national flag.

The high politics of European technology policy remain lively in large part because concerns about cohesion dominate the policy agenda in a way that was difficult to foresee in the early 1980s. At that time, before Spain and Portugal were EU members, and long before eastern enlargement was even remotely on the agenda, Community research programmes seemed a fairly straightforward pay-back to the rich, northern, net contributors to the Community's budget. By the late 1990s, the picture had changed. On one hand, globalisation and Europe's *collective* competitiveness problems made national interests in technology policy harder to identify. On the other, richer and poorer EU member states still perceived themselves as having very different interests and thus pursued very different priorities. These differences were reflected, for example, in league tables ranking European firms according to their abilities to use technology effectively. All of the top firms had headquarters in northern European countries; but none in less-favoured regions (see Table 10.1). This clash of interests between the relatively rich and poor was reflected, too, in Spain's refusal even to consider the Commission's proposal for Framework V until it received assurances about how much funding would be earmarked for cohesion (Commission 1997d).

The wider point is that EU technology policy has not managed to wriggle free from the exigencies of high politics. Despite the highly technical nature of technology policy-making, the European Council often has had to step in to take crucial decisions on the Framework programme, as intergovernmentalist theory would predict.

At the same time, the Framework programme has become an accepted part of the EU's policy *milieu*. The Commission has gone to great and often dubious lengths to justify increased funding for EU programmes, but it has also shown considerable leadership in making research one of the most developed of all EU policies. Once the big decisions on the Framework programme's overall budget are

TABLE 10.1

European firms: most effective use of technology (1996)

Based on the *Financial Times*–Price Waterhouse survey of 1451 European firms in 18 states.

Firm	Nationality	Sector(s)
1. Nokia	Finland	Electronics
2. Reuters	UK	Media, printing, advertising
3. Ericsson	Sweden	Electronics
4. ABB	Sweden/Switzerland	Engineering
5. BMW	Germany	Automobiles
6. Siemens	Germany	Electronics
7. Philips	Netherlands	Electronics
8. SAP	Germany	Computers, office equipment

Source: *Financial Times* (1996).

taken, the politics of the detailed technological content usually become far less intergovernmental.

Since the 1980s, when the EU emerged as a system of government in its own right (as opposed to just another international organisation), it has developed a systemic level of decision-making, where policy choices are taken after bargaining between member states and EU institutions. In RTD as elsewhere, important policy decisions are taken according to the so-called 'Community method' of decision-making: that is the Commission proposes, the Council disposes, and so on. At this level of analysis – one step removed from high politics – the new institutionalism helps us explain how programmes with track records and dedicated constituencies have tended to persist without much change. The systemic level of RTD policy-making features consensus building, package-dealing and 'path dependency': once a path is set, the EU's programmes tend to stay on it. However, when the EU does alter its path in RTD policy, it is usually to broaden the scope of its activities. The result is that already limited EU funding is diluted and spread over too wide an area to have much impact. It is difficult to dispute the Commission's (1991b: 21) own *cri du coeur* that 'compromises almost always operate in the same direction – that of the widening of the field of action'.

At the same time, the Commission *does* have considerable power over RTD policy once overarching political deals are struck and the range of the EU's activities are defined by intergovernmental bargains. The problem for the Commission is less one of defending its autonomy in RTD policy than of getting its own internal act together. By the late 1990s, research accounted for a serious chunk of the small amount of 'discretionary' funding available to the Commission (the CAP and structural funds being generally less discretionary), thus making it logical that it should be used at the service of more general EU strategies. One upshot was that the Framework programme was becoming the concern of a range of Commission services, beyond the dominant trio of DGs III (Industry), XII (Research) and XIII (Telecoms). Inter-Commission rivalries over research were nothing new, but they appeared to be intensifying.

'Below' the systemic level, decisions are prepared, policies are shaped, and the EU's research programmes (as well as EUREKA) actually operate. It is here, at the sub-systemic level, that many detailed technical and distributional RTD decisions are taken about which projects actually to fund. In technology policy, the policy networks that operate at this level of decision-making are sometimes quite insular and even incestuous. Collaborative R&D programmes could be viewed as the epitome of how pooling resources at the European level often fragments accountability and makes it more difficult to hold the private beneficiaries of public money to account (see Peterson 1997b).

However, technology policy features a unique convergence of innovation networks that allow private actors to innovate and compete and policy networks that help public policy-makers to determine who gets what. Moreover, RTD policies at the *national* level, in Europe and elsewhere, have always tended to be dominated by élite networks of officials, firms and scientists. Subjecting them to normal political controls is inherently difficult, because it requires lay people to judge technical issues whose outcomes are in any case very uncertain, especially in fast changing fields of technology. If European technology policy seems a clear manifestation of the EU's 'democratic deficit', it must be recalled that national research policies in Europe have never been subjects of very open or inclusive democratic debates. In this context, Cresson's attempts to initiate a wider public debate about the goals of RTD policy are laudable, even if also politically motivated.

As for the question of who really controls European technology policy – national governments or élite supranational networks – the answer must be hedged. Even neofunctionalists concede that supranational EU action always operates within a framework that is constrained, often tightly, by intergovernmental politics (Stone Sweet and Sandholtz 1997). EU research policy sometimes becomes a matter of high politics, but policy networks of like-minded actors, often organised and led by the Commission, have considerable scope to set the agenda and influence outcomes. In this context, it is worth dusting off Haas's (1976: 72) own notorious hedge of theoretical certainties about European integration:

> there is no tenable distinction between 'high' and 'low' politics, political and technical issues . . . R&D – the technical issue par excellence – has appeared in fundamental choices involving national identity. But not always and not inevitably. Such a distinction makes sense only in the context of a fixed set of national

purposes – a long-range teleology of action – and not in a setting of uncertainty and hesitation concerning the future of industrial society.

Certainly, the EU has no fixed set of purposes in technology policy, and it faces massive and perhaps unprecedented 'uncertainty and hesitation concerning the future of industrial society'. The result is that there remains no clear distinction between high and low politics in European technology policy.

What is clear is that the Commission tries hard to keep technology policy from becoming politicised. Increasingly, it has presented itself not as a power-and-resource-hungry federative agent of a centralised technology policy, but more as a sort of think tank. In this context, it has tried to influence *national* technology policy choices in ways that served the causes of European solidarity and enhanced competitiveness. One example was Cresson's expressed enthusiasm for coordination of the Framework programme and EUREKA. Two others were the Commission's sponsorship of technology policy studies and its exhortation about taking the 'needs of society' into account in the design of technology policies (see André 1995).

Part of the rationale behind EU-sponsored studies on science and technology issues is that European and national technology policies are likely to work at cross-purposes unless there is agreement on where Europe is innovating and where it is not. Reliable data are required to get all to sing the same tune. Moreover, governments will always be tempted to make technology policy decisions on purely political grounds (so that political supporters are rewarded), unless they are confronted publicly with data that suggest where technology policy can be used to promote innovation and competitiveness. However, the rationale is broader than that: if EU member states remain reluctant to increase the Union's own RTD resources, then at least the Commission's studies act to remind governments of the links between research (regardless of who funds it), innovation and competitiveness. Unless governments are constantly reminded of these links then *national* technology policies are likely to be downgraded and suffer cuts in funding in an era of fiscal austerity.

In spite of the mandate it received in the Maastricht Treaty to propose measures to coordinate national policies, the Commission has relatively little in the way of coordination for which to take credit in the post-Maastricht period. The Task Force initiative was originally conceived with coordination – of national, EUREKA and EU research efforts – in mind. Again, however, the Commission's first problem of coordination remains its own internal rivalries. It is difficult to see where RTD policy has been coordinated effectively with other EU policies – such as energy, transport, agriculture, the environment, or industry – despite the vastly increased importance of science and technology in all these sectors.

By the late 1990s the Commission *did* appear to be essentially united in a campaign to 'sell' EU research policy as beneficial to European society at large. Edith Cresson, a French technocrat schooled in the purest tradition of *dirigisme*, urged that the EU's research policy should 'exert a genuine impact on the economy and quality of life in Europe' and 'put the EU's scientific resources and industrial potential of Europe even more at the service of its citizens' (Commission 1994: i). The emphasis on societal needs as a basic starting point for designing technology policies may be traced back to the 1993 Delors White Paper, with its emphases on fighting unemployment and protecting the environment. Subsequently, public R&D budgets came under strain as governments struggled to meet EMU convergence criteria (with serious knock-on effects for EUREKA). Research budgets were often relatively easy places to cut

TABLE 10.2

Average R&D – sales ratios (%, 1996)

State	Ratio
Sweden	7.4
Switzerland	6.2
Japan	4.9
Germany	4.7
USA	4.3
France	4.0
Italy	2.3
UK	2.3

Note: Figures show ratios for firms included in the world's largest 300 spenders on R&D headquartered in each state shown.

Source: DTI 1997.

without provoking too much of a political backlash. Thus, the Commission tried to nurture a constituency to support public spending on R&D.

Meanwhile, the EU's largest private sector firms – leaving aside those from Sweden or Germany (see Table 10.2) – tended to let spending on R&D stagnate. Data on the private sector's performance in the UK presented, in the words of the Labour government's science and industry minister, John Battle, a 'worrying picture' (quoted in *Financial Times*, 26 June 1997). The world's 300 largest companies invested an average of 4.4 per cent of sales in R&D in 1996, but the 18 British companies in this group cut their R&D spending to 2.3 per cent, down from 2.5 per cent in 1995 (DTI 1997).

The increased complexity of new technologies and the importance of knowledge as a factor of production led leading lights such as Baruch Blumberg (1995), former Nobel prize winner, to lament the 'remarkable lack of understanding among non-scientists of what the scientific world is up to'. A clarion call for 'greater dialogue . . . involving companies, labour, consumers, the academic community and the whole knowledge base' was taken up the Ciampi Group (1995) on competitiveness, a group of senior executives representing each EU member state, formed by the Commission after the 1993 White Paper. More generally, the Commission spent progressively less time and effort trying to convince member states to increase EU policy resources, and instead tried to stimulate national actors to protect their technology policy prerogatives and resources.

At the level of EU technology policy, two classic problems persisted. First, national governments tended to remain captives of 'techno-nationalism', and rarely appeared even to consider what might be in their collective interests at the EU level. In the words of a senior DG XII official, 'when we ask the member states what they want us to do for them, the response a lot of the time is deafening silence' (interview, November 1995).

Second, governments continued to avoid hard choices about where limited EU funds should be concentrated. For example, just weeks after the British Labour government came to power in 1997, Battle welcomed the Commission's proposals for a more focused Framework V programme. At the same time, he confessed that he had 'suggested 24 more themes' that it should embrace (quoted in *Financial Times*, 26 June 1997).

In short, the EU's programmes and EUREKA cannot, by any criteria, be regarded as having made Europe's research effort a truly collective one. Nevertheless, they have survived and even flourished into the late 1990s. They have continued to induce governments to commit a small but significant share of public spending to collaborative R&D. They have fostered a significant (and growing) amount of collective action within a research élite that increasingly thinks and acts 'European', and is influential within national research communities. In its role as a think tank, the Commission has continued to harangue member states to think about what they can usefully accomplish through the EU that they cannot accomplish by themselves. Research policy is not a powerful or pervasive engine for integration, but there are few other sectors of public policy where Europe acts with more unity.

Europe and globalisation

A good indicator of the extent to which globalisation had touched the world of research and science by the end of the 1990s was the fact that the biggest user of CERN, the European particle physics laboratory based in Geneva, was the United States. More generally, foreign direct investment (FDI) continued to grow about four times faster than GNP in the world economy. The shift abroad by major companies of their sales, production and R&D activities continued unabated. Globalised firms persisted in both 'widening' and 'deepening' their activities in places to which they previously had simply exported.

One upshot is that science and technology has become far more geographically fluid. The actual benefits of RTD – in terms of jobs, sales, tax revenues, and so on – no longer necessarily remain where the research activities are undertaken. However, Europe is still far from having placeless firms, which are decoupled from their national roots. One former national EUREKA official admits:

> Frankly, I don't know what globalisation is. Sometimes I think that it's the intention of bigger companies to blackmail all the national authorities that they can blackmail to get the lowest price for their activities. Lowest price, biggest profit . . . [But] EUREKA cannot be a fortress Europe any more, it should open to the bigger world.

We should not close our eyes to Japanese collaboration. We should do things together with Israel . . . The craziness of these Europeans sitting together is that we would rather work together with the Romanians than with the Israelis. When I complain, I am told: 'that's politics, my dear guy, that's politics'. (Interview, September 1996)

The point is that Europe faces new pressures to adjust its technology policies to suit a more globalised world. On one hand, globalisation was a major theme of the 1996–7 British chairmanship of EUREKA, which organised (with the Netherlands) a major 'brokerage event' in the US to bring together European and American firms in environmental technology. The subsequent Portuguese chairmanship planned a similar event to take place in Macao in 1998. On the other, only about 8 per cent of all EUREKA projects included a non-European participant by this time. Past internal squabbles over the participation of so-called 'third countries' in EUREKA had sometimes been quite fierce, with the Commission, in particular, indulging in considerable 'techno-nationalism' and opposing projects that included non-European participants. Nevertheless, consensus was reached in 1997 with surprisingly little difficulty on new rules that made it easier for non-European firms to participate in EUREKA.

Attempts to open up EU-funded research to other countries generally were not very successful. A steering committee created in 1992 to bring together the Commission, Japan, the USA, Canada and Australia to study ways of working together, particularly on advanced manufacturing technologies, failed to get very far. Similarly, exchanges between JESSI and the American Sematech project 'brought fewer benefits than expected', according to one evaluation, which also speculated that '[a] stronger European industry would allow in theory a more balanced communication but political obstacles from the American side would remain' (EUREKA Secretariat 1995a: 8).

However, even in the Commission where 'little European' attitudes were well entrenched, attitudes were changing. For example, after the take-over of the British firm ICL (International Computers Limited) by Japan's Fujitsu in the 1980s, it was expelled from most high-level consultations between the Commission and industry. By 1994, in a complete about-face, the Commission was appointing

ICL's Chairman, Peter Bonfield, to its High Level Group on Information Technology (IT). By this time, it was clear that EU technology producers who wished to remain on the cutting edge of technology needed to attack markets beyond European shores, and develop collaborative links with non-EU producers who offered complementary assets.

The clear trend is to *global* networks of innovation, in which links to the USA are crucial. Nye and Owens's (1996) trumpeting of America's 'information edge' might be somewhat reckless, but it is clear that the US holds a commanding lead in most industries that are crucial to the emerging 'information society'. In hard security terms, massive Cold War investments in America's military–industrial complex have given the USA intelligence collection, surveillance and reconnaissance capabilities that no other state or group of states had the resources to duplicate. In economic terms, the Nye and Owens (1996) argument needs only a bit of stretching to produce the conclusion that the development of the Internet and America's 'information edge' combine to produce a result, in terms of global economic competition, that mirrors the effect of the Cold War's end on *military* competition. In both cases, we are left with a US-dominated, unipolar world.

There is no reason for Europe to feel threatened by America's technological prowess, as long as US firms continue to invest heavily in Europe, and, even more crucially, the EU retains the world-class technological skills needed to facilitate rapid and widespread dissemination of innovations. However, the rationale for subsidising R&D consortia that only include European partners has weakened considerably. European firms clearly need links to American firms, markets and technology, as well as to those of other 'third countries'.

Another clear change from the 1980s is that fears of Japanese technological hegemony have receded. In the 1990s, Japan's economy suffered from relatively low growth rates and an overvalued currency. Even after a substantial devaluation of the yen in 1995, underlying economic problems remained: radically depressed asset prices, which caused a banking crisis and conservatism among Japanese firms, and a huge surplus in industrial capacity, which squeezed the profit margins of many large technology firms. Many of Japan's top global firms invested heavily in new facilities with cash borrowed at rock-bottom rates in response to the downturn, and, by the late 1990s, had become far more efficient. However, the looming threat from China attracted far more attention, with many in the West wondering what would happen once China came on-line and developed its own high-tech firms. Was the millennium going to mark the start of the 'Chinese century?'

In many respects, such warnings have become anachronistic plati-tudes. It is still possible to argue that '[c]ontrol over technology mat-ters. It can be used both defensively, as a way of building up a nation's economic competitiveness, and aggressively, as a means of market penetration' (Taylor 1995: 19). Yet, globalisation means that more firms must collaborate and compete globally in order to sur-vive and innovate. Public policies need to encourage firms to act globally, but to ensure that the benefits of their innovation are felt locally. It is tricky balancing act for governments. Ultimately, states (and the EU) have only very limited means to control technology or the firms that are at the leading edge of the fastest-growing indus-tries. In a globalised world, the best governments can do is to create sensible regulatory frameworks, open markets through trade liberali-sation, and, above all, invest in modern infrastructures and in the abilities of their citizens to use and diffuse new technologies.

What next for European technology policy?

Just as disagreement persists about what has been achieved by European collaborative programmes, controversy abounds about what direction European technology policy should take in the twenty-first century. Advocates of a *status quo* approach can point to evidence that Europe's IT companies nearly doubled their spending on research after the mid-1980s, not least in response to new oppor-tunities available through collaborative programmes. Critics can argue that EU subsidies are spread too thinly and do not address the EU's major weakness: its proclivity for thinking that laboratory breakthroughs can substitute for efficient manufacturing or aggres-sive marketing. For many, the problem is rooted in pre-competitive shackles placed on EU research at the insistence of UK and Germany along with their powerful internal ally: DG IV of the Commission.

When research serves a clear social need, concerns about distor-tion of competition tend to be less prominent. The new and wider focus of EU-funded research on 'societal needs', such as fighting unemployment and protecting the environment, may be a way to escape these shackles. Cynically, one might conclude that tighter competition for public funds has forced Europe's research community to find a new rationale for the burden they impose on public coffers. Yet, proposals to 'keep politicians out of it' and give technology policy over to 'an enormous European research council with the most outstanding scientists who have the freedom to spend the money' (Haarder 1997: 347) are difficult to reconcile with the fact that a large portion of research will always be funded with public money. A key feature of the new political economy of RTD is that, more than ever before, new technologies must be widely accepted by societies if they are to become genuine innovations.

Moreover, the principle that European technology policies should be geared to public needs is a welcome antidote to the entirely contradictory obsessions with, on one hand, keeping EU-funded research pre-competitive, and, on the other, linking EU programmes and EUREKA to competitiveness. The former director of the EU's FAST programme speaks for many when he complains that competitiveness 'has ceased being a means and become an end in itself' (Petrella 1995: 2). Research, particularly basic or pre-competitive research, should be viewed as a sort of insurance policy to ensure that Europe has the technology and high-level skills base to compete in the long term.

European technology policies clearly have not succeeded in pushing EU firms and institutes into leading positions in the development and application of all new technologies. However, they *have* succeeded in encouraging collaboration between firms and research institutions across the EU. They also have opened up opportunities for upgrading European knowledge and skills, widening horizons and improving understanding and information flows. In these ways, European programmes have played an important role in shifting European firms and institutes out of their 'bunker' mentality of the 1970s and early 1980s.

By the late 1990s, the focus of policy was shifting. The debate over the Framework V programme revealed that the Commission (1997e) was sensitive to the need for policy change. In particular, it was concerned to simplify and concentrate the focus of the Framework V programme on a narrower range of objectives. The Commission promised that Framework V would emphasise diffusion and help for SMEs, and would do more to coordinate action between the Union and its member states. In particular, the Task Forces would coordinate research performed under different EU programmes and by different tiers of government, helping to shift research towards downstream applications that were relevant to SMEs. The Commission's (1997a) *Action Plan for Innovation* contained a series of proposals aimed at creating a true culture of innovation.

Meanwhile, EUREKA's 'Medium-Term Plan' (for 1996–2000) embraced much of the same agenda. It pledged EUREKA member states to identify measures to encourage the diffusion (or 'exploitation') of results, 'strengthen the position of SMEs', and remove obstacles to the synchronisation of public funding mechanisms (EUREKA Secretariat 1996b: 5–7). After years of rhetoric at the political level, there finally appeared to be commitment at the operational level to enhanced synergy with EU programmes.

Still, the forces of inertia within these programmes are formidable. Both Council and Commission have tended to pander to special-interest groups and perpetuate fragmentation rather than seek focus or simplification. The Commission in particular has built up a formidable army of experts, which can be wheeled out to justify its ways. Likewise, EUREKA's industry-led methodology is treated as precious and inviolable, to the point where too many poor-quality projects are tolerated, and insular, exclusive networks may actually discourage diffusion.

The 1997 Davignon review of the Framework programme concluded: 'it's time for a change, because times have changed' (Commission 1997c). Most of its proposed reforms were sensible, as were most of the Commission's and the ideas contained in EUREKA's Medium Term Plan. Yet none went far enough. Our own programme for reform is built upon four main arguments.

(1) *The ESPRIT model has outlived its usefulness.* Generally, collaborative research programmes do not have direct, measurable economic effects. Where direct benefits in terms of competitiveness may be found, it is usually the result of collaboration between SMEs and academic research organisations. Some collaborative projects, in the environmental or energy sectors, may produce important public goods. In other industries (such as aerospace), important imbalances in access to technology still remain between large companies in different countries. In these cases, state intervention may be justified. However, the ESPRIT model is essentially a technology gap

model. It is based on the assumption of important first-mover advantages, and the need to encourage former national champions to collaborate. In the late 1990s, former national champions are either global oligopolists or have disappeared. In a world of intense competition and global oligopoly, any MNC worth its salt should be spending heavily on R&D anyway. One of Europe's top high-tech firms, Ericsson, spends as much as 18 per cent of its sales on R&D. Ericsson is headquartered in Sweden but it, along with most globally competitive firms, has links and alliances on a worldwide basis. High-tech MNCs can access technology wherever they need it. There is no need to pay them to do what they are already doing. Subsidising their R&D raises suspicions about 'the use of research policy as a substitute for an undeclared industrial one' (Larédo 1996: 10).

(2) *Europe's competitiveness remains a problem, but the proper focus for technology policy is diffusion.* As in the early 1980s, the competitiveness debate of the late 1990s has featured distortion and even nonsense. Taken by themselves, Germany and Sweden (and Switzerland) have, by any measure, a better record on civilian R&D expenditure than the USA. Europe's strength in middle-tech sectors such as chemicals and mechanical engineering usually has been downplayed or under-estimated. Comparisons have rarely taken account of the effect of including the new eastern Länder alongside the (much better) performance of the old West Germany. Europe's poor innovation record has as much to do with cyclical factors, especially Europe's slow recovery from recession in the early 1990s and pre-EMU austerity, as it does with underlying science and technology structures or inflexible labour markets.

Nevertheless, European firms generally have been slower to pick up and use new technologies than their counterparts in the US and Japan. Moreover, Europe has failed to develop dynamic and creative small firms in either IT or biotechnology on anything close to the same scale as the US. These problems are rooted in the slow diffusion of new technologies, especially among firms in MNC supply chains. The general problem that technology policy needs to solve concerns EU industrial structures, and their lack of creativity and dynamism.

(3) *New means must to be found to ensure genuine coordination between European and national programmes.* We have focused on technology policy at the European level, but nearly all research on national systems

of innovation indicates that patterns of innovation vary quite markedly from country to country and firm to firm, reflecting past history and cultures (Lundvall 1992; Nelson 1993). National 'research cultures' still matter, and nationally based institutions and policies are not withering away, to be replaced by a new 'European system of innovation'. European technology policy has to learn to live with and even nurture these national research cultures, especially where they have been shown to generate innovation.

Measures at the European level must add some kind of value to national systems of innovation. Where EU, national, and regional programmes work in concert to achieve mutually agreed goals, the effect of mutually reinforcing policies is powerful. The same point applies to European level programmes themselves. Coordination between different arms of the Commission is critical to the success of the EU's programmes. The general lack of synergy between the Framework programme and EUREKA is striking, but so are the results in the few cases (such as JESSI) where synergy has been achieved. The broader point is that technology policy has become too important to be undermined by 'techno-nationalism', 'little Europeanism', or bureaucratic rivalries.

(4) *Globalisation means that technology policy must focus on immovable factors: labour and infrastructure.* In a competitive climate that features global oligopolies, mobile capital and technology, and intense competition between MNCs to innovate, the key assets that any state (or group of states) possesses are the quality of its labour force and its infrastructure to support innovation. As Reich (1991) and Strange (1998) have argued, it is silly to worry about who owns these large companies. The prime concern should be how and how much they add to national income. A well-educated population with high skill levels and a good quality infrastructure attract MNC investment and bring high-paying jobs. The key technology policy issues thus become: education, training and skills; the quality of the public research system; modern telecommunications and transport infrastructures; and a flexible and innovative small-firm sector. The problem for the European Union is that most of these issues are traditionally and rightly the responsibility of national/regional governments, not the EU itself.

Our four propositions lead to four policy prescriptions.

(1) *Earmark more resources for basic research.* Traditionally the funding of basic research has been the responsibility of national governments, not the EU. The case for greater EU involvement arises both from the argument that the quality of the labour force is a key factor attracting high-value-added jobs, and from the increasing recognition that basic research is not just about producing new ideas but about training and technology transfer in state-of-the-art knowledge and techniques (Pavitt 1997). Given the acknowledged spillovers inherent in basic research, there are in any case strong arguments for financing it at higher rather than lower levels of government, as is the case in the United States where basic research is the responsibility of the federal government.

It would be wrong to suggest that the current European programmes do not support basic research. Many of those in the medical and life sciences field have a strong basic research element to them. Even in the seemingly more applied areas, as Larédo has observed, many large firms share ideas and assets within networks (which often include large numbers of public laboratories), but they do *not* conduct research that is 'near market' or even pre-competitive. Rather they undertake what he calls 'basic technological research':

It is mainly devoted to the elaboration of new methods and a large share of its outputs is made [up] of computer models and the simulations which go with them. This establishes a new relationship between theoretical work and experimental activities: instead of realising complicated and costly experiments, the validation of the concept and the design studies are carried out through the development and use of mathematical models.
(Larédo 1996: 8; see also Gibbons *et al.* 1994)

Clearly, it is highly desirable that European firms should collaborate in such activities. Research consortia allow them to share ideas and develop their in-house capabilities to assimilate and apply new technologies. Giving research organisations themselves more scope to set objectives and deliberately targeting resources towards 'basic technological research' might be advantageous.

(2) *Put more resources into the mobility programmes.* Programmes that encourage the mobility of researchers between national systems of innovation are one of the most effective ways of diffusing new ideas

and technologies, especially to the cohesion countries (see Pavitt 1997). There is a tendency on the part of the richer northern member states to dismiss the EU's mobility programmes as 'job schemes for Mediterranean boys and girls'. However, these programmes help expand markets for innovations, including those that originate in the more technologically advanced north. At the leading edge of science and engineering, people carry knowledge and technology with them and pass it on to others through discussion and hands-on experimentation. Looking ahead to eastern enlargement, training and mobility programmes will become even more important EU policy tools. They will act not only as political tools to extend the EU's technology policy *acquis* to the east. They also will allow EU research networks to expand and benefit, for example, from Hungarian excellence in mathematics or even Russian expertise in software, which developed during the Cold War largely because Russia's military hardware worked so badly!

(3) *Place more emphasis on upgrading technical standards.* High-level European standards, such as the GSM standard for mobile phones, offer double benefits. First, they help standardise technologies across the Union and thus reinforce the single market. Second, if they are tough enough (as with GSM), they can themselves help to drive innovation. Both the EU and EUREKA (through its supportive measures) could do more to promote and then disseminate high technical standards.

(4) *Above all, make diffusion the EU's most prominent technology policy goal.* There is near unanimous agreement that *the* key technology issue facing the EU is now upgrading the performance of its SMEs. It needs to be easier for new firms with new ideas to set up in business and find risk capital. Existing small firms need to have easier access to new technologies, especially ICT, which can improve their performance. These priorities are now widely accepted. The question is whether the delivery mechanisms are right. The Task Forces are meant to be 'applications-oriented' as they coordinate actions towards the development of 'the car of the future', new clean water technologies, and so on. They have the potential, at least, of helping to pull together national efforts with EU-funded actions. However, it is not clear that they will be truly diffusion-oriented. There are obvious dangers that they will attract – in the typical style of the EU – the European 'great and the good' in the sectors targeted for their work. If they do, they risk becoming subject to 'industrial capture',

particularly by large firms, failing to reach down the supply lines to the SMEs.

The problem is that the sorts of measures needed are more seed-corn funding for new enterprises, assistance with management training and making best use of ICT, and reinforcing supply chains. These measures do not lend themselves to the EU model of shared-cost, collaborative frameworks designed by the Commission and its allied policy networks in Brussels. Most of these measures are best designed and delivered at the regional or even subregional level of government. What are needed from Brussels are programmes that provide a catalyst for actions but, as with the structural funds, essentially promote such action at lower tiers of government. European technology policy must truly add value to national and local initiatives, as opposed to replacing them.

Conclusion

We have assessed European technology policy with a critical eye, and found much to criticise. We also have argued that the EU and its member states learned important lessons from the early days of the Framework programme. Most of the Union's programmes were better run and targeted by the time the Framework V proposal was tabled than was the case ten or even five years earlier. EUREKA had begun to generate tangible results, with four of five participants reporting that new products or processes would emerge from their projects (British EUREKA Chairmanship 1997: 2).

We have argued that collaborative European programmes must be evaluated according to objectives set. Yet, what is perhaps most striking about these programmes is the very high value placed by their participants on collaboration *per se*, as opposed to public funding or effects on their competitiveness. As such, *the* most important benefit of collaborative programmes from the point of view of those who actually take part in them appears under-appreciated by those who *design* them.

As we have seen *juste retour* still rules in all the big decisions, and even in many little ones. Europe still lacks anything approaching a collective RTD effort. We have posed hard questions about the EU's proper role in technology policy, and have suggested that much of what it does now – subsidising exclusively European collaboration –

may not be an effective use of European taxpayers' money. And while collaborative programmes clearly have created a vast, complex and impressive array of links between governments and industry – something like a 'European Technological Community' – the political spillovers have been minimal.

A separate problem is that Cresson and her predecessors have been guilty of overselling the potential of EU programmes. But this exuberance is excusable and perhaps even necessary as a means for sustaining a European Technological Community. Promoting its existence and development is justified by the reality that many of Europe's innovation problems are shared, *collective* problems. In particular, the EU is handicapped by a worrying complacency about Europe's ability to continue to generate levels of wealth, prosperity and quality of life which, traditionally, have been envied around the world. One study of manufacturing practice and performance indicated that 75 per cent of the European managers *thought* their firms could compete with the best of their international rivals, even though only one in 50 European factories was genuinely 'world-class' (Hanson and Voss 1994).

Arguably, such complacency is even more damaging in the public sector. The big European political economy story of the late 1990s was the way in which governments sacrificed a range of public policy ambitions – including many technology policy ambitions – in their headlong and headstrong rush to create a single European currency. As national research budgets fell or stagnated, something like a nascent European Technology Community warned governments of the long-term costs of failing to invest in research and science. These warnings often seemed to fall on deaf ears. At least, however, the European Technological Community had a voice by this point, and governments could not ignore it altogether.

Guide to Further Reading

Chapter 1

The Commission's (1994; 1997f) two reports on 'Science and Technology Indicators' provide a treasure trove of data on nearly all aspects of Europe's scientific, technological and competitive performance. The Commission's (1993) White Paper on 'Competitiveness, Growth and Employment' and its (1995a) Green Paper on Innovation are essential guides to the current state of EU technology policy. Reich (1991) and Strange (1998) offer provocative treatments of the policy implications of globalisation, while Zysman and Schwartz (1998) analyse the emergence of new industrial structures and production networks.

Chapter 2

Guzzetti (1995) manages an overview of the history of European collaboration which is both user-friendly and comprehensive. Krige and Guzzetti (1997) offer a number of insiders' accounts of the history of European programmes. Layton (1969) and Williams (1973) remain essential works on early collaborative experiments.

Chapter 3

The most stimulating book on the economics of technology policy is undoubtedly Freeman and Soete (1997). On systems of innovation, the two classic texts are Lundvall (1992) and Nelson (1993). On networks, Callon (1989) provides a sociological perspective, while Mytelka (1991) offers a practical guide to strategic alliances. On the EU as a multi-level system of government, see Marks et al. (1996a, 1996b). The classic neofunctionalist works are Haas (1958) and

Lindberg (1963), and they are worth revisiting alongside Moravcsik's liberal intergovernmentalism (1991; 1993; 1995). The new institutionalism is applied to the EU by Pierson (1996) and Amstrong and Bulmer (1998). On policy networks, see Peterson (1995a; 1995c). The best theory-based treatment of EU technology policy is Sandholtz (1992).

Chapter 4

Sharp and Shearman (1987) was one of the first texts to be written about EU technology programmes and it formed the basis for this chapter. Since that time, much else has been written. Sandholtz (1992) is strong on the development of ESPRIT and RACE (if less strong on EUREKA), while Cowles (1995) examines links with the single market programme. Guzzetti (1995) and Krige and Guzzetti (1997) both give good coverage to events in the 1980s. Sharp (1993) expands on the twin-track approach of the 1992 project.

Chapter 5

Information on EUREKA's evolving project list is available from EUREKA's web-site: http://www.eureka.be. The EUREKA Secretariat publishes a quarterly bulletin called *EUREKA News*, and the UK's Department of Trade and Industry publishes a similar *EUREKA Bulletin*. For academic analyses of EUREKA, see Peterson (1993a; 1993b).

Chapter 6

The Commission's (1992b) *Research After Maastricht* marks an essential turning-point in the evolution of EU technology policy. Peterson (1995b) offers a detailed analysis of the Framework IV negotiations. Bangemann (1992) gives a good picture of the Commission's vision of EU industrial policy in the early 1990s. Fagerberg and Verspagen (1996) examine the interface between cohesion and EU funding for research.

Chapter 7

The core material on which the early part of this chapter is built comes from the Commission (1994). Its Green Paper on Innovation (1995a) and the follow-up *Action Plan for Innovation* (1997b) illuminate the innovation debate. The Framework V programme is documented in the Commission's consultation paper (1996b) and subsequent proposals (1996c), all of which are available (along with many comments on them) on the Internet (http://www.cordis.lu/cgi.en/fifth_papers). The House of Lords (1997) and POST (1996) reports both provide useful background material, albeit biased to a British perspective.

Chapter 8

On EU decision-making generally, see Peterson and Bomberg (1998) and Peterson (1995a). Cawson (1987; 1992) and Cawson and Holmes (1995) offer clear analyses of the politics of advances in television technologies. On JESSI, see EUREKA secretariat (1995a) and Hobday (1995). Elizalde (1992) and Docksey and Williams (1995) offer useful treatments of 'sub-systemic' EU decision-making. The national approaches of larger EU Member States to issues of RTD collaboration are examined in Peterson (1996).

Chapter 9

There is a plethora of published evaluations of the EU programmes and EUREKA. Given their size, they are probably the most over-monitored, over-evaluated programmes in the world. Useful overviews are provided by the Commission (1994; 1997f), while Luukkonen (1997) and Pavitt (1997) offer welcome perspectives on European technology policies and competitiveness. For assessments of EUREKA, see Peterson (1993a) and EUREKA Secretariat (1995b). The UK Impact Study (Georghiou *et al* 1993) and the French Impact Study (Larédo 1995) are both good examples of country-based evaluations of the Framework programme. The Ledoux *et al.* (1993) study on BRITE-EURAM makes interesting reading, but has its own particular methodology. The Davignon assessments of the Framework programme (Commission 1997c) and EUREKA (Davignon Group 1996) offer a broad-ranging view of current developments.

Chapter 10

At least glimpses of the future of European technology policy may be found in the Commission's (1997a) *Action Plan for Innovation* and EUREKA's most recent 'Medium-Term Plan (EUREKA Secretariat 1996b). On America's 'information edge', see Nye and Owens (1996). On the competitiveness debate, see Petrella (1995).

Bibliography

André, M. (1995) 'Thinking and debating about science and technology at the European level', *Science and Public Policy*, vol. 22, no. 3, pp. 205–7.

Aigrain, P., Allen, G., Oliviera, E. d'a., Colombo, U., Mark, H. and Ruscoe, J. (1989) *The Report of the Framework Review Board*. Brussels, DG XII, July.

Armstrong, K. and Bulmer, S. (1998) *The Governance of Single European Market*. Manchester University Press.

Arnold, E. and Guy, K. (1986) *Parallel Convergence: National Strategies in Information Technology*. London, Pinter.

Bangemann, M. (1992) *Meeting the Global Challenge: Establishing a Successful European Industrial Policy*. London, Kogan Page.

Belgian EUREKA Chairmanship (1995) 'The programme of work of the incoming Belgiam Chairmanship'. Brussels.

Blumberg, B. (1995) 'The importance of basic research', *Financial Times*, 23 June, p. 17.

British EUREKA Chairmanship (1986) 'Procedures for EUREKA projects: note by chairman of the Ministerial Conference'. London, DTI, 21 May.

British EUREKA Chairmanship (1997) 'The continuous and systematic evaluation of EUREKA: interim annual impact report 1997 (summary)'. London, DTI.

Bulmer, S. (1994a) 'The governance of the European Union: a new institutionalist approach', *Journal of Public Policy*, vol. 13, no. 4, pp. 351–80.

Bulmer, S. (1994b) 'Institutions and policy change in the European Communities: the case of merger control', *Public Administration*, vol. 72, no. 3, pp. 423–44.

Bush, V. (1945) *Science: the Endless Frontier*. Washington, DC, National Science Foundation.

Callon, M (ed.) (1989) *La science et ses réseaux: genèse et circulation des faits scientifiques*. Oaris, La Découverte.

Callon, M., Laredo, P. and Rabeharisoa, V. (1990) 'The management and evaluation of technological programmes and the dynamics of techno-economic networks: the case of Agence Française de la Maîtrise de l'Energie (AFME)', Centre de Sociologie de l'Innovation, Ecole des Mines, Paris.

Cantley, M. (1995) 'The regulation of modern biotechnology: a historical and European perspective', in H. J. Rehn *et al.* (eds) *Biotechnology – Legal, Economic and Ethical Dimensions*, vol. XII. Weinheim, VCH.

Cawson, A. (1989) 'European consumer electronics: corporate strategies and public policy', in M. Sharp and P. Holmes, (eds) *Strategies for New Technologies: Six Cases from Britain and France*. Oxford, Phillip Allan.

Cawson, A. (1992) 'Interests, groups and public policy-making: the case of the European consumer electronics industry', in J. Greenwood, J. R. Grote and K. Ronit (eds) *Organized Interests and the European Community*. London, Sage.

Cawson, A. and Holmes, P. (1995) 'Technology policy and competition issues in the transition to advanced television services in Europe', *Journal of European Public Policy*, vol. 2, no. 4, pp. 650–71.

Cawson, A., Morgan, K., Webber, D., Holmes, P. and Stevens, A. (1990) *Hostile Brothers: Competition and Closure in the European Electronics Industry* Oxford, Clarendon.

Cecchini, P. (1988) *The European Challenge: The Benefits of the Single Market*. Aldershot, Wildwood House.

Chesnais, F. (1988) 'Technical cooperation agreements between firms', *STI Review*, no. 4, pp. 51–110. Paris, OECD.

Ciampi Group (1995) *Enhancing European Competitiveness: First Report to the President of the Commission, the Prime Ministers and Heads of State*. Luxembourg, European Commission, Competitiveness Advisory Group, June.

CIRCA (1993) *Thematic Evaluation of the Impact of the CSFs for Research and Technology in Greece, Ireland and Portugal. Report to the Commission*. Brussels, European Commission, DG XII and XVI.

Clark, F.G. and Gibson, A. (1976) *Concorde: The Story of the World's Most Advanced Passenger Plane*. London, Phoebus.

Clay, N., Creigh-Tyte, S. and Storey, D.J. (1996) 'Public policy towards small firms: spreading the jam too thinly?', *Journal of European Public Policy*, vol. 3, no. 2, pp. 253–71.

Coase, R. (1937) 'The Nature of the Firm', *Economica*, vol. 4, no. 3, pp. 386–405.

Cockfield, Lord Arthur (1994) *The European Union: Creating the Single Market*. London, Wiley Chancery Law.

Cohen, W.M. and Levinthal, D.A. (1989) 'Innovation and Learning: the Two Faces of R&D', *Economic Journal*, vol. 99, September, pp. 569–596.

Colombo, U. (1997) 'Report by panel of experts under Umberto Colombo on workings of Framework programme IV', Brussels, European Commission.

Commission of the European Communities (1967) *Opinion on the Applications for Membership Received from the UK, Ireland, Denmark and Norway*. Brussels, European Commission.

Commission (1970) Commission Memorandum to the Council, *La Politique Industrielle de la Communauté*, COM (70) 100 (final). Brussels, Commission of the European Communities, 1970.

Commission (1982) 'Towards a European strategic programme for research and development in information technology'. Luxembourg, CEC.

Commission (1983) *Forecasting and Assessment in Science and Technology (FAST) A Community Strategy for Biotechnology in Europe*, FAST Occasional Papers, no. 62. Brussels, European Commission, DG XII.

Commission (1984) *RACE – A Proposal for an Action Plan*, Luxembourg, OTR 25, no. 1.

Commission (1985) *Towards a European Technological Community*, COM (85) 350 (final). Brussels, European Commission, June.

Commission (1987) *Towards a Dynamic European Economy: Green Paper on the Development of the Common Market for Telecommunications Services and Equipment* COM 290 (final), June 1987. Brussels.

Commission (1989) *RACE '89*. Brussels, March.

Commission (1990) *Innovation and Technology Transfer*, 11/1.

Commission (1991a) *The European electronics and information technology industry: state of play, issues at stake and proposals for action*, Communication from the Commission. Brussels, SEC (91) 565 (final), 3 April.

Commission (1991b) 'European Industrial Policy for the 1990s', *Bulletin of the European Communities*, 3/91, document based on COM (90) 556, SEC (91) 565 and SEC (91) 629. Luxembourg, 1991

Commission (1992a) *Eurobarometer: Public Opinion in the European Community. Trends 1974–91. Brussels*, DG X, European Commission, April.

Commission (1992b) *Research After Maastricht: an Assessment, a Strategy*, Communication from the Commission to the Council and European Parliament, Bulletin supplement 2/92 (SEC (92) 682 (final).

Commission (1993) *Growth, Competitiveness and Employment: the Challenges and Ways Forward into the 21st Century*, COM (93) 700 (final).

Commission (1994) *The European Report on Science and Technology Indicators 1994*, Report EUR 15897 EN, Luxembourg, DG XII, European Commission.

Commission (1995a) *Green Paper on Innovation*, COM (95) 688 (final), December.

Commission (1995b) 'Intervention de Mme. Edith Cresson devant la CERT', Commission Européenne, *Porte Parole Note d'Information*, 22 November.

Commission (1995c) *Telework 95: New Ways to Work in the Virtual European Company*. Brussels, DG XIII, European Commission, March.

Commission (1996a) *First Report on Economic and Social Cohesion*, Luxembourg, Office of Official Publications of the European Commission.

Commission (1996b) *The Integrated Programme: a General Framework for All Community Actions in Favour of SMEs. Brussels*, COM (96) 329 (final), 10 July.

Commission (1996c) *Inventing Tomorrow: Preliminary Guidelines for the Fifth Framework Programme*. Brussels, July.

Commission (1996d) *Position Paper of the German Federal Government on the Fifth Framework programme*, 1998–2002, DG XII, July

Commission (1996e) *Research and Technological Development Activities of the European Union: Annual Report*. Brussels, COM (96) 436 (final), 9 September.

Commission (1997a) *Amended Proposal for a European Parliament and Council Decision concerning the Fifth Framework Programme*. Brussels, 11 August COM (97) 439 (final).

Commission (1997b) *First Action Plan for Innovation: Innovation, Growth and Employment*, Luxembourg, DG XIII, Office of the Official Publications for the EC.

Commission (1997c) Five Year Assessment of the European Community RTD Framework Programme, *Report of an Independent Panel chaired by Vicomte Davignon*, DG XII, February.

Commission (1997d). Spanish comments on the Commission Working Paper COM (97) 47, March, DG XII.

Commission (1997e) *Towards the 5th Framework programme: Scientific and Technological Objectives*, Luxembourg, DG XII, Office for the Official Publications of the EC.

Commission (1997f) *The European Report on Science and Technology Indicators 1997* Report EUR 17639 EN, Luxembourg, DG XII, European Commission.

Corbett, Richard (1994) 'Representing the people', in A. Duff, J. Pinder and R. Pryce (eds) *Maastricht and Beyond: Building the European Union.* London, Routledge.

Council of Europe, *Scientific and Technological Aspects of the Extension of the European Communities,* Doc 2279 Strasbourg, Council of Europe, 1967.

Court of Auditors (1991) 'Special report: the utilisation of the results of Community research work, accompanied by the replies of the Commission, *Official Journal,* no. 133, 23 May.

Court of Auditors (1994) *Annual Report Concerning the Financial Year 1993* (OJ 327), 24 November.

Court of Auditors (1995) *Annual Report Concerning the Financial Year 1994* (OJ C303) 14 November.

Court of Auditors (1996) *Annual Report Concerning the Financial Year 1995* (OJ C340) 12 November

Cowles, M. G. (1995) 'Setting the agenda for a new Europe: the ERT and EC 1992', *Journal of Common Market Studies,* vol. 33, no. 4, pp. 501–26.

Cowles, M. G. (1996) 'German big business and Brussels: learning to play the Euorpean game', *German Politics and Society,* vol. 14, no. 3, pp. 73–107.

Cram, L. (1994) 'Breaking down the monolith: the European Commission as a multi-organisation – social policy and IT policy in the EC', *Journal of European Public Policy,* vol. 1, no.1, pp. 135–46.

Cram, L. (1997) *Policy-Making in the EU: Conceptual Lenses and the Integration Process.* London, Routledge.

Cresson, E. (1997) 'Intervention de Mme Edith Cresson', *15ième Conférence Ministérielle EUREKA. London,* 19 June.

Dang Nyugen, G. (1985) 'Telecommunications: a challenge to the old order', in M. Sharp (ed.) *Europe and the New Technologies.* London, Pinter.

Dang Nguyen, G. and Arnold, E. (1985) 'Videotext – Much Ado About Nothing?' in Sharp, M. (ed.) *Europe and the New Technologies: Six Case Studies of Adjustment and Innovation.* London, Pinter.

Davignon Group (1996) *The Role and Medium Term Future of EUREKA: An Assessment and Recommendations.* Brussels, EUREKA Secretariat.

Docksey, C. and Williams, K. (1995) 'The Commission and the execution of Community policy', in G. Edwards and D. Spence (eds) *The European Commission.* Harlow, Longman Current Affairs.

Dosi, G. (1983) 'Semi-conductors: Europe's precarious survival in high technology' in G. Shepherd, F. Duchêne, and C. Saunders (eds) *Europe's Industries: Public and Private Strategies for Change.* London, Pinter.

DTI (1997) *The R&D Scoreboard.* (London, DTI Innovation Unit).

Duff, A.N. (1986) 'Eureka and the new technology policy of the European Community', *Policy Studies,* no. 6, pp. 44–61.

Dutch Eureka Chairmanship (1991) *The Report of the EUREKA Assessment Panel,* The Hague.

The Economist (1993) 'Europe's technology policy: how not to catch up', 9 January, pp. 19–22.

Edwards, G. and Spence, D. (eds) (1995) *The European Commission*. Harlow, Longman Current Affairs.

EITO (1996) *EITO Update 1996*, Frankfurt, European Information Technology Observatory.

Elizalde, J. (1992) 'Legal aspects of Community policy on research and technological development (RTD)', *Common Market Law Review*, vol. 29; pp. 309–46.

Ergas, H. (1984) *Why Do Some Countries Innovate More Than Others?*, CEPS Paper no 5. Brussels.

ESF (1996) *Position Paper of the European Science Foundation (ESF) on the Fifth Framework Programme Proposals*. Brussels, Commission of the European Communities, DG XII (mimeo), October 1996.

Esser, J. (1994) 'Technological Development in the Triad: Consequences for the European Technological Community', paper presented to the ESRC Conference on the Single European Market. Exeter, 8–11 September 1994.

EUREKA Secretariat (1985) *Declaration of Principles Relating to EUREKA Adopted at Hanover*, 6 November. Brussels.

EUREKA Secretariat (1991) *The Report of the EUREKA Assessment Panel*. Brussels.

EUREKA Secretariat (1993) *Evaluation of EUREKA Industrial and Economic Effects*. Brussels.

EUREKA Secretariat (1995a) *Assessment of JESSI Programme – European Report*. Brussels, Coordination Group Final Report, 31 May.

EUREKA Secretariat (1995b) *EUREKA Evaluation Report*. Brussels, November.

EUREKA Secretariat (1996a) *Communiqué of the XIVth Session of the EUREKA Ministerial Conference*, 28 June 1996. Brussels, Document EUREKA 14 MC 8, 5 July.

EUREKA Secretariat (1996b) *EUREKA Medium Term Plan 1996–2000*. Brussels, June.

EUREKA Secretariat (1996c) *Statistics: Ongoing Projects*. Brussels, 28 June.

EUREKA Secretariat (1997) *Ongoing EUREKA Projects by 19 June 1997 London Ministerial Conference*. Brussels.

European Round Table of Industrialists (1993) *Beating the Crisis*. Brussels, 3 December.

Eurotechnology (1996) 'Data on EU budget and research funding', no. 76, December.

Fagerberg, J. and Verspagen, B. (1996) 'Heading for divergence? Regional growth in Europe reconsidered', *Journal of Common Market Studies*, vol. 34, no. 3, pp. 431–48.

Farge, Y. *et al.* (1988) *Evaluation of the First BRITE Programme 1985–88*. Luxembourg, European Commission.

FAST (1984) *Eurofutures: the Challenges of Innovation*, (Forecasting and Assessment in Science and Technology). London, Butterworth.

FAST (1992) *Archipelago Europe and Islands of Innovation: A Synthesis Report*, U. Hilpert, vol.18, Prospective Dossier no. 1: Science, Technology and Social and Economic Cohesion in the Community. Brussels.

Finnish EUREKA Chairmanship (1992) *NPC Office Functions*. Tampere, 22 May.

Flamm, K. (1990) 'Semi-conductors', in G. C. Hufbauer (ed.) *Europe 1992: An American Perspective*. Washington, DC, Brookings Institution.

Freeman, C. (1982) *The Economics of Industrial Innovation*. London, Pinter.

Freeman, C. (1987) *Technology Policy and Economic Performance: Lessons from Japan.* London, Pinter.

Freeman, C. and Soete, L. (1997) *The Economics of Innovation.* London: Pinter.

Galimberti, I. (1993) 'Large Chemical Firms in Biotechnology: Case Studies of Learning in a Radically New Technology', DPhil Thesis, SPRU, University of Sussex.

Gambardella, A. and Garcia, W. (1995) 'Regional linkages through European research funding, *Economies of Innovation and New Technologies*, vol. 4, no. 2, pp. 123–38.

Gamble, A. (1990) *Britain in Decline.* 3rd edition. London, Macmillan.

Georghiou, L., Stein, J., Janes, M., Senker, J., Pifer, M., Cameron, H., Nedeva, M., Yates, J., and Boden, J. M. (1993) *The Impact of European Community Policies for Research and Technological Development upon Science and Technology in the UK.* London, HMSO.

Gibbons, M., Limoges, C., Nowotny, H., Schwartzman, S., Scott, P., and Trow, M. (eds) (1994) *The New Production of Knowledge: The Dynamics of Science and Research in Contemporary Society.* London, Sage.

Grieco, J.M. (1995) 'The Maastricht Treaty, Economic and Monetary Union and the neo-realist research programme', *Review of International Studies*, no. 21, pp. 21–40.

GTS (1993) *Quantitative Study of the Biotechnology Action Programme (1985–9)*, Final report, no. 91123. Brussels, European Commission, DG XII.

Guzzetti, L. (1995) *A Brief History of European Union Research Policy.* Brussels, European Commission, DG XII.

Haarder, B. (1997) 'Commentary on the History of EUREKA' in J. Krige and L. Guzzetti (eds) *History of European Scientific and Technological Cooperation* Luxembourg, European Commission, European Science and Technology Forum.

Haas, E. (1958) *The Uniting of Europe: Political, Social and Economic Forces, 1950–1957.* 2nd edn, 1968, Stanford University Press.

Haas, E. (1976) *The Obsolescence of Regional Integration Theory.* Berkeley, CA Institute of International Studies.

Hanson, P. and Voss, C. (1994) *Made in Europe: A Four Nations Best Practice Study Guide.* London, IBM Consulting Group.

Hayward, K. (1989) *The British Aircraft Industry.* New York, St Martin's Press.

Hayward, K. (1994) *The World Aerospace Industry: Collaboration and Competition. London*, Duckworth and RUSI.

Hayward, K. (1997) *Towards a European Weapons Procurement Process.* Paris, West European Union Institute for Security Studies, Chaillot Paper 27.

Herman, R. (1995) 'Biotech squeezes project funding', *Research Fortnight*, vol. 2, no. 2, p. 12.

Hicks, D. and Katz, S. (1997) 'The Changing Shape of British Industrial Research', *STEEP Special Report*, no. 6, SPRU, University of Sussex.

Hinder, S. (1987) 'EUREKA: a UK Perspective'. M.Phil thesis, University of Manchester.

Hobday, M. (1995) 'The Technological Competence of European Semiconductor Producers', *Sussex European Institute Working Papers in Contemporary European Studies*, no. 11. Brighton.

House of Lords Select Committee on the European Communities (1985) *European Research and Development in Information Technology*, Session 1984–5, 8th Report. London, HMSO.

House of Lords (1997) *EU Framework Programme for European Research and Technological Development*, Select Committee on Science and Technology. Session 1996–7, 2nd Report. London, HMSO.

Humphreys, P. (1991) The state and telecommunications modernization in Britain, France and West Germany' in U. Hilpert (ed.*) State Policies and Techno-Industrial Innovation*. London, Routledge.

IDS Consultants (1989) 'Audit opérationnel du programme Eurêka en France: point clés de la synthése'. Levallois.

IFO Institute (1997) *Monitoring the Evolution of the Competitiveness of the EU Mechanical Engineering Industry*. Munich, July.

IFT Marketing Research (1989) *EUREKA Survey*. London, Department of Trade and Industry.

Johnson, C. (1984) (ed.) *The Industrial Policy Debate*. San Francisco, Institute for Contemporary Studies.

Judge, D., Earnshaw, D. and Cowan, N. (1994) 'Ripples or waves: the European Parliament in the European Community policy process', *Journal of European Public Policy*, vol. 1, no. 1, pp. 27–52.

Katz, J. (1996) 'Democracy and the information society', in F. Spufford and J. Uglow (eds) *Cultural Babbage: Technology and the History of Culture*. London, Faber.

Keliher, L. (1987) *Policy-making in information technology: a decisional analysis of the Alvey project*, PhD thesis. London School of Economics.

Kline, S. J. and Rosenberg, N. (1986) 'An Overview of Innovation: The Positive Sum Strategy' in R. Landau and N. Rosenberg (eds) *Harnessing Technology for Economic Growth*. Washington DC, National Academy Press.

Krige, J. and Guzzetti, L. (eds) *History of European Scientific and Technological Cooperation*. Luxembourg, European Commission, European Science and Technology Forum.

Krige, J., Russo, A. and Sebasta, L. (1997) 'A Brief History of the European Space Agency' in J. Krige and L. Guzzetti (eds) *History of European Scientific and Technological Cooperation*. Luxembourg, European Commission, European Science and Technology Forum.

Krugman, P. (ed.) (1987) *Strategic Trade Policy and the New International Economics*. Cambridge, Mass. MIT Press.

Krugman, P. (1994) 'Competitiveness: A Dangerous Obsession', *Foreign Affairs*, vol. 73, no. 2, pp. 28–44.

Larédo, P. (1995*) The Impact in France of the European Community Programmes for RTD*. Paris, Presses de l'Ecole des Mines.

Larédo, P. (1996) 'The effects of EU research programmes: towards a reappraisal of the formulation and implementation of the EU research policy', paper presented to the Triple Helix Conference, Amsterdam, 4–6 January.

Larédo, P. and Breitenstein, A. (1993) *Les Effets industriels de l'initiative EUREKA en France*. Paris, CSI.

Larédo, P. and Mustar, P. (1996) 'The techno-economic network: a socio-economic approach to state intervention in innovation', in R. Coombs, P. Saviotti, A. Richards, and V. Walsh (eds) *Networks and Technology Collaboration*. Cheltenham and Brookfield, VT, Edward Elgar.

Layton, C. (1969) *European Advanced Technology: A Programme for Integration*. London, Allen & Unwin.

Layton, C. (1986) 'The High-Tech Triangle', in R. Morgan and C. Bray (eds) *Partners and Rivals in Western Europe: Britain, France and Germany*. Aldershot, Gower for the Policy Studies Institute.

Ledoux, M. J., Bach L., Conde Molist, N., Frantz, C., Matt, M. (1993) *Economic Evaluation of the effects of BRITE-EURAM on European Industry. Final Report to DG XII*. Strasbourg, CNRS-BETA, Université Louis Pasteur, January.

Liebenstien, H (1987) *Inside the Firm: The Inefficiencies of Hierarchy*. Cambridge Mass., Harvard University Press.

Lindberg, L.N. (1963) *The Political Dynamics of European Economic Integration*. Oxford and New York, Oxford University Press.

Lundvall, B-A. (1992) *National Systems of Innovation: Towards a Theory of Innovation and Interactive Learning*. London, Pinter.

Luukkonen, T. (1997) 'The limits of our knowledge on the impacts', paper presented to the conference on the Past and Future of EU Research Funding – Framework Programmes under consideration, Helsinki.

Macilwain, C. (1996) 'EU–US cooperation talks may hinge on access to research programmes', *Nature*, vol. 4, no. 1, p. 14.

Magien, E. and de Nettancourt, D. (1993) 'What Drives European Biotechnology Research?', *International Journal of Technology Management*, pp. 47–58.

March , J.G. and Olsen, J.P. (1989) *Rediscovering Institutions: the Organizational Basis of Politics*. New York and Oxford, Free Press.

Marcum, J. (1986) 'The technology gap: Europe at a crossroads', *Issues in Science and Technology*, Summer, pp. 28–37.

Marks, G., Hooghe, L. and Blank, K. (1996a) 'European integration from the 1980s', *Journal of Common Market Studies*, vol. 34, no. 3, pp. 341–78.

Marks, G., Nielson, F., Ray, L. and Salk, J. (1996b) 'Competencies, cracks and conflicts: regional mobilization in the European Union', in G. Marks, F.W. Scharpf, P.C. Schmitter and W. Streeck (eds) *Governance in the European Union*. London and Thousand Oaks, Sage.

May, R. M. (1995) 'The force behind a dramatic century', *Financial Times*, 18–19 November, pp. I, XI.

Metcalf, I.S., Georghiou, L., Stein, J., Jones, M., Senker, J., Pifer, M., Cameron, H., Nedeva, M., Yates, J. and Boden, M. (1991) *Evaluation of the Impact of European Community Research Programmes upon the Competitiveness of European Industry – Concepts and Approaches*. University of Manchester, PREST, EUR 14198.

Micossi, S. (1996) 'By the people, for the people?', *I & T Magazine*, no. 19, April, p. 1.

Middlemas, K. (1995) *Orchestrating Europe: The Informal Politics of European Union 1973–1995*. London, Fontana.

Ministére de la Recherche and l'Espace de la France (1992) *Projet de loi de finances pour 1993: état de la recherche et du développement technologique*, Activités 1991–92 et Perspectives 1993, Paris, Imprimerie Nationale.

Moravcsik, A. (1991) 'Negotiating the Single European Act' in R. O. Keohane and S. Hoffmann (eds) *The New European Community*. Boulder and Oxford, Westview.

Moravcsik, A. (1993) 'Preferences and power in the European Community: a liberal intergovernmentalist approach', *Journal of Common Market Studies*, vol. 31, no. 4, pp. 473–524.

Moravcsik, A. (1995) 'Liberal intergovernmentalism and integration: a rejoinder', *Journal of Common Market Studies*, vol. 33, no.4, pp. 611–28.

Mowery, D. C. (1992) 'Finance and corporate evolution in five industrial economies', *Industrial and Corporate Change*, vol. 1, no. 1, pp. 1–36.

Mytelka, L. (1991) *Strategic Partnerships in the World Economy*, London: Pinter.

Nelson, R. R. (1993) *National Systems of Innovation: A Comparative Study*. Oxford University Press.

Neven, D. and Seabright, P. (1995) 'European industrial policy: the Airbus case', *Economic Policy*, 26, October, pp. 315–44.

Nye, J. S., Jr., and Owens, W. A. (1996) 'America's information edge', *Foreign Affairs*, March/April, pp. 20–36.

Oakley, B. and Owen, K. (1989) *Alvey: Britain's Strategic Computing Initiative*. London, MIT Press.

OECD (1971) *The Conditions for Success in Technological Innovation*, Paris, OECD.

OECD (1985) *The Semi-conductor Industry: Trade Related Issues*, Paris, OECD.

OECD (1996) *Information Infrastructure Convergence and Pricing: the Internet*, Paris, OECD, June.

OECD (1997) *Main Science and Technology Indicators, Volume 2*, Paris, OECD.

Office of Technology Assessment (OTA) (1991) *Competing Economies: America, Europe and the Pacific Rim*. Washington, Government Printing Office.

Oliver, S. G. *et al.* (1992) 'The complete DNA sequence of yeast chromosome III', *Nature*, vol. 357, no. 7, May, pp. 38–46.

Patel, P. (1995) 'Localised production of technology for global markets', *Cambridge Journal of Economics*, no. 19, pp. 57–85.

Pavitt, K. (1997) '*The inevitable limits to EU research funding*', paper presented to the conference on the Past and Future of EU Research Funding – Framework Programmes under consideration, Helsinki.

Pavitt, K. and Patel, P. (1991) 'Technological strategies of the world's largest companies', *Science and Public Policy*, vol. 18, no. 6, pp. 363–8.

Peterson, J. (1993a) 'Assessing the performance of European collaborative R&D policy: the case of Eureka', *Research Policy*, vol. 22, no. 3, Summer, pp. 243–264.

Peterson, J. (1993b) *High Technology and the Competition State: an Analysis of the Eureka Initiative*. London, Routledge.

Peterson, J. (1993c) 'Towards a common European industrial policy? The case of high definition television', *Government and Opposition*, vol. 28, no. 4, pp. 496–511.

Peterson, J. (1995a) 'Decision-making in the European Union: towards a framework for analysis', *Journal of European Public Policy*, vol. 2, no. 1, pp. 69–93.

Peterson, J. (1995b) 'EU research policy: the politics of expertise', in C. Rhodes and S. Mazey (eds) *The State of the European Union Volume 3: Building a European Polity?*, Harlow and Boulder, Longman and Lynne Rienner.

Peterson, J. (1995c) 'Policy networks and European Union policy making', *West European Politics*, vol. 18, no. 2, pp. 389–407.

Peterson, J. (1996) 'Research and development policy', in H. Kassim and A. Menon (eds) *The European Union and National Industrial Policy*. London, Routledge.

Peterson, J. (1997a) 'EUREKA: a historical perspective', in J. Krige and L. Guzzetti (eds) *History of European Scientific and Technological Cooperation*. Luxembourg, European Commission, European Science and Technology Forum.

Peterson, J. (1997b) 'The European Union: Pooled Sovereignty, Divided Accountability', *Political Studies*, vol. 45, no. 3, pp.559–78.

Peterson, J. and Bomberg, E. (1998) *Decision-Making in the European Union*. London, Macmillan.

Petrella, R. (1995) (ed.) *Limites à la Compétitivité*. Brussels, Labor.

Pierre, A. (1987) *A High Technology Gap? Europe, America and Japan*, New York, New York University Press and Council on Foreign Relations.

Pierson, P. (1996) 'The path to European integration: an historical institutionalist pespective', *Comparative Political Studies*, no. 29, pp. 123–63.

Pollack, M. (1995) '*The new institutionalism and EC governance: the promise, and limists, of institutionalist analysis*', paper presented to the annual meeting of the American Political Science Association, 31 August–3 September.

Porter, M. E. (1990) *The Competitive Advantage of Nations*. London, Macmillan.

Porter, M. E. amd Fuller, M. B. (1986) 'Coalitions and Global Srategy', in M. E. Porter (ed.) *Competition and Global Strategy*. London, Macmillan.

POST (Parliamentary Office of Science and Technology) (1996) *The European Union and Research – the EU Framework Programmes and National Frontiers*. London, House of Commons.

Powell, W. W. (1990) 'Neither market nor hierarchy: network forms of organisation', in B. N. Straw and L. L. Cummings (eds) *Research in Organisational Behaviour*, vol. 12, no. 2.

Reger, G. and Kuhlmann, S. (1995) *European Technology Policy in Germany. The Impact of European Community Policies on Science and Technology Policy in Germany*. Heidelberg, Physica-verlag.

Reich, R. (1991) *The Work of Nations: Preparing Ourselves for 21st Century Capitalism*. New York, Alfred Knopf.

Rhodes, R. A. W. (1990) 'Policy networks: a British perspective', *Journal of Theoretical Politics*, vol. 2, no. 1, pp. 293–317.

Rhodes, R. A. W. (1996) 'The New Governance: Governing Without Government', *Political Studies*, vol. 44, no. 1, pp.652–67

Rifkin, Jeremy (1996) *The End of Work*. Berkeley, Putnam Books.

Ross, G. (1995) *Jacques Delors and European Integration*. Cambridge and New York, Polity.

Ruberti, A. (1997) 'Preface' in J. Krige and L. Guzzetti (eds) *History of European Scientific and Technological Cooperation*. Luxembourg, European Commission, European Science and Technology Forum.

Sale, K. (1996) *Rebels Against the Future*. London, Quartet Books.

Sandholtz, W. (1992) *High-Tech Europe: the Politics of International Cooperation.* Berkeley and Oxford, University of California Press.

Sandholtz, W. and Zysman, J. (1989) '1992: recasting the European bargain', *World Politics*, vol. 42, no. 1, pp. 95–128.

Scharpf, F. (1988) 'The joint-decision trap: lessons from German federalism', *Public Administration*, vol. 66, no. 3, pp. 239–78.

Schumpeter, J. A. (1947) *Capitalism, Socialism and Democracy.* New York, Harper & Row.

Senker, J., Joly, P-B. and Reinhard, M. (1998) 'Biotechnology and Europe's chemical/pharmaceutical multinationals', in J. Senker (ed.) *Bioechnology and Competitive Advantage: Europe's Firms and the US Challenge.* Cheltenham and Brookfield, VT, Edward Elgar.

SEPSU (1989) *European Collaboration in Science and Technology II: Pointers to the Future for Policymakers.* London, Science and Engineering Policy Studies Unit of the Royal Society and Fellowship of Engineers.

Servan-Schreiber, J-J. (1967) *Le Défi Américain*, Paris, Denoël.

Sharp, M. (1991) 'Europe – a renaissance?', *Science and Public Policy*, vol. 18, no. 6, pp. 393–400.

Sharp, M. (1993) 'The Community and new technologies' in J. Lodge (ed.) *The European Community and the Challenge of the Future.* London, Pinter.

Sharp, M. and Holmes, P. (1989): *Strategies for New Technologies: Six Cases from Britain and France.* Oxford, Philip Allan.

Sharp, M. and Pavitt, K. (1993) 'Technology policy in the 1990s: old trends and new realities', *Journal of Common Market Studies*, vol. 31, no. 2, pp. 129–51.

Sharp, M. and Shearman, C. (1987) *European Technological Collaboration.* London, Routledge & Kegan Paul for the Royal Institute of International Affairs.

Shaw, E. N. (1997) 'Joint European Torus' in J. Krige and L. Guzetti (eds) *History of European Scientific and Technological Collaboration.* Luxembourg, European Commission, European Science and Technology Forum.

Shearman, C. (1986) 'Cooperation in fast reactors – lessons from the European experience', *Physics in Technology*, vol. 17, no. 1.

Shearman, C. (1997) 'Airbus industry' in J. Krige and L. Guzzetti (eds) *History of European Scientific and Technological Cooperation.* Luxembourg, European Commission, European Science and Technology Forum.

Smith, M.J. (1993) *Pressure, Power and Policy: State Autonomy and Policy Networks in Britain and the United States*, New York and London, Harvester Wheatsheaf.

Stone Sweet, A. and Sandholtz, W. (1997) 'European integration and supranational governance', *Journal of European Public Policy*, vol. 4, no. 3, pp. 297–317.

Strange, S. (1998) 'Who are EU? Ambiguities in the concept of competitiveness; confusion concerning causes and consequences', *Journal of Common Market Studies*, vol. 36, no. 1, pp. 101–14..

Taylor, M.Z. (1995) 'Dominance through technology', *Foreign Affairs*, November/December: 14–20.

Taylor, P. (1989) 'The new dynamic of European integration in the 1980s', in J. Lodge (ed.) *The European Community and the Challenge of the Future.* London, Pinter.

Taylor, T. (1994) 'Western European Security and Defence Cooperation: Maastricht and Beyond', *International Affairs*, no. 70 (January), pp. 1–16.

Tranholm-Mikkelsen, J. (1991) 'Neofunctionalism: obstinate or obsolete? A reappraisal in light of the new dynamism of the European Community', *Millennium*, no. 20, pp. 1–22.

Tyson, L D.(1992): *Who's Bashing Whom: Trade Conflict in High Technology Industries*. Washington, DC, Institute for International Economics.

UK EUREKA Chairmanship (1997a) 'XV session of the EUREKA Ministerial Conference, London, 19 June 1997'. London, 19.6.97, Document EUREKA 15 MC 6.

UK EUREKA Chairmanship (1997b) 'Synergy between EUREKA and the programmes of the European Union'. London, 19.6.97, Document EUREKA 15 MC 5.

UK Government (1965) *Report of the Committee of Enquiry into the Aircraft Industry (The Plowden Report)*, C. 2583. London, HMSO, December.

van Tulder, R. and Junne, G. (1988) *European Multinationals in Core Technologies*. New York, Wiley.

Vogel, D. (1997) *Barriers or Benefits? Regulation in Transatlantic Trade*. Washington DC, Brookings Institution Press.

Von Hippel, E. (1988) *The Sources of Innovation*. Oxford and New York, Oxford University Press.

Wallace, H. and Young, A. (1996) 'The single market: a new approach to policy' in H. Wallace and W. Wallace (eds) *Policy-Making in the European Union*. Oxford University Press.

Walker, W. and Gummett, P. (1993) *Nationalism, Internationalism and the European Defence Market*, Paris, West European Union Institute for Security Studies, Chaillot Paper 9.

Watts, S. (1989) 'Esprit gives Brussels a good name', *New Scientist*, 16 December, pp. 16–17.

Williams, R. (1973) *European Technology: the Politics of Collaboration*. London, Croom Helm.

Williams, R. (1989) 'The EC's Technology policy as an engine for integration', *Government and Opposition*, vol. 24, no. 2, pp. 158–76.

Williams, S. (1991) 'Sovereignty and accountability in the European Community' in R. O. Keohane and S. Hoffmann (eds) *The New European Community*. Boulder and Oxford, Westview Press.

Williamson, O. (1975) *Markets and Hierarchies*, New York, Free Press.

Williamson, O. (1985) *The Economic Institutions of Capitalism*, New York, Free Press.

Wilson, H. (1971) *The Labour Government 1964–70*. London, Weidenfeld & Nicolson and Michael Joseph.

Ziegler, N. (1998) *Governing Ideas*. Ithaca, NY, Cornell University Press.

Zysman, J. and Schwartz, A. (1998) 'Reunifying Europe in an Emerging World Economy: Economic Heterogeneity, New Industrial Options, and Political Choices', *Journal of Common Market Studies*, vol. 36, no. 3, forthcoming.

Index